THE GREAT
JAZZ
PIANISTS

Speaking of Their Lives and Music

LEN LYONS

PHOTOGRAPHS BY VERYL OAKLAND

A DA CAPO PAPERBACK

Library of Congress Cataloging in Publication Data

The great jazz pianists: speaking of their lives and music / Len Lyons;
photographs by Veryl Oakland.
    p.   cm. — (A Da Capo paperback)
    Reprint. Originally published: New York: W. Morrow, 1983.
    Includes discographies and index.
    ISBN 0-306-80343-7
    1. Pianists — Interviews. 2. Jazz musicians — Interviews. I. Lyons,
Leonard.
ML397.G68   1989
786.1′092′2 — dc19   88-38603
[B]   CIP

Most of the interviews in Part Two (with the exception of the Dave Brubeck interview)
appeared in different form in *Keyboard* magazine, *Down Beat* magazine, and *Musician* magazine. Most of the interviews, however, have been supplemented and preceded by new introductions. Some interviews are actually composites of several conversations with a pianist. The
author is grateful to these publications for granting permission to reprint portions of the
interviews as they originally appeared.

Reprinted by permission of *Keyboard*, Cupertino, California, are portions of the interviews
with Teddy Wilson, Mary Lou Williams, Sun Ra, George Shearing, Ahmad Jamal, Horace
Silver, Oscar Peterson, Red Garland, Jimmy Rowles, Paul Bley, Marian McPartland, Billy
Taylor, Jaki Byard, Ran Blake, Ramsey Lewis, Randy Weston, Steve Kuhn, McCoy Tyner,
Toshiko Akiyoshi, Herbie Hancock, Joe Zawinul, Keith Jarrett, and Cecil Taylor.

Reprinted by permission of *Down Beat*, Chicago, Illinois, are portions of the interviews with
Oscar Peterson, Paul Bley, Bill Evans, and McCoy Tyner.

Reprinted by permission of *Musician*, Gloucester, Massachusetts, are portions of the interviews with Chick Corea and Joe Zawinul.

This Da Capo Press paperback edition of *The Great Jazz Pianists* is an unabridged
republication of the edition published in New York in 1983.
It is reprinted by arrangement with the author.

Copyright © 1983 by Leonard S. Lyons

Published by Da Capo Press, Inc.
A Subsidiary of Plenum Publishing Corporation
233 Spring Street, New York, N.Y. 10013

THE GREAT
JAZZ
PIANISTS

For Louis E. Siagel,
who taught me the
most important lesson of the piano:
how to enjoy it

PREFACE

Jazz piano has always seemed to me to be a single language of a thousand different dialects. It embraces a multiplicity of styles, yet has a strong underlying continuity that its artists study formally or absorb naturally through their listening and playing. It has been six years since it first occurred to me that the jazz piano tradition was an autonomous subject deserving book-length treatment. My original idea was to write a collection of journalistic stories about the pianists I had interviewed over the years for magazines and newspapers, contrasting their individual differences with their commonly shared heritage. The project was slow to start. It was superseded by my ongoing work as a freelance journalist and the time-consuming process of writing a listener's guide to jazz, published in 1980 as *The 101 Best Jazz Albums.*

Then, in May 1982, while organizing my portfolio, I began rereading my transcribed interviews with jazz pianists, which, by that time, exceeded three dozen. An hour later I was still reading, finding their stories delightful (even the second time around) and their insights enlightening and thought-provoking. Suddenly I realized I had the key to presenting the jazz piano story: The pianists must speak for themselves. Their opinions, reminiscences, and anecdotes reveal intimately who they are, and their comments on playing jazz, and on their unique heritage, ring truest in their own words. In short, the focus of the book I was imagining shifted from jazz piano to the jazz pianists, who are, after all, the lifeblood of the music.

The book has finally taken shape in two parts. Part One is a survey of jazz pianists from 1900 to today. It places these musicians in the context of the overall history of jazz and its changing instrumental styles. There were some intimidating challenges involved in composing this overview. First, there is the inevitable overlapping of some material in this section with information provided in the introductions and interviews of Part Two. Having interviewed many of the key figures in the history of jazz piano, I could not very well survey the field without referring to them and their work. Repeating certain points seemed preferable to ignoring them. (As they are introduced into the survey, the names of pianists interviewed in Part Two are followed by an asterisk [*].)

Secondly, it was clear that some excellent jazz pianists were going to be omitted from the survey. Anyone who has written about jazz from a historical viewpoint and has spent a lot of time "in the trenches," knows that not every worthy artist plays a significant historical role. Unfortunately this means excluding some of the musicians one admires and enjoys, while including a few well-known pianists whose historical significance outweighs their artistry. These decisions must be made and adhered to, if only to preserve adequate space for the major figures.

Thirdly, organizing and describing the crazy quilt of the world of jazz piano were no simple tasks. After all, there are more than eighty noteworthy artists. Nevertheless, my goal throughout has been to keep both the whole fabric and the individual pieces in view for the reader, while illustrating where and how each of the pianists fits in.

The interview material in Part Two (except for the Dave Brubeck interview, which was arranged with this volume in mind) was gathered for magazine publication between 1974 and 1979. In many cases the interviews herein are expanded versions of the articles that first appeared in print. Whenever possible, they have been supplemented and updated with this book in mind, to allow the pianists an opportunity to express themselves fully on crucial subjects.

Generally I have transcribed the pianists' remarks verbatim, but I have not indulged in the tiresome practice of documenting every "er" and "uh" uttered, nor have I attempted to reflect dialects or to preserve patently ungrammatical sentences. Most of the pianists requested that I render their answers in the most readable manner possible. I have done so, with scrupulous concern for their meaning, emphasis, and choice of words.

The introductions to the interviews have been kept brief to avoid duplicating topics discussed during the interviews themselves and in the survey in Part One. My own speeches in the dialogues have also been pared down to a minimum, except where the pianist is responding to my opinions or hypotheses. Considering my ubiquitous presence in Part Two as the interviewer, it seemed advisable to cut myself out of the picture whenever possible.

The selected discographies following each interview will provide the reader with a sampling of the musician's best, or most representative, recordings from each period of his or her career. As a rule, I have selected albums that are in print, but I have occasionally identified some essential listening that is now out of print and may therefore be difficult to find. These titles are marked with an asterisk (*) to indicate their problematic status.

The Appendix lists recommended albums for most of the pianists mentioned in Part One and even for a few pianists not included there. The names of the twenty-seven pianists interviewed in Part Two do *not* appear in the Appendix because their discographies follow the interviews.

Finally, I must reveal what may be the deepest impetus for this book—my own love affair with jazz piano and its artists, many of whom I idolized long before I contemplated the idea of meeting and writing about them. Like many writers on music, I began by loving it, playing it, and ultimately by realizing that my own talents are best expressed at the keyboard of a typewriter. Though I cannot make a contribution to the great legacy of jazz piano, I do hope that this book will increase the understanding, appreciation, and enjoyment of it.

Berkeley, 1982

ACKNOWLEDGMENTS

WITH MY GRATEFUL THANKS TO:

Amy Louise Shapiro and Kristina Lindbergh for their editorial skill and insight;

Veryl Oakland, a distinctive photographer and understanding collaborator, for making my work look so much better over the years;

Tom Darter, editor of *Keyboard* magazine, for making helpful suggestions on Part One and for making possible so many of the interviews in Part Two;

Bob Kahn for making available the keyboard of his word processor; and

Maxine, Gila, and Ami for a happy home.

The author also wishes to acknowledge his gratitude to the Ralph J. Gleason Memorial Fund Awards Committee of the Monterey Jazz Festival for a grant during the early stages of this project. This award was both a deeply felt honor and a practical asset.

A long-deserved thank-you as well to the various editors of *Keyboard, Down Beat*, and *Musician* magazines for assisting and supporting the author's work in jazz journalism.

CONTENTS

PRELUDE

The piano is the most versatile and autonomous of all the musical instruments. No more perfect tool (and that, ultimately, is all an instrument really is) for expressing music has ever been developed. The piano has been a central instrument in the evolution of jazz from the music's infancy, and pianists have always been among jazz's great improvisers, composers, and bandleaders.

The piano was invented in about 1698, by Bartolomeo Cristofori, the keeper of the instruments in the Medici Court of Florence. Its main advantage over its principal predecessor, the harpsichord, was its great versatility of expression. "Piano" is an abbreviation of the instrument's full name, *piano e forte* (later pianoforte), which means "loud and soft." The players of the ubiquitous harpsichord could not control the volume of sound or the tone by striking the keys because this keyboard is a plectrum instrument—its strings are plucked and with precisely the same force each time a note on the keyboard is played. The piano, however, is a percussion instrument. Felt hammers strike its strings, but with a force that varies with the way the player depresses the keys. The piano's sensitivity to touch makes it the ideal keyboard for personal expression, one of the hallmarks of good jazz.

The piano is an expansive, emotional sounding board capable of extraordinary dynamics (dramatic changes in tone and volume). It can whisper, crash, tinkle, and thunder simultaneously in different areas of the keyboard. It speaks harshly and sharply or with a soothing, honey-coated voice. Its only limitation for jazz players is that unlike stringed and wind instruments, its notes (or technically speaking, its pitches) cannot be altered, smeared, or "bent" to produce the vocalized intonation common to these other instruments. Although pitch variation is an important element of jazz, the piano's advantages overshadow this single drawback.

The piano keyboard allows for innumerable combinations and permutations of its notes, and considering that rhythm, tone, dynamics, and the sustaining or damping of notes with the pedals can be varied as well, the number of sounds the piano can create is infinite. Besides the fact that its eighty-eight keys produce a range of pitches that exceed any other instrument's span, more than ten notes, perhaps twelve or fourteen, can be played simultaneously without abandoning precision.

Most important, the pianist has at his fingertips all the elements of complete musical expression: rhythm, melody, and harmony. For this reason, most musicians consider the piano the fundamental instrument of Western music. For jazz musicians the piano's self-sufficiency has been one of its major assets, for it allows them to study, experiment, and perform alone.

PART · ONE

A SURVEY OF THE JAZZ PIANISTS AND THEIR TRADITION

A Piano in Every Parlor

At the turn of the century—before the age of radio, television, high-fidelity recording, and computerized video games—the piano was one of the focal points of American family life in the home. The image of Mother seated at the keyboard with the children gathered around her and Father in his pinstriped shirt and suspenders looking on proudly epitomized the American dream. White American families purchased moderately priced "uprights" at the rate of nearly 250,000 per year.

In black family life the piano was one of the first major purchases made by those who could afford it. Although they were less likely than white families to own instruments, blacks frequently heard piano music in churches, which were the center of community life, or in the urban "tonks" and "juke" houses (the ancestors of the jukebox). Indeed, black pianists were largely responsible for the instrument's acceptance as "part of the family." The music they played and composed during the late 1890's, eventually known as ragtime, was a major source of the piano's popularity in the two decades that followed.

Ragtime was the earliest documented form of jazz piano, although pianists also played in such various prejazz idioms as stomps, struts, blues, and gospel music. Ragtime, like jazz itself, evolved from diverse sources, adopting the harmony of European classical music, the thematic divisions of marching band music, the rhythms of ethnic dances like the cakewalk and the two-step, and the spirit of the early black music played on banjos and in itinerant brass bands. Its origins are reflected in titles like "Combination March," "Ragtime Two-Step," and "A Real Slow Drag." The piano was ideal for playing ragtime because it could capture, in the interplay of the two hands, the rhythms of both the dances and their banjo accompaniment. Other piano pieces were condensed versions of the way the brass bands played, the left hand taking the trombone, guitar, and tuba parts, while the right hand approximated the clarinet or cornet. In this sense, the pianist was virtually a one-man band. Composers wrote rags in 2/4 meter (two quarter notes per measure) capturing the rhythmic feeling of marches, the era's most popular music.

Ragtime was more European than the later forms of jazz piano. The music was usually composed note for note, rather than improvised, and although a performer often added flourishes and embellishments to give his version a distinctive, personal touch, the variations never violated the basic melody or the order and repetition of the rag's three or four themes. This style was later called classical ragtime, because it was written down and because its composers intended it to serve as America's answer to the nineteenth-century sonata, étude, and polonaise.

Syncopation was ragtime's primary contribution to jazz piano and was an unprecedented development in Western music. A syncopated rhythm is one whose accents occur on, or fall around, the weak beats of the measure. On the keyboard, the left hand establishes *one* and *two* as strong beats by playing a bass note, usually followed by a chord played in the middle register. The right hand, however, plays a melody with accents that fall between the two distinct beats. (Listening to the music of the pianists and composers mentioned in the next few pages is, of course, the surest way to understand syncopation.) The slightly off-center or "ragged" rhythm was so novel and electrifying that it produced a "rag-time" craze. Genuine ragtime, and the imitations of it churned out by the prolific Tin Pan Alley tunesmiths, became the most popular music in America from 1900 to 1918. Published in sheet music form, ragtime pieces might sell 50 to 100,000 copies. The piano "rolls" of the pianola, or player piano, cranked out the same music, rather stiffly, in the homes of those who were unable to play the instrument. These player pianos with their exchangeable rolls were the "record players" of the day.

The greatest composer of classical ragtime was Scott Joplin (1868–1917), who was born to former slaves in Texarkana, Texas. Until his considerable talent earned him a scholarship to study with a classical teacher in a nearby white community, Joplin was self-taught. In his teens he entertained in the honky-tonks of St. Louis, and later worked as a cornetist, traveling with a band that played marches, popular songs, and symphonic music. In 1895 he settled in Sedalia, Missouri, and attended George Smith College, where he learned to transcribe his piano pieces, so far as that was possible, into conventional notation. (Although the tens of thousands of pianists who played from sheet music were reluctant to admit it, the lilting swing of ragtime could only be approximated on the written page.)

Joplin's second published composition, "Maple Leaf Rag" (1899), named for a saloon on Main Street in Sedalia, made him a famous and relatively wealthy man. Joplin, however, was an uncomfortable performer. He shied away from the bravado and flashy technique of his contemporaries, who liked to dazzle audiences with sweeping *arpeggios* and breathtaking "runs" up and down the keyboard. One of the popular forums for these barroom "professors" was the "cutting contest," where madcap tempos and complicated "fingerbusters" often won accolades over musical content and originality. Many pianists built their reputations on little more than technical prowess. Joplin did not have a performer's panache, nor did he seek it. Instead, he retired from performing altogether and devoted himself to composing. A few years later he followed his friend and publisher John Stark to New York, where he composed dozens more melodic, bittersweet rags and two operas before his death at forty-nine.

Joplin's contemporaries revered him as the master of classic ragtime, though many of them also composed moving and exciting music for the piano, if not with Joplin's consistency. Most of these composers were in some way involved with Joplin, justifying his place at the center of the pantheon. James Scott was Joplin's protégé. Scott Hayden was related by marriage and lived with Joplin in St. Louis. Arthur Marshall had been a classmate and confidant at George Smith College. Louis Chauvin, a dissolute *bon vivant* who died at age twenty-five, was also a student of Joplin's. Three-hundred-pound Tom Turpin was a flamboyant virtuoso who took delight in outplaying Joplin at the cutting contests he staged in his own saloon, the Rosebud Café.

There were only a few white pianists who contributed to the ragtime style in the early years, and although they all lived on the East Coast, they were strongly influenced by the Sedalia circle. Joseph Lamb, who spent his life in New Jersey, was a diffident composer with an aversion to show business. His few published rags, however, were of high quality and won Joplin's admiration. Brun Campbell and Ben Harney, on the other hand, were known for their playing, rather than for their original music.

A ragtime revival in the 1970's renewed its prestige as a classical, strictly composed genre. An album of Joplin's compositions by pianist Joshua Rifkin inaugurated the revival, which gathered steam when Joplin's piece "The Entertainer" was adopted as the theme for the movie *The Sting*. Pianists Max Morath, Dick Hyman, William Bolcom, and Bob Darch also reinterpreted classic ragtime during the seventies.

Although classic ragtime served jazz by developing the art of syncopation, high standards of virtuosity, and a repertoire of thematic music, its contribution was limited by its dependence on composition and its remoteness from the blues. Improvisation and the sentiments embodied in the blues are central to black American music, and these basic elements began to find expression during the early 1900's in New Orleans and on the eastern seaboard.

Eastern and New Orleans pianists made use of the classic repertoire. Historical accounts of the period and *post facto* recordings by pianists who had performed in the early 1900's show that the easterners had a more robust, earthy style than the midwesterners and took more liberties with the composed music. Rather than imitate Europeans, whose piano playing had become the darling of the concert hall and salon, these pianists sought to leave their mark in the brothels, dance halls, and tonks of the cities.

At the turn of the century the piano had not yet gained importance as a band instrument because of its size. The early brass bands, which played primarily at picnics, parades, and funerals, relied more on portable chord-based instruments such as guitars or banjos. Thus, the aim of the East Coast pianists was to pack all the sound and excitement of a full brass band into each piece.

One of the most fascinating of the New Orleans pianists was a pool hustler, sharpshooter, pimp, and inveterate braggart named Ferdinand La-Menthe, Jr., who began playing during his teens in the red-light district of New Orleans. After his own father (a trombonist) left home, he took his stepfather's name, Morton, and later acquired the nickname Jelly Roll.

Jelly Roll Morton (1885–1941) became a highly paid "professor," playing stomps, blues, struts, and "naked dances" in the "mansions" of the French Quarter (also known as Storyville) of New Orleans. When the Navy Department shut down Storyville in 1917, Morton headed out to California and traveled throughout the Southwest before he finally settled in Chicago. There, in the mid-twenties, he formed and recorded with the Red Hot Peppers, a band that epitomized the complex and colorful sound of New Orleans jazz.

With his Creole background, Morton was familiar with opera as well as European classical piano music, and his playing reflected both classical ragtime and the more earthy, ethnic styles of New Orleans. One of his major influences was an unrecorded pianist and local entertainer named Tony Jackson (1876–1921), whose "Naked Dance" and "Michigan Water Blues" remained in Morton's repertoire for years. Morton's abilities as a player were highly controversial, and his incurable boasting provoked his critics to particularly vocal and vicious assaults. Morton enraged people by claiming adamantly to have "invented" jazz himself in 1902 and by accusing others of stealing his songs. Nevertheless, his recordings show him to have been highly effective and inventive within his style, even if he was not the virtuoso many of his contemporaries were.

Morton's music transcends the limited forms of blues and rags, although it contains elements of both. For this reason, he is thought of as the first composer to have written in an idiom clearly identifiable as jazz. His composing was first acknowledged with the sheet music publication of some of his early material, including "King Porter Stomp" (one of the big band chestnuts of the swing era) and "Tiger Rag" (a Dixieland standard), "Frog-i-More Rag" and "New Orleans Joys." Morton's piano scores are, even more than are those of midwestern composers, microcosms of how he heard the brass bands of his day. Conversely, his brilliant Red Hot Peppers scores, such as "Grandpa's Spells" and "Black Bottom Stomp," were based on his piano style.

Eubie Blake (1883–1983), who performed with energy and wit until his one hundredth birthday, was a self-taught ragtimer and composer. By fifteen he was earning a living in his hometown, Baltimore–as Morton had in New Orleans–by playing in "sporting houses." Blake's ambition to make his mark and fortune in music drew him to Atlantic City and eventually to New York, which was even then one of the proving grounds (along with Chicago) for jazz musicians. In 1915 he teamed up with lyricist Noble Sissle and wrote several hit songs, among them "I'm Just Wild About Harry," "Memories of You," and "Lucky to Be Me." Unlike Morton, Blake was celebrated for his technique and his ability to play comfortably in all twelve keys, a rare accomplishment even among the better-schooled contemporary pianists. Blake was all but forgotten from about 1930 until the late 1960's. But during that time he studied the Schillinger system of composition and earned a degree in music from New York University. Then, after a successful concert at the Newport Jazz Festival in 1969, Blake was rediscovered, and he began recording prolifically.

After 1910, ragtime piano on the East Coast, especially in New York, took a turn away from the classical style and from the stomps and struts that were part of Morton's and Blake's repertoires. The pianists in the great urban centers began entertaining at all-night gatherings known as rent parties, where partygoers donated money to raise rent money for the host. It was not unusual to have a roomful of pianists at these parties, and they played as much to impress each other as for dancing and listening. The competition between them, which delighted the other guests, was fierce.

The rent party style was still called ragtime by its practitioners (and Harlem ragtime by historians), but it soon evolved into an idiom aptly dubbed stride–after its rhythmic momentum and the action of the left hand. As in ragtime, it would leap from a bass note (or a two-note interval, such as a fifth or an octave), to a chord in the middle register. It is a fast-paced music more likely to be in 4/4 than 2/4 meter; the listener feels four quarter notes per measure instead of only two. This difference in meter is usually attributed to the fact that while early ragtime was based to a great extent on marches and, for that reason, sounded relatively stiff, stride descends from the ring shout, an early black American circle dance of great vitality.

These are not the only differences between stride and early ragtime. The stride pianists use fuller harmonies and chromatic chord progressions, and their right-hand melodies are more improvisational and more likely to include blues-related phrases. The right hand also imitates the guitar's "bent" notes with "grace" notes—tones played a split second before the main melody notes. The music is robust, complex, and often played at a breakneck tempo. And as the tendency to improvise increased, so did the need for better technique to meet that challenge.

The evolution of stride from ragtime was, of course, gradual. There were pianists who could be classified in either style and who could play comfortably in both. Charles Luckeyeth "Luckey" Roberts (1895-1968) and Willie "The Lion" Smith (1897-1973) were important transitional figures. Roberts, who started out in vaudeville as a child acrobat, became a popular bandleader and was adored by members of high society. During the 1920's he was hired to play at private parties for some of America's best-known millionaires, such as the Astors and Vanderbilts. He was also a successful composer of musical comedies. As a "tickler" (the term that had replaced "professor"), Roberts dazzled audiences with cascades of notes in the right hand while his left hand pumped away, stoking the burning tempo. Luckey did not have the melodic gifts of those who followed him, but he demonstrated the degree of excitement that could be generated with keyboard precision and power.

Willie "The Lion" Smith was a more inventive pianist than Roberts, and he was among the reigning royalty of the rent parties. His stylish clothes, ever-present cigar, and regal manner prompted James P. Johnson to comment that Smith's "every move was a picture." Smith slid easily between the ragtime and stride styles, but it was his right hand that set him apart from his colleagues. Smith could improvise charming impressionistic melodies, many of which were formalized in compositions like "Morning Air" and "Echoes of Spring." Using the higher tones of the scale (such as ninths and elevenths), Smith's harmonies were bold and ahead of their time. One of Smith's ardent admirers at the rent parties was twenty-year-old Duke Ellington, whose piano solos often revealed Smith's direct influence. Smith's chords also stimulated the magnificent harmonic imagination of Art Tatum, a titan of the keyboard who will be discussed later.

James P. Johnson (1891-1955), often called the father of stride piano, had a lasting impact on other pianists. He played strong and imaginative stride, distinguished by his own clever, uniquely phrased melodies. Johnson received private piano lessons as a boy and, unlike his predecessors, had a good knowledge of the European classics. He had mastered the East Coast ragtime repertoire in his teens, during which he became close friends with Luckey Roberts. Some of Johnson's first jobs as a pianist in New York were in the rough barrooms of the waterfront, where fighting and dancing competed with the sound of the piano. Johnson had to develop an aggressive style that had the power of the shout as well as the appeal of popular dances. One of those original dance tunes was included in his Broadway show *Runnin' Wild* (1923) and subsequently became America's most famous dance number of all, "The Charleston." However, more typical of the power and elegance of Johnson's composing are his "Carolina Shout" and "Snowy Morning." Johnson, like the Lion, was an early influence on Duke Ellington, but his impact can be felt even farther down the line in the work of such pianists as Thelonious Monk and Cecil Taylor.

Johnson's career as a solo pianist was short-lived. He began to write film scores for Hollywood, accompanied singers, including Bessie Smith, and tried to create an idiom of black American symphonic music, but with little success. These pursuits drew him away from playing. He also suffered a series of strokes that slowly deteriorated his keyboard facility. Nevertheless, he remained an active player and late in his career returned to performing composed rags.

One of Johnson's greatest contributions to jazz piano was his private tutoring of Thomas "Fats" Waller (1904-1943), a gifted and facile pianist whose popularity, for a time, rivaled that of Louis Armstrong. A *bon vivant,* who could party and jam all night, Waller was famous for showing up at a recording session with a hangover and without the required original music. Then, sitting down at the piano, he would miraculously come up with gems that have yet to lose their brilliance and appeal. He wrote hundreds of songs in this fashion, some of them conjured up spontaneously, literally within minutes.

Waller, the son of a minister, became familiar with the pipe organ, which his mother played in church. He was one of the few keyboardists to play successful jazz on that instrument, and wrote the first jazz piece in 3/4 time for it—"Jitterbug Waltz." While in his teens, playing the organ for silent movies at the Lincoln Theater in Harlem, Fats gave lessons and encouragement to a young fan who came from New Jersey to hear him, Bill (later "Count") Basie. Waller influenced a great number of other pianists through his performances at rent parties, his solo recordings, and countless after-hours sessions. Like his teacher, Johnson, Waller had conscientiously practiced much of the classical piano literature, which honed and sharpened his talent to a fine virtuoso's edge.

Waller improvised more complex, sophisticated, and symmetrical right-hand melodies than any of his predecessors. His solos sparkle the brightest on many lesser-known compositions, such as "Numb Fumblin'," "Handful of Keys," "Smashing Thirds," and "Clothes Line Ballet." Some of Waller's more popular compositions are "Ain't Misbehavin'," "Honeysuckle Rose," and "I'm Gonna Sit Right Down and Write Myself a Letter." He had the speed and power of his contemporaries, but his music was unusually light and intricate at the same time. Virtually all of the pianists who dominated the thirties are indebted to some extent to Waller, as they are, indeed to all the stride artists.

Stride piano was disseminated by dozens of pianists around the country throughout the twenties. Some of the later pianists who have kept the stride idiom alive are Joe Sullivan, Johnny Guarnieri, Art Hodes, Dick Wellstood, and Ralph Sutton.

The Swing Era

The great virtue of ragtime and stride was self-sufficiency. But since jazz is an improvisational, personal, and restless music, it was inevitable that other pianists would alter, reinterpret, and explore ideas beyond those they had inherited. By the mid-twenties the party piano of the ragtime era had moved onto the bandstand and into the recording studio. Recording technology had, until that time, been unable to capture adequately the range and dynamics of the piano. Once that limitation was overcome, however, the piano replaced the guitar (which had been thought of as strictly a rhythm instrument in those days) in most studio and dance bands. The pianist's horizons reached beyond the "one-man-band" concept of piano playing.

Earl "Fatha" Hines (1905–), the "father of jazz piano," expanded the piano's capabilities on every front: rhythmic, harmonic, and melodic. Born in Pittsburgh, Hines studied classical piano and gave several local concerts in his early teens. He had visions of becoming a concert artist but soon realized that black musicians could not expect to earn a living that way. After working in local nightclubs, Hines moved to Chicago in 1922, working for singer Lois Deppe. A few years later he joined the Carroll Dickerson Orchestra and met trumpeter Louis Armstrong and drummer Zutty Singleton. These men became friends and would later form the nucleus of Armstrong's sensational Hot Five and Hot Seven recording bands.

Hines's innovations began to appear on the Hot Five and Hot Seven recordings, and it was through them that both Hines's and Armstrong's soloing influenced the course of jazz. Hines would vary the ordinarily regular, pistonlike action of the left hand with broken rhythms, implied rhythms, double-timed passages, and some almost indescribable acrobatics of tempo and meter. Though he kept the 4/4 feeling of stride, he varied it enormously with displaced accents. Like the circus clown who plays at tripping and falling (but deftly lands on his feet every time), Hines would "lose" both rhythm and chord changes within a song only to bring them together perfectly at the end of the phrase or chorus.

Hines also used harmonies more creatively than his contemporaries. His chromatic (half-step) progressions were a signpost to future pianists, pointing the way, for example, to Art Tatum's reharmonizing of song material. While ragtime and stride were pianistic styles, Hines gave the piano an added tonal color approximating the brilliance of a trumpet. He played his melodies in "trumpet style," using right-hand octaves, sometimes with a tremolo or a grace note in the upper octave. The bright and forceful tone projected the piano's melody over the backdrop of the other instruments, and although Hines was profoundly impressed by Armstrong's soloing, he has claimed that the trumpet-style right hand predates their association. Ironically, Hines was best known the next twelve years, not for his keyboard innovations, but for the big bands he led at the Grand Terrace Hotel in Chicago from 1928 to 1940.

During the thirties, as America tried to dance its way out of the Depression, big bands became the country's most popular musical groups. And there was no shortage of pianists to lead them. Fletcher Henderson (1898–1952), whose main distinction behind the keyboard was in accompanying singers Ethel Waters and Bessie Smith, left his native Georgia for New York in 1922. There he started out as the house pianist for a record company owned by composer W. C. Handy, but his real importance to jazz was as an arranger and a bandleader. He helped define the big band style in the mid-twenties.

William "Count" Basie (1904–) was also best known as a bandleader, but along the way he developed an original and influential piano style of his own. As noted earlier, Basie studied organ informally with Fats Waller and was a proficient ragtimer. In his early years he played with all the speed, power, and agility that the style demanded. But after settling in Kansas City in the mid-thirties, he came under the influence of blues pianists Bennie Moten and Jay McShann (also important bandleaders in the Midwest) and the boogie-woogie stylist Pete Johnson. Basie also began to accommodate his piano style to the needs of his seven-piece band, which demanded a rhythmic, light, and lean accompaniment. Under Basie's guidance, his early rhythm section (which included bassist Walter Page, drummer Jo Jones, and guitarist Freddie Green) drove the band like a compact, quiet, but powerful motor.

Edward Kennedy Ellington (1899–1974), who led his celebrated orchestra from 1923 until his death, contributed to the piano's development by exploiting the instrument's percussive capabilities. Until about 1930 "Duke," an epithet Ellington acquired in high school, was little more than a talented copy of Willie Smith, James P. Johnson, and Fats Waller – the pianists he followed after he moved to New York in the early twenties from his hometown of Washington, D.C. Eventually, however, Ellington's compositional genius began to enrich his piano playing. Integrating the sound of his piano with that of the full band, Duke would splatter the music's tonal "surface" with biting, dissonant chords in the piano's higher register and with drumlike bass notes. He used novel-sounding runs and arpeggios built on the pentatonic scale to lace together melodic ideas. If stride piano was fun-loving and high-spirited, Ellington transformed it into something stark, strong, and much more mysterious. His Spartan approach to playing, his impeccable selection of notes and chords, and his sharp keyboard attack inaugurated a percussive strain in the jazz piano legacy that found expression later in the work of Thelonious Monk and Randy Weston *. Although it does not share Duke's economy of notes, the work of McCoy Tyner * and Cecil Taylor * also descends from Ellington's percussive approach to the keyboard.

The subsequent stage of the piano's development in jazz was introduced by Teddy Wilson *, whose entire aesthetic sense differed significantly from that of his peers. Basically, Wilson adopted the left-hand action of stride but eliminated most of its accents. He also introduced the idea of using a series of tenths in lieu of the broken figures of stride, to keep the music moving. His right-hand lines were long, intricate, and precisely articulated. Abandoning Hines's forceful trumpet-style octaves, he increased his mobility in the melody line. He could also afford to play more delicately, thanks to the invention of the electronic microphone, which enabled the piano to project over the other instruments without his playing loudly or in octaves.

Wilson took the rocking, rollicking sound of the party piano and clothed it in elegant attire. He emphasized discipline and control, rather than the fire and ice of the ragtime and stride eras. This was in part the result of his love for the European classics and in part an extension of his temperament. And while he sacrificed the visceral excitement which thus far had been the pianist's calling card, he gained a more objective kind of beauty.

Wilson's lack of the obvious emotionality of other pianists was supplied in abundance by his band-mates. As part of the Benny Goodman "chamber quartet," he was heard in the company of very physical players like drummer Gene Krupa and vibraphonist Lionel Hampton. During the mid-thirties Wilson was also the music director of impromptu bands that drew their musicians from the Basie and Ellington orchestras and featured vocalist Billie Holiday. As can be seen in the music of those who have followed Wilson, his artful, exquisite improvising tapped a subtler kind of emotional response that played an increasingly greater role in jazz.

A Fertile Milieu

From roughly 1935 until the early 1940's most jazz pianists worked with some combinations of the elements heard in the playing of Johnson, Waller, Hines, and Wilson. Although the basic approach to playing jazz on the piano had reached, at least temporarily, a point of definition, there were many pianists who created original and influential styles out of these basic building blocks.

By all accounts it was Art Tatum (1910–1956) who cast the longest shadow among them. There has been no more complete master of the instrument, and to no other pianist does the cliché "a legend in his own time" apply more readily. Born in Toledo, Ohio, Tatum played in local clubs and on the radio until he went to New York in 1932 as the accompanist for singer Adelaide Hall. The cornerstones of his music were the harmonies of Hines, the driving left hand of Waller, and the flowing, legato melody and moving left-hand tenths that he heard in the playing of young Teddy Wilson.

The most obvious difference between Tatum and the other pianists was his conspicuous virtuosity. Despite his extremely limited vision in one eye (to the extent that he was judged legally blind), Tatum seemed to play everything twice as fast as his peers, while increasing the level of swing and harmonic variety. His influence on other pianists was profound, if not devastating. It is said that he intimidated many of them into taking up other instruments. But Tatumesque passages are evident in the music of many undaunted pianists who followed him, especially in the music of Bud Powell (in his ballads), Oscar Peterson *, Billy Taylor *, and Hank Jones, though these are only a few of the most obvious examples.

Tatum's repertoire was vast but not otherwise unusual. Some of the songs he played early in his career—such as "Tea for Two," "Tiger Rag," "Someone to Watch over Me," dozens more standards, and a few light classics—he continued to record in the 1950's. Yet he rarely repeated himself in his treatment of the material. His harmonic variations were startling, especially when he soloed. Where another pianist might go directly from one chord to the next, Tatum's left hand would walk crablike through a cycle of four to six new chords between the original two. Meanwhile, his right hand would spin out a web of interconnecting lines of thirty-second notes. Tatum could keep up these magnificent circumlocutions for eight bars or more and never drop a beat. Jazz pianists idolized Art Tatum, as did several classical virtuosos. Leopold Godowsky, Vladimir Horowitz, and Walter Gieseking, for example, were known to have come down to marvel at the phenomenal Tatum in the Onyx Club on Fifty-second Street, one of his favorite places to hold court.

During the forties Tatum worked frequently with a trio that included Slam Stewart on bass and Tiny Grimes on guitar. The group was celebrated for the intuitive communication among the players as well as for Tatum's blistering speed, as they achieved a unity of sound that was rare at any tempo.

While Tatum was virtually without deficiency as a pianist, his improvising sometimes amounted to ornate, if not rococo, interpretations of his material. There was no doubt that those ornaments were gorgeous, but they were at times more decorative than creative. Most of Tatum's music, however, is genuine artistry amplified by awesome virtuosity. Moreover, those who knew him claim that he played best of all beyond the reach of recorded history and without the inhibiting presence of the public or recording microphones, at private, after-hours parties.

While the Tatum legend will live on and rightfully, history does not always pay its debts in full. There are two men, for example, whose far-reaching influence on jazz pianists is seldom acknowledged. One of them, Milt Buckner, who played with Lionel Hampton's band from 1941 to 1948, invented the locked-hands technique, a means of playing melody and harmony together in "block" chords. By this method the melody is doubled by being played with both the thumb of the left hand and the little finger of the right hand one octave higher, leaving four fingers of the right hand free to fill in the chord. After perfecting this technique, Buckner could play complicated melodic passages in rhythm, making the piano sound like the reed section of a big band. Nat Cole, George Shearing, and Red Garland are only a few of the pianists who have adapted Buckner's technique to their own styles.

The second of these underrated pianists was Nat "King" Cole, whose velvety voice made him one of the top popular singers of the fifties. His celebrated career as a vocalist has obscured his historical contribution to the piano. Cole began his career as a swinging, Hines-influenced jazz pianist, who was also influenced by the single-note melody lines of Wilson and, as noted above, by Buckner's locked-hands chording. Cole's originality was in the swing feeling he generated and in his light touch. Cole was widely admired and imitated by pianists, largely as a result of the King Cole Trio he formed with guitarist Oscar Moore and bassist Wesley Prince in 1939. Cole's light and airy improvising, combined with his ability to swing without the heavy undercurrent of drums, set the pattern for the piano/bass/guitar trios of Art Tatum, Oscar Peterson, and Ahmad Jamal *. Peterson and Jamal both acknowledge Cole as one of their major influences.

There are, of course, other prominent figures of this period, whom history has treated with even less fanfare. For one, Jess Stacy, who was self-taught, played with Goodman's orchestra between 1935 and 1939. His spot in Goodman's band was then taken over a couple of years later by Mel Powell, who was known for his remarkable sense of swing. Powell later became a professor of composition at Yale University in the mid-fifties and soon dropped out of jazz.

Billy Kyle, who played in the bands of Lucky Millinder and bassist John Kirby, was derivative of Hines and had considerable talent as an improviser of single-note lines. Nat Jaffe, one of trombonist Jack Teagarden's favorite accompanists, was a prominent soloist in the Fifty-second Street clubs in New York, until his premature death at age twenty-seven. Eddie Heywood, Jr., was first noticed as the pianist in Benny Carter's band, but temporary paralysis of his hands, as well as his digressions into popular music, interfered with his career in jazz. Bob Zurke became popular through his performances with the Bob Crosby Band and through his mastery of the boogie-woogie style. Joe Bushkin began in the neo-Dixieland style popular in Chicago of the late twenties. Moving to New York, he played in guitarist Eddie Condon's bands from 1936 to 1939, and later he worked briefly with Goodman, Armstrong, and his own quartet. By the mid-fifties, however, Bushkin was identified with show business rather than jazz.

Mary Lou Williams * was the first woman to become an accomplished, all-around jazz musician. Through her association with Kansas City musicians, including Basie, she absorbed a strong feeling for swing and the blues. Williams was one of the few swing pianists who was equally at home in bebop, and she was one of the first of the traditional players to befriend Thelonious Monk and Bud Powell. During the 1970's, when pianists began to separate themselves into commercial, electronically inclined camps, on one side, and avant-garde, acoustic players, on the other, Williams became a crusader for the pristine values of bebop, which she exemplified in a vigorous, driving style.

Interlude in Eight

Boogie-woogie, also known as blues and barrelhouse piano, was a fascinating but short-lived phenomenon whose development occurred tangentially to that of jazz piano. Although the blues scale (or, more accurately, mode) is one of the central elements of jazz, boogie-woogie adopts the blues overtly and exclusively, creating a kind of "folk" piano idiom. The stride pianists of the Northeast, for example, might have played some barrelhouse now and then to please the crowd, but down deep they considered it beneath them as artists. Boogie-woogie pianists did not have the classical training or technique of the stride players, and their use of harmony seldom went beyond what was required to play the blues. For the most part, they used the piano in the same limited role as their rural predecessors had the guitar.

Nevertheless, the short-lived style has an interesting history. The blues flourished most readily in the big cities like Chicago and Kansas City, to which blacks migrated from the rural South in search of better jobs. There the appeal of boogie-woogie was its blues message and its powerful, relentless rhythm, created by repetitive bass figures that usually consisted of eight notes. These bass lines were often no more than measures of eight eighth notes that made use of the flatted-third or flatted-seventh notes of the blues scale. Of course, there were variations, but the boogie-woogie feeling was generally one of acceleration and regularity, like that of a freight train clacking down the track with its throttle wide open. The right hand played riffs (or short phrases) that were reminiscent of blues guitar and, in Kansas City, of the riffs improvised by the horn sections of the great swing bands.

The good boogie-woogie players—and the jazz pianists, such as Art Tatum and Oscar Peterson, who liked to toy with the idiom—could play with terrifying speed and accuracy, summoning up instantaneous excitement in their audiences. But the problem was what to do next. Jazz piano music is enduring, and its tradition is long-lived because of its variety, subtlety, nuances, and shading. In these qualities, however, boogie-woogie is noticeably deficient.

The height of boogie-woogie's popularity was the period from 1935 to 1939, when Columbia Records producer John Hammond brought many of the top players to New York, recorded them, and put them on the concert stage. But the style had developed primarily in the early 1920's and had come into existence even before World War I in the music of Jimmy Yancey. Born in Chicago in 1894, Yancey was a self-taught pianist, singer, and tap dancer. He toured America and Europe with a vaudeville act and once gave a command performance in London for King George V. Later Yancey played blues piano at rent parties in Chicago and was greatly admired by the younger pianists in town. But he decided to leave the music business at the end of the war and thus had to wait until the boogie boom of the mid-thirties to record his music.

One of Yancey's better-known protégés was Clarence "Pinetop" Smith. Smith grew up in Birmingham, Alabama, and in his teens moved to Pittsburgh, where he performed as a pianist, dancer, and comedian in vaudeville. "Pinetop's Boogie-Woogie," recorded by Cleo Brown in 1935, was one of the genre's first hit records, although Smith had recorded it himself in 1928. Smith died in 1929, the victim of a brawl in Chicago's Masonic Hall. Charles "Cow Cow" Davenport was another early pianist who spent most of his professional life in Chicago. Starting out as a student of theology, he was thrown out of the seminary, the story goes, for playing ragtime piano. Davenport traveled the vaudeville circuit, composed "Cow Cow Boogie," along with several other songs, and formed a band called the Chicago Steppers. Unable to support himself, he dropped out of music in about 1935 and took up residence in Florida, where he worked under the Depression Works Progress Administration.

It was during the twenties in Chicago that two taxicab drivers, Albert Ammons and Meade Lux Lewis, set the stage for boogie-woogie's brief heyday. Inspired by Pinetop Smith, they soon began to dominate the rent parties. Lewis recorded sporadically during that period but then decided to give up professional playing. Ammons left Chicago to tour with his own band in the South and Midwest. But several years after Lewis had retired, John Hammond came across his 1929 recording of "Honky Tonk Train Blues," perceived, in its rumbling bass lines and simple bluesy melodic figures, the next musical fad, and soon rescued these legendary practitioners from obscurity.

After a determined search for the mysterious pianist Hammond finally located Meade Lux Lewis washing cars in a Chicago garage. Before long,

Lewis, Ammons, and the Kansas City boogie-woogie master Pete Johnson all were recording and performing in New York. They became major concert attractions and often performed together or with the blues singer Big Joe Turner. Jimmy Yancey was also brought with haste to New York, having been retrieved from Comisky Park, where he had been working for years as a groundskeeper for the Chicago White Sox.

Boogie-woogie's rolling rhythms, clever right-hand riffs, and frequent emotional climaxes then thrilled the public for about five years, during which time its stock-in-trade bass lines crept into the playing of Count Basie, Art Tatum, and countless others. The boogie beat, however, was not flexible enough for jazz musicians, nor did the style offer a sufficiently varied diet to its fans. By 1940 the public's fascination with boogie-woogie had disappeared as suddenly as it had arisen.

Modern Jazz Piano

Modern jazz piano began to emerge in the mid-1940's as a result of broad-based changes occurring throughout jazz. There is, of course, no fixed starting point for modernity. The changes were gradual, like the changes of an ocean tide, with waves overlapping one another and their waters inevitably mixing.

Until about 1940 the piano functioned supportively in big bands or as a solo instrument. Then, in the forties, the piano also became an effective ensemble, or small combo, instrument in an evolutionary step that led to considerably more interplay between the piano and the other instruments. Prior to that, small combo jazz had been foreshadowed by Teddy Wilson and the Benny Goodman Quartet of 1936 and to a greater degree by the Nat "King" Cole Trio of 1939. In Cole's group the bassist took over some of the chores of the pianist's left hand, giving rise to a transformation that was completed by modern ensemble pianists.

Unlike swing, modern jazz is intended for listening rather than for dancing. The music involves chord structures that use unusual intervals from the root tone of the chord, including "altered" tones such as flatted fifths and flatted ninths. The music's improvised lines are based on these chords and related chord progressions; and its fast-paced rhythmic pulse has an eighth-note (rather than quarter-note) feeling. Modern jazz acquired the onomatopoetic name "bebop," a word whose sound seemed to capture a typical melodic pattern in the players' repertoires.

The seeds of bebop were first sown in New York, and then nourished by certain historical events and individuals between 1939 and 1945.

One of the historical factors that encouraged the small combo format was the military draft, which thinned out the ranks of the big bands. Another was the 20 percent New York City cabaret tax on clubs that had floor shows or dancing. The added expense motivated nightclubs to furnish music that appealed to listeners—the more complex, intimate, and expressive music that jazz musicians had been working on since 1940 in their famous jam sessions at Minton's Playhouse in Harlem.

Central among the individuals who contributed to bebop was Charlie Parker, the alto saxophonist who started his professional career in the bands of pianists Jay McShann and Earl Hines. Parker's inspired melodic improvising— in which he used seldom-heard scale tones—suggested an entirely new set of harmonic changes. Pianists were soon trying to emulate Parker's innovative saxophone lines, which then led them to a new emphasis on fluency and dexterity in the right hand. The guitarist Charlie Christian provided a similar influence in the melodic arena, although his premature death in 1941 reduced his potential impact on other musicians. Thus in the modern era, the essence of the pianist's personality at the keyboard shifted from the left hand to the right.

The left hand became even less prominent in bebop combos as other instruments took over its functions. The bassist Jimmy Blanton, for example, whose duets with Ellington in 1940 were a high point of Duke's career as a pianist, was the first to begin to use the bass more melodically. The "walking" bass lines that grew out of Blanton's approach gave the pianist's left hand a respite from its rhythmic tasks. Modern drumming also took shape at Minton's in the early forties at the hands of Kenny Clarke, who kept the 4/4 feeling going on the ride cymbal with occasional accents (or bombs) on the bass drum and snare. Similarly, pianists began to accompany their own right-hand lines, as well as the horn soloists, with short, stabbing chords in the left hand. This abbreviated style of accompaniment became known as comping.

The first house pianist at Minton's was Thelonious Sphere Monk (1917–1982), who, through his composing and original harmonic ideas, contributed enormously to the development of modern jazz. Monk was an incomparable individualist. He was a self-taught pianist who played church organ in his youth and accompanied a gospel-singing evangelist in his teens. Except for his ballads, most of Monk's compositions are based on the twelve-bar blues. But unlike most blues-based tunes, they demand rhythmic and harmonic precision,

even down to the way each chord is structured (or voiced). Monk's compositions are intended not as songs or tunes, but as *pieces* to be rendered with
unerring accuracy.

After working at Minton's with Dizzy Gillespie, Kenny Clarke, Charlie
Christian, and dozens of other early beboppers, Monk went on the road briefly
with Lucky Millinder's big band in 1942. He made his recording debut with
saxophonist Coleman Hawkins in 1944 and there revealed his indebtedness to
stride pianist James P. Johnson. By the late forties Monk's piano playing had
become idiosyncratic and contrasted sharply with the qualities that typified
other pianists of the bebop years. While the others were imitating the flowing
lines of horn players, Monk played angular, sparse melodies punctuated by
dissonant minor seconds or "clusters" that defied normal chord structure. At a
time when virtuosity was being defined by the number of notes per measure a
pianist could articulate meaningfully, Monk pared down his improvisations to
bare bones and even used silence as a positive force in his music.

To many critics, listeners, and even musicians of the forties, Monk sounded
as if he could barely play the instrument. But in fact, he was using it to speak
his own incisive, abstract, and witty language. Monk was also unique in improvising thematically, making frequent references to the original melody line,
while other pianists tended to use the song material as a point of departure to
which they never returned.

Although musicians had recognized the importance of Monk's influence by
1950, the public's appreciation lagged behind. To make matters worse, he was
arrested in New York in 1951, and his cabaret card, a license to perform where
liquor was served, was revoked. Monk did not begin to receive the acclaim he
deserved until 1957, when he opened at the Five Spot Café in New York with
a quartet fronted by the saxophonist John Coltrane. Monk's captivating compositions and the highly personal keyboard idiom he had developed drew
waiting lines outside the club.

When playing solo, Monk retained the stride left hand of James P. Johnson, scattering the whole-tone-scale runs of Duke Ellington throughout his
playing. Monk's keyboard attack, however, had no precedent. He played with
flat, extended fingers, instead of in the accepted curved-finger position. And his
percussive technique knew no bounds, leading him on occasion to strike the
keys with his elbows. Despite these eccentricities, it was Monk who really used
the piano *pianistically*—as a percussion instrument—while his contemporaries
tried to imitate the flowing lines of the saxophone. Monk endured ridicule for
his technical quirks and for his habit of dancing around the piano while his
sidemen soloed. But criticism had no effect on him. He was an artist who

focused his attention on his own creative needs rather than on the reactions of his audience.

The influence of his music extended even beyond pianists to saxophonists like Coltrane and Eric Dolphy, to bassist and composer Charles Mingus, and to the drummer in Monk's early Blue Note band, Art Blakey. Among pianists, the traces of his style are clearly evident in his early protégé Bud Powell, who became the quintessential bop pianist. Elements of Monk's left-hand style were swallowed whole by Randy Weston * and Ran Blake.* Cecil Taylor's atonal clusters descend in part from Monk's dissonances in the right hand. Equally profound was Monk's impact as a composer. A partial list of his enduring compositions includes "Round Midnight," "Pannonica," "In Walked Bud," and "Straight, No Chaser."

Most bebop pianists crossed paths at some point with Charlie Parker and Dizzy Gillespie, either on the bandstand or in the recording studio. Among them, Clyde Hart was one of the first to free the left hand from striding and to imitate the phrasing of horns in the right hand. He worked with trumpeter Roy Eldridge and bassist Oscar Pettiford, two frequent participants in the Minton's jam sessions. Then, in 1944, Hart accompanied Parker and Gillespie on "Blue and Boogie" and "Groovin' High," which were generally regarded as the first mature bebop recordings. But Hart was dead within a year, at age thirty-five, of tuberculosis. The pianist Herbie Nichols (1919–1963), an early associate of Monk's, was one of the lesser-known early bop pianists. Nichols, however, became involved with some popular rhythm-and-blues bands during the forties and had few opportunities to display his abilities until he recorded for Blue Note in 1953.

Among the other prominent bebop pianists was Irving "Duke" Jordan, who had worked for saxophonist Coleman Hawkins and was leading his own trio at the Three Deuces when Charlie Parker heard him. Jordan played for Parker on and off between 1945 and 1948. Pianist Tadd Dameron, a composer and arranger, wrote for Gillespie's band and taught Parker some of the theory behind the chords Parker was using instinctively. George Wallington was a Sicilian-born New Yorker who played with Gillespie and drummer Max Roach in the Fifty-second Street clubs. Argonne Thornton, who changed his name in 1947 to Sadik Hakim, accompanied Parker on the recording of "KoKo," one of the saxophonist's crowning achievements of that period.

Michael "Dodo" Marmarosa was a talented melodic improviser who developed under the influence of clarinetist Buddy DeFranco, from 1940 to 1944. Joe Albany, another good melodic player, worked with Parker and trumpeter Howard McGhee in 1946 but soon afterward moved to Los Angeles, where he lived the life of a recluse. Lou Levy, a college-trained musician, accompanied the young Sarah Vaughan, who had recently debuted with the Earl Hines Band and subsequently recorded with Parker and Gillespie. During the fifties Levy gave up full-time playing for the advertising business. Finally, Billy Taylor,* who came to New York in 1942 with a music degree from Virginia State College, absorbed the influences of Tatum and Parker simultaneously and applied elements of both styles to the keyboard.

Further distancing their music from that of the big band era, the beboppers built an entirely new repertoire for themselves. Many of the new tunes were complex melodies that had been improvised on the blues and then codified. These tunes used the altered tones and unusual intervals that had become part of the jazz idiom. The altered tones were also incorporated into the pianists' harmonic vocabulary in "passing" and "substitution" chords.

Other bebop compositions were based on the chord progressions used in standard popular songs such as "Cherokee," "All the Things You Are," and "I Got Rhythm." According to one reckoning, there were more than three dozen bebop tunes that were based on the altered chords to "I Got Rhythm." At a jam session or club date, the leader might simply call out, "Rhythm changes," and a new tune would be born if the improvising was good enough.

The Paragon of Modern Piano

Bud Powell (1924–1966) seemed to epitomize everything jazz pianists were trying to achieve during the forties, although it should be pointed out that many of the pianists mentioned above had assimilated features of modern jazz at the same time he did, and in some cases before him. But Powell's passion, his energy, his flawless and fluid hornlike lines (when he was at his peak), and his overflowing imagination established him as the bop pianist par excellence. His influence on the pianists who followed him was profound.

Powell began studying piano at six years old and quickly developed an excellent technique by playing the European classics. At fifteen he was playing in his older brother's band and frequenting Minton's, and it was there that he met Monk, who took the talented, troubled youngster under his wing. Powell was impressed by the economy of notes in Monk's left hand and his use of harmony. Powell was also influenced by Art Tatum, and adopted Tatum's harmonic modulations on ballads.

Powell played with trumpeter Cootie Williams's band in 1944, with saxophonist Dexter Gordon in 1946, and with Parker in 1947 – the year in which his style began to coalesce. At the same time, however, Powell was fighting another battle that would dominate his life. His emotional problems, variously diagnosed as depression and schizophrenia, drove him to mental institutions several times between 1945 and 1955.

After nearly a year of hospitalization and several electroshock treatments in 1948, Powell emerged to find that he was looked to as a central figure of the new piano idiom. Powell was offered his own record dates on Blue Note and on Verve. His recordings between 1949 and 1953 reveal his astonishing reservoir of ideas and a precise, intuitively sensitive technique for executing them. Powell could make the piano wail with the nuances and inflections of a horn. His phrases would shift, twist, pause, and turn back on themselves rhythmically. Weaving in and out of chord progressions, Powell's lengthy lines were distinctly articulated, yet certain groups of notes seemed to melt together in a white-hot stream of sound. More than a few of these spontaneous lines evolved into lasting compositions, such as "Bouncing with Bud," "Dance of the Infidels," "Wail," "Tempus Fugue-It," "Celia," and "Hallucinations." Powell spent most of the sixties in Europe, where he hoped to escape the pressures at home, but his health remained fragile until the end.

The pianist Elmo Hope was one of Powell's close childhood friends. The two youngsters listened to classical records together, and their early musical development was parallel. In the midst of his career Hope (like Monk's friend and contemporary Herbie Nichols) became involved with rhythm-and-blues and curtailed his jazz playing for years. Later, however, he returned to jazz, working with trumpeter Clifford Brown (who later used Bud's younger brother, Richie, on piano) and saxophonist Sonny Rollins. While Hope's playing grew more personal and more harmonically sophisticated as the years progressed, he had chronic health problems that forced him into an early retirement. He died in Los Angeles in 1967.

There was a multitude of Powell-inspired pianists during the fifties, but there were also a few significant modernists who made their presence felt in the late forties. John Lewis,* encouraged by drummer Kenny Clarke to come to New York in 1945, worked as a pianist and arranger for the Dizzy Gillespie Big Band. In 1948 he accompanied Charlie Parker and the next year played on, and arranged for, Miles Davis's *Birth of the Cool* recording session. Lewis became well known for his role as the musical director of the Modern Jazz Quartet. Though influenced by Powell, Lewis tempers his emotional intensity with the discipline of European classical music, and compared to other pianists of the forties, his playing is more ordered, sedate, and restrained. With the MJQ, Lewis brought the piano into extraordinary interplay with Milt Jackson's vibes, using contrapuntal and fugal elements.

One of the mavericks of modern jazz piano was the impish, energetic, and imaginative Erroll Garner (1921–1977). Entirely self-taught, Garner never learned to read music. If Lewis was serious and genteel at the keyboard, Garner was a fun-loving ruffian. Born in Pittsburgh, Erroll was friendly with Billy Strayhorn and Dodo Marmarosa during his schooldays. In 1944 he moved to New York and played at many of the Fifty-second Street clubs. Although Garner's improvising and chord progressions were characteristic of the bebop era, his guitarlike left-hand chords, which fell evenly on all four beats of the measure, derived from the swing beat of bands like Count Basie's and, equally, from the regularity of stride. Garner's right hand always lagged slightly behind the beat, generating a delayed-action effect that set in motion two contrasting but delightfully compatible rhythmic patterns.

Garner would occasionally break up his "strummed" chords with crashing left-hand octaves and would vary his right-hand lines with tremolos and lush, rolling, romantic chords. And though most impressionistic pianists have a gentle touch, Garner was rough and percussive. No pianist is likely to have admired his technique, but many envied his witty and melodic improvising, which seemed to flow from a bottomless reservoir. Garner was extensively recorded from the late forties until his death. His increasingly pop-oriented repertoire earned him a following that spilled over the customary boundaries of the jazz audience, and in 1958, he wrote the hit song "Misty."

Lennie Tristano (1919–1978) was also a product of bebop who developed an intensely personal style—one that in many ways was the opposite of Garner's. Tristano was born in Chicago during an influenza epidemic, which presumably affected his eyesight. Though he was able to play piano by ear from the age of four, his deteriorating vision was an obstacle to formal musical training. By age ten, Lennie was blind, and his parents enrolled him in an institution where he spent the next decade of his life. Undaunted, he led a Dixieland band there and learned to play clarinet, piano, sax, and cello. Because of Lennie's obvious talent, the institution's visiting music teacher had him enrolled in Chicago's American Conservatory of Music, where he earned his degree in three years. Though Tristano composed in the European classical forms at the conservatory, he pursued jazz privately and, by the time of his graduation, was an accomplished pianist and sounded something like an amalgam of Hines and Tatum.

When Tristano moved to New York in 1946, he was swept up in the bebop movement and, like most young pianists, fell under the influence of Charlie Parker and Bud Powell. But Tristano had an intellectual and experimental streak that ran deep. Participating in his experiments were a coterie of followers who were in many respects his students. These included saxophonists Lee Konitz and Warne Marsh, guitarist Billy Bauer, and bassist Arnold Fishkin. With these men Tristano recorded "Intuition," an exercise in spontaneous, atonal, collective improvising that predated Ornette Coleman's more celebrated *Free Jazz* session by eleven years. Not surprisingly Tristano's playing had little commercial appeal, and few musicians were eager, or able, to work out these demanding concepts with him. Except for a few performances and a precious few recordings for Capitol and Atlantic, Tristano's career was devoted to teaching.

Tristano continued to grow as a pianist. The independence of his hands was his technical forte. He sometimes played in different time signatures with each hand, and while most pianists grouped notes in triplets or fours or sixes in their melodic lines, Lennie used groups of five, nine, or eleven notes. He tended to play a "walking" bass line in the left hand, but when he used chords, they were dense and abundant with colorful tones. Tristano was also the first musician to overdub, or record a second piano part on top of his first, when he recorded "Turkish Mambo" and "Requiem" for Atlantic in 1955. Though Tristano was usually a "cool" or even cerebral pianist, he could also play with great warmth and could swing, as in "Line Up," and play a poignant blues, such as "Requiem," a piece he improvised for Charlie Parker's funeral.

Two other players who appeared during the late forties, Jimmy Jones and Ellis Larkins, were known for their harmonic originality. Jimmy Jones, who was Sarah Vaughan's accompanist from 1947 to 1952, was never well known because he almost never soloed. Single-note lines, which were the essence of solos in those years, interested him little, compared with the structure of chords. Jones also had a very gentle touch which made him, along with Jimmy Rowles,* one of the superb natural accompanists for jazz singers. Ellis Larkins, who grew up in Baltimore, was trained in the classics at the Peabody Conservatory and the Juilliard School of Music. He was prominent as a Tatum-inspired soloist and accompanist in the New York clubs of the forties and fifties. Larkins's style was delicate, subtle, and harmonically rich, and like Jones he was compatible with modern jazz but did not subscribe to its linear, melodic bias.

The Funky Fifties: Hot and Cold

The piano enjoyed a prominence in jazz of the 1950's that it would not see again until the early 1970's. During the previous decade the bebop pianists, except for the passionate Powell, had been eclipsed from public view by the attention lavished upon trumpeters and saxophonists. The spectacular accomplishments of Parker and Gillespie, especially, focused the limelight on the band's front line. In the fifties, however, even the great horn stylists—trumpeters Miles Davis and Clifford Brown, saxophonists Sonny Rollins, Sonny Stitt, and a blossoming John Coltrane—had to share center stage with piano players, many of whom led bands themselves.

There was very little solo piano performed in this decade, except for the prodigious Art Tatum, who was creating a legacy of masterpieces on recording tape in the studios of producer Norman Granz. Some of the great pianos of past years were temporarily silent: Earl Hines was living in semiretirement in Oakland, California, and Teddy Wilson was teaching (when he was not confined to a functional role in the CBS radio studio orchestra in New York). By the mid-fifties Bud Powell's mental problems had reduced his performances to substandard and sometimes took him out of action altogether. Although there were still soloists who played "intermission piano" in small clubs and in after-hours settings, the art of soloing was to remain relatively dormant for some time.

There was, however, a crop of pianists who reached maturity in the fifties and carved out a new and prominent role for their instrument. Many of them led trios. At first the favored combination was piano, bass, and guitar, a light, fast unit popularized by the King Cole Trio and, a few years later, by Art Tatum's group. The bass, of course, was a potent extension of the pianist's left hand, and so was the guitar in that it could provide harmonic changes. Before long, the drums replaced the guitar, giving the pianist a stronger rhythmic background and more freedom in selecting harmonies. The left hand's comping replaced the guitar chords. As ensemble soloists, the pianists who played in, or led, quartets and quintets were more articulate than before, thanks to the liberation of the right hand that had taken place during the forties.

During the 1950's modern jazz splintered into stylistic camps that can be divided rather roughly into the hot and the cool. The cool side of jazz found expression in an orchestrated approach that often used European principles of composition and instrumentation. This trend grew into the progressive and third stream movements, which attempted to fuse jazz with modern classical music. Cool jazz also included the relaxed and sometimes genteel improvisational form that was developed by West Coast musicians (or at least easterners who had migrated to California). On the East Coast the musicians gravitated to a hotter style, exploiting the rhythmically aggressive, blues-based elements of bebop. This style became known as hard bop, probably for its rhythmic drive. Rather than looking to Europe for inspiration, the pianists in the hard bop style drew upon the Afro-American reservoirs of blues, soul, and gospel music. Although the boundaries between hot and cool jazz are often vague, and were easily crossed by many players, the distinction will help clarify certain important differences among pianists of the fifties.

The first of the noteworthy postbebop players were George Shearing * and Dave Brubeck,* each of whom made his name as the leader of a small combo. Shearing, who had emigrated from England in the forties, was primarily a stride pianist when he arrived. He was modernized in part, however, by listening to Bud Powell and working with clarinetist Buddy DeFranco. Shearing grew into a melodic, tasteful, single-note improviser, but his most distinctive sound was a result of his adaptation of Milt Buckner's locked-hands style to the playing of medium tempo ballads. A sweet and gentle player, Shearing inclined toward the values of cool and West Coast jazz.

Brubeck, on the other hand, was a paradigm of the cool pianist. Through studying composition with the composer Darius Milhaud, he enriched his harmonies with polytonal chords (chords involving more than one tonal or key center). He also developed a very early interest in exploring alternative rhythms and meters during his first recording period in 1949. Brubeck was in some ways an anachronism. In finger dexterity and melodic improvising, he lagged behind the standards of his contemporaries, but in using the harmonic discoveries of modern European composers, he was ahead of his time. The Dave Brubeck Quartet, featuring the cool saxophonist Paul Desmond, was the source of his extraordinary popularity during the fifties.

In retrospect, it is clear that jazz piano of the early fifties was one of the tributaries that flowed into the third stream later in that decade. At the time of Brubeck's emergence, for example, the disciplined music of John Lewis was being nourished by the fertile milieu of the Modern Jazz Quartet. Although Lewis was more closely aligned with the Powell-style players than Brubeck was, these men both had an affinity for the European compositional approach. It was at about this time that Lennie Tristano opened his studio in New York and began teaching and that the band of pianist Stan Kenton (1912–1979), which had been a hard-swinging unit in the forties, was expanded to forty members in an ambitious attempt to mix classical and jazz ideas.

The antithesis of this European bias was the driving, blues-based style of hard bop. The most influential pianist of soul jazz, as it was then known, was Horace Silver.* Other pianists began to notice Silver in 1954, when he joined the powerful drummer Art Blakey in a band that was later known as the Jazz Messengers. Silver formed his own quintet the following year. Beyond his prolific composing, Silver showed pianists that bebop could be simplified by a deeper commitment to the blues and that good melodic improvising could aim at funkiness rather than at complexity. He also proved that pianists could fire up a band with aggressive, percussive comping. His own comping, which borrowed its propulsive momentum from gospel music and rhythm-and-blues, was often more exciting than the solo he was accompanying.

There were other pianists who excelled at transforming the tortuous improvised lines of bebop into sharp-edged, blues-based lines. Red Garland,* who worked with the Miles Davis Quintet from 1956 to 1958, improvised lines that, while they were not as Spartan as Silver's, were less complex than Powell's. He also added thick, assertive block chords, derivative of Buckner's locked-hands technique, to the hard bop repertoire. Bobby Timmons (1935–1974) elevated block chords to a stylistic high point in solos that also echoed the gospel music of the black church. Timmons came to be known for his playing in the Jazz Messengers and in the Cannonball Adderley Quintet. His composition "Moanin' " became a jazz standard, and his "Dis Here" and "Dat Dere" helped popularize the Adderley quintet in the early sixties. Wynton Kelly (1931–1971) also belongs in this group of hard bop pianists, although his playing was quieter and more elegant. He is best known for his work with the Davis quintet in 1959 and, during the 1960's, with guitarist Wes Montgomery. Ray Bryant (1931–) is another prominent soul jazz artist, who worked during the fifties with various bands and has since led his own trio and performed as a soloist.

There was also a more popular side to the soul jazz piano style that involved the overt use of gospel and rhythm-and-blues elements. Singer Ray Charles (1932–), who accompanied himself on piano, is the most prominent example. Although Charles is famous for his uniquely resonant voice and his emotion-packed vocals of the late fifties, he began his career as a trio pianist influenced by Tatum, Powell, and Nat Cole. Ray Charles helped provide the impetus for a bluesy, funky brand of jazz piano that was destined for wide public appeal. Jimmy Smith (1925–), originally a pianist, took up Hammond organ in the early fifties. After forming his own trio in 1955, his soulful and articulate improvising, which borrowed conspicuously from rhythm-and-blues, electrified both jazz and popular audiences. Shirley Scott (1934–), another organist, based her hard-swinging approach to the instrument largely on Smith's, as did Richard "Groove" Holmes (1931–). Not since Fats Waller had there been pianists like Smith, Scott, and Holmes, who transferred their fluent techniques to the keys, stops, and foot pedals of the organ.

Other pianists, such as Ramsey Lewis * and, beginning in 1960, Les McCann (1935–), also used their jazz backgrounds in a funky, rhythmic brand of piano. And Mose Allison (1927–), heavily indebted to boogie-woogie pianists like Albert Ammons and Freddie Slack, played a mixture of bebop and blues that served as the background for his witty, satirical vocals.

From Funk to Finesse

Although most jazz pianists were affected to some extent by hard bop's affinity for the blues, the values of subtlety, technique, and harmonic sophistication found very worthy champions. Oscar Peterson * and Ahmad Jamal * patterned their trios in the early fifties after the piano/bass/guitar combos of Nat "King" Cole and Art Tatum. By the mid-fifties they had replaced their guitarists with drummers in keeping with the growing preference for more strongly felt rhythms, and Peterson, who represented a hybrid of the Tatum and Powell styles, had inherited Tatum's status as jazz's leading virtuoso. Though he occasionally displayed more technique than imagination, most of the time Peterson's music was harmonically rich, clean, and swinging. His unmatched dexterity unleashed all the rhythmic potency inherent in the hard bop rhythm section. By contrast, Jamal, a more delicate player than Peterson, taught pianists the value of understatement. Poignant silences became part of the Jamal aesthetic. His playing was light, tasteful, and unhurried. Despite a strong following among musicians in the early fifties, Jamal was not widely known until about 1958, when he recorded the much-admired *Live: At the Pershing*.

For a short time, Phineas Newborn, Jr. (1931–) approximated the style of Oscar Peterson and even rivaled him technically. From 1956 to 1958 Newborn was lauded for his flawless execution at breakneck tempos, although he did not have the warmth of touch or emotional range of Peterson. Unfortunately Newborn's career was cut short after 1960 by illness. Hampton Hawes (1928– 1978) also played in the Powell and Peterson tradition, especially in his use of harmony. But with his background in the black church, Hawes injected the echoes of blues, spirituals, and gospel music into hard bop. His penchant for a funkier style of hard bop piano was partly inspired by the Los Angeles-based Carl Perkins (1928–1958).

From the late forties into the sixties the city of Detroit produced a succession of pianists that shared an affinity for both Powell and Tatum. Hank Jones (1918–), Barry Harris (1929–), Tommy Flanagan (1930–), and Roland Hanna (1932–) have all been known for tasteful accompaniment and the sophisticated use of modern jazz elements in their soloing and trio works.

Some of the new pianists of the fifties adhered more closely to traditional piano styles. Marian McPartland,* who had emigrated from England in 1946, is the most eclectic of them. While she has continued to absorb the evolving piano styles, the continuity of tradition is always reflected in her own work. Dave McKenna (1930–), another traditionalist, started out as a big band pianist working for Woody Herman, Charlie Ventura, and Gene Krupa. But McKenna's real talents lie in solo performing, where he elicits compelling momentum with a strutting single-note bass line. McKenna's recordings of the late seventies have finally brought his self-sufficient playing the attention it deserves.

Radical Revisions

Around 1960 there were some radically new approaches to playing jazz that affected the piano and, briefly, even threatened its role in small combos. These changes were foreshadowed by experiments with pianoless groups that began in 1952 with the Gerry Mulligan/Chet Baker Quartet. This group caused a small sensation with its open, free-sounding instrumentation and Mulligan's artful arranging. Then, in 1957, tenor saxophonist Sonny Rollins performed at the Village Vanguard in New York with only drums and bass. Rollins's improvised lines were sufficient to establish a harmonic framework, leaving the rhythm and melody more exposed. These events, however, were isolated precursors of a more sweeping revelation that was brought into focus by a controversial Texas-born alto saxophonist, Ornette Coleman.

Ornette Coleman had a pervasive and far-reaching impact on jazz. His quartet's performances at the Five Spot Café in New York in 1959 caused a shock wave that shook jazz to its foundations. Coleman's approach to improvising was to play without prior commitment to specific chord changes. His band, which included trumpet, bass, and drums, also took license with meter, pitch, and tempo. And the piano was rigorously excluded as if it were an obstacle in the way of freeing the group from harmonic preconditions.

The immediate result of severing the improviser's link to chord changes was an emphasis on melodic content and spontaneity, the same values being sought at that time by Miles Davis, John Coltrane, and Charles Mingus in the form of improvising on modes. Basically, modes are scale patterns upon which various melodic lines can be built. Although jazz musicians experimented with new combinations of modes, they did not invent them. Modes actually predated the invention of the piano by centuries. There were many musicians who took an active interest in developing the existing modes as vehicles for improvisation. Coleman and the other "free" jazz players of the avant-garde realized at that point that without chord changes the improviser had more freedom to invent melodic lines.

Pianists were among those working with modes during the late fifties. The pianist and composer George Russell (1923-) had been working since the forties on his *Lydian Concept of Tonal Organization.* He argued in a published thesis that the Lydian mode was the one used most frequently in jazz and that by exploring it chromatically (using each of the twelve tones in an octave), improvisers could expand upon the melodic possibilities that were open to them. In the experimental climate of the early sixties Russell had the opportunity to try out his methods and his intriguing compositions in recording sessions that included the imaginative saxophonist Eric Dolphy. As the popularity of jazz waned later in the decade, Russell moved to Scandinavia, where he devoted himself to composing and teaching.

One of the foremost students of modal improvising was Bill Evans,* who had worked with Russell in Chicago in the late forties. No pianist since Bud Powell has had as great an impact on his colleagues. Evans was a sensitive, self-critical pianist, schooled in the European classics. He meticulously analyzed the theoretical basis of whatever he heard and played, whether it was Bach or Bud Powell. Evans also set new standards for touch, harmonic richness, and the potential for interplay between piano, bass, and drums. Evans contributed both conceptually and as a pianist to the Miles Davis recording session that produced the LP *Kind of Blue,* a triumphant proof that there was a bright future for improvising on modes instead of on chord changes.

The adventurous Canadian-born Paul Bley,* who had hired Ornette Coleman in Los Angeles in 1958 (before Coleman formed his own pianoless group) was another early modal explorer. As one of the first to recognize the importance of Coleman's ideas, Bley learned how to let go of preset chord changes and generally how to apply Coleman's free approach to the keyboard. In so doing, he influenced many younger pianists, most notably Keith Jarrett. Mal Waldron (1926–) became involved with modal ideas as early as 1956 as part of Charles Mingus's jazz workshops and was the pianist on the recording of "Pithecanthropus Erectus"–one of the first improvised pieces to employ modes, free passages, and atonality. Later in the fifties Waldron became Billie Holiday's accompanist, but he returned to a freer style in the sixties with Eric Dolphy's bands and as an expatriate soloist living in Munich.

McCoy Tyner * applied modal concepts to the keyboard as a member of the John Coltrane Quartet from 1960 until 1965. Inspired by Coltrane's brilliant use of alternative scales built on unusual modes, Tyner cultivated the use of harmonies built on intervals of a fourth, clusters of notes, and pedal point (a continuous root tone in the bass register). Tyner went on to become an even more influential pianist during the 1970's, when he expanded his harmonic ideas and employed a highly percussive technique in a style more dense and intense than he had been capable of during the Coltrane years.

Alice McLeod Coltrane (1937–), who married John Coltrane in 1963, became the quartet's pianist in 1966. Since her husband's death in 1967, Alice Coltrane has continued to explore new modes, many of which are derived from Indian music. Originally influenced by Bud Powell, she has an active and intensely melodic right hand, and her left hand plays strong chords and a droning pedal point. In the seventies she also began to improvise on the Wurlitzer organ in a searching, mystical style that radically departs from Jimmy Smith's use of the instrument in the sixties. Steve Kuhn * is another pianist who was touched directly by Coltrane, at least for a few months in 1960, when he preceded McCoy Tyner in the quartet. Kuhn, who worked for trumpeters Art Farmer and Kenny Dorham before moving to Scandinavia in 1967, excels at producing a singing, dramatic tone from the piano. He has led several bands since the late seventies, when he returned to New York.

Herbie Hancock,* who was influenced by both Tyner and Evans, joined the Miles Davis Quintet in 1962. A talented composer, Hancock wrote a number of mode-based pieces that have since become jazz classics. Like Horace Silver, Hancock proved that accompaniment could be as vital to pianists as the ability to solo. As part of the rhythm section, he used harmony in a personal way and, inspired by Tony Williams's drumming, learned to accent creatively with chords, giving each measure a powerful thrust. As will be noted in Part Two, during the 1970's Hancock was involved in exploring the use of electronic keyboards, especially synthesizers, in a style heavily influenced by rhythm-and-blues.

Beyond Modality

While Ornette Coleman's innovations in ensemble playing involved bypassing the piano altogether, the bold ideas of Cecil Taylor * were augmenting the notion of the piano's role and the kinds of sounds it could produce. In the Cecil Taylor Unit, Taylor brought the piano into full, improvisational dialogue with the other instruments, expanding its traditional functions as either an accompanying or a solo instrument. Influenced equally by modern European classical composition and by Ellington and Monk, Taylor explored atonal ideas within "constructivist" compositions that, while carefully planned, left room for spontaneity. Rhythmically he used the piano to create waves of motion, instead of the customary swing beat that characterizes most modern jazz. Like Bill Evans (and despite their contrasting aesthetic preferences), Taylor demonstrated that pianists could work with "texture" as well as with melody, harmony, and rhythm, and by the 1970s he had become a soloist with a percussive keyboard approach of pyrotechnical proportions. Atonal clusters exploded off the sounding board with the frequency of single notes, and the piano had achieved a new level—unnerving at times—of emotional intensity.

Sun Ra * was another pianist and bandleader whose bold innovations began to coalesce during the 1960's. Though personally attached to the stride and swing styles, Sun Ra used his band as a laboratory for experiments in free jazz. During the seventies he experimented with electronic keyboards and highly unorthodox ways of playing them. Ran Blake,* one of the foremost proponents of third stream music, also has an affinity for traditional styles. Blake's style is influenced by sources as diverse as Monk and Greek music, and his trademarks are economy of expression and humor.

Not all the sixties pianists were immersed in experimentation and modal playing. Many relied primarily on the bebop tradition, while they incorporated new harmonic ideas and a greater sense of interaction among piano, bass, and drums into their styles. Soloing was still a thing of the past, except for unheralded "cocktail" jobs, the same species of work that had been termed intermission piano during the forties. As in the bebop years, jazz pianists felt they belonged in bands.

Jaki Byard * worked with bassist Charles Mingus's groups for most of the sixties and has grown increasingly eclectic over the years. He reflects, in his own work, the continuity of the jazz piano tradition. By continuing to solo in the cocktail lounges around New York, Byard helped keep other pianists aware of the instrument's soloing potential. Toshiko Akiyoshi,* who emigrated from Japan in 1956, was influenced primarily by Bud Powell. During the seventies she contributed to jazz by composing and arranging for her own big band, into which she integrated Japanese instruments and a supportive piano accompaniment. Josef Zawinul * arrived in the United States in 1959 from Austria and quickly established himself as a soulful and original pianist and composer in the Cannonball Adderley Quintet. Zawinul's career evolved dramatically when he discovered electronic keyboards and cofounded the fusion band Weather Report.

Cedar Walton (1934–), who worked with Art Blakey's Jazz Messengers and led several of his own quartets, plays with exceptional rhythmic drive. Walton experimented with electronic keyboards and rhythm-and-blues during the mid-1970's but soon returned to the acoustic piano and the bebop tradition. Stanley Cowell (1941–) expresses the influence of stylists from Art Tatum to Cecil Taylor. Displaying taste and musicianship across the spectrum of styles at his command, Cowell seems most at home in the swinging, hard bop idiom. Kenny Barron (1943–) worked for years with trumpeters Dizzy Gillespie and Freddie Hubbard. He became less active as a player after joining the faculty of Rutgers University in New Jersey in 1973 but returned to performing in the late 1970's. During the late sixties George Cables (1944–) worked with saxophonists Sonny Rollins and Joe Henderson. A sensitive player who can respond to a variety of moods, Cables was in demand as an accompanist throughout the seventies.

Plugging into a New World

By 1973 the keyboard had become a focal point for some stylistic changes that were taking place in jazz. Pianists captured the public's enthusiasm even more than they had in the glorious stride era. There were two reasons for the attention. The first—though not the most enduring—was the consequence of electronic keyboards and the spectacular popularity of rock and roll.

Rock and roll so dominated the sixties that many jazz pianists, in order to make a living, had to play commercial music, flee to Europe, or quit music altogether. Among its multiple effects, rock was responsible for popularizing electronic instruments. Electric guitars, which had been used in jazz since the thirties, were advantageous to rock musicians because they could be amplified, a distinct advantage in performing for the enormous rock and roll crowds.

They were also easier to play than acoustic guitars, which required greater finger pressure and control.

Electric pianos followed swiftly in the wake of electric guitar mania. Ray Charles traveled with a Wurlizter electric in the mid-sixties, and in 1967 Josef Zawinul played the Wurlitzer on a hit recording of his song "Mercy, Mercy, Mercy," by the Cannonball Adderley Quintet. Sun Ra also experimented with electric pianos and organs during the sixties. Pianists began to take the electric keyboard more seriously in 1968, when Miles Davis insisted that Chick Corea,* Herbie Hancock, and Josef Zawinul use this new "toy" (as it was dismissed by most pianists) on the albums *In a Silent Way* and *Miles in the Sky* and in concert on the road. When Davis used the electric piano again in 1969 on the immensely popular and controversial jazz–rock album *Bitches Brew,* the instrument attracted some very vocal partisans and critics. By 1970 portable electric keyboards, sitting on their own amplifiers or plugged into external speakers, were commonplace, and the brand names of Fender Rhodes, Wurlitzer, and RMI were suddenly upstaging Steinway and Baldwin.

The electric keyboard was popular for a variety of reasons. The sound itself was novel and easily amplified, making the instrument ideal for the jazz–rock style. It also offered an alternative to the unpredictable quality of the pianos a musician would encounter on the road. Despite its limited touch control and, consequently, expressiveness, the electric was an insurance policy against the legendary battered, out-of-tune upright with its sprinkling of unplayable keys. And, as with the guitar, the electric keyboard made it easier to play loud and fast.

Electric pianos were only the beginning of the proliferation of electronic keyboards that would come into use in the seventies. Synthesizers–keyboards that could be instructed (or programmed) to produce electronically (or synthesize) a variety of sounds, to "bend" and alter pitches, and even to repeat, sequence, or echo those sounds automatically–were the next to be introduced. The first synthesizers were built in the early 1960's for use in composed electronic music. Their size and cost were prohibitive for improvising musicians. But by 1968 technology had advanced sufficiently for Paul Bley and vocalist Annette Peacock to perform a synthesizer concert at Town Hall in New York City. The next year Herbie Hancock was experimenting with synthesizers under the guidance of Patrick Gleeson, a San Francisco pianist and producer who is conversant with electronics. Denny Zeitlin (1938–), who had a dual career as a pianist and psychiatrist during the sixties, abandoned the piano completely (although he later returned to it) for electronic music. The synthesizer offered the pianist a new palette of tonal colors and the opportunity to bend pitches in imitations of horns, bass, and guitar. The keyboardist could also create totally new instrumental sounds by reprogramming the synthesizer—opportunities that could not be ignored by a music as eclectic and experimental as jazz.

During the seventies many jazz pianists began to call themselves keyboardists or even multikeyboardists to call attention to their new tools. Herbie Hancock, for one, used a variety of synthesizers with a new funky band, The Headhunters, as well as keyboards like the ARP String Ensemble to provide simulated backgrounds. Jan Hammer (1948-) enhanced the mystical quality of the Mahavishnu Orchestra with his adroit use of synthesizers in tandem with John McLaughlin's guitar lines and Jerry Goodman's violin. Chick Corea, whose important role as a solo pianist will be discussed later, played electric piano and synthesizer in his popular jazz-rock band Return to Forever. George Duke (1946-) took up synthesizers when he joined Frank Zappa's rock band, Mothers of Invention, and he returned to jazz in about 1973 with a mastery of multiple electronic keyboards. After working with Cannonball Adderley and accompanying singer Flora Purim, Duke led a fusion band with drummer Billy Cobham.

In the meantime, synthesizers had metamorphosed from monophonic instruments, capable of playing one note at a time, into polyphonic instruments, capable of playing up to sixteen different notes simultaneously. If the piano was a one-man band, the synthesizer had the potential to be a one-man orchestra. Josef Zawinul, co-leader of Weather Report, integrated the orchestral dimension of synthesizers into jazz in a more systematic way than most keyboardists by composing scores that notated each synthesizer voice. By comparison, Hancock emphasized the synthesizer's rhythmic potential; and Corea, its melodic and pitch-bending capabilities. Significantly there was no one who developed the synthesizer—or even a bank of synthesizers—as a self-sufficient solo instrument. The technology was there, at least judging by successful recorded performances in nonimprovised music, such as Walter Carlos's *Switched-On Bach* and Patrick Gleeson's adaptation of Gustav Holst's *The Planets*.

The new class of keyboardists were angrily denounced in some quarters for abandoning the purity of the piano for the commercial appeal of rock, soul, and funk. To be sure, using electric keyboards in the fusion style had commercial benefits, but there were other reasons for using them. As noted above, the eclectic, experimental, and creative nature of jazz demanded that the potentials of these new keyboards be explored. Ultimately, however, they made little difference to the way jazz (or the piano) was played. Like the electric piano and organ, the mighty synthesizer appears destined for a minor, supporting role in the unfolding drama of jazz.

The Piano, Center Stage

The second reason for the renaissance in jazz piano during the seventies was the bold return by postbebop players to the solo tradition. (The notoriety brought to the jazz pianists by the multikeyboard phenomenon was, in this case, a great asset.) The revitalized solo piano presupposed the rhythmic and harmonic freedom inaugurated in the work of Ornette Coleman, Cecil Taylor, and those who followed similar paths. Thus, by the mid-1970's there were many pianists who could play effectively alone, yet without the rhythmic left-hand stride and preordained harmonic patterns that their predecessors had relied upon. Although Coleman's free-form groups had dispensed with the piano, and perhaps, in that way, called its worth into question, the piano ultimately adapted magnificently to the assumptions, techniques, and spontaneity inherent in avant-garde jazz.

The pianists began building on experiments in free jazz in diverse ways. They alluded more frequently and more conspicuously to modern European music, probably because of their higher level of academic training. In some cases these pianists' left hands adopted the even, pulselike rendering of chords that typifies European music. Others continued to develop a polyrhythmic feeling. Almost every pianist grew more sophisticated in the use of harmony, modes, and atonality. Chick Corea and Keith Jarrett,* among the first of the new generation to attempt free-form soloing, demonstrated how intimately the European traditions can be integrated into jazz piano. Corea, who had extensive classical training, has played virtually every type of jazz and excels at the driving hard bop and modal styles of the fifties and sixties. At the outset of the seventies he was part a group called Circle, which experimented with free, collective improvisation, and he applied that experience to spontaneous solo playing in 1971. His *Piano Improvisations, Vol. I* was a series of open-ended compositions that recalled strains of Ravel, Debussy, Bartók, and Spanish flamenco music, along with jazz. His keen melodic gift and crisp technique made this recording a memorable and influential event.

Keith Jarrett had less formal training than Corea, but his soloing makes it obvious that he has an intimate knowledge of keyboard literature, from Bach to Charles Ives. Jarrett started out working with his own quartet, whose music was based on Coleman's innovations and in fact included two former Coleman sidemen—bassist Charlie Haden and saxophonist Dewey Redman. Like Corea, Jarrett tended to swing much harder with a group than when playing alone. Jarrett took up the challenge of soloing in 1972 with the album *Facing You,* but he found his style in *Concerts: Bremen/Lausanne* of 1973 and *The Köln Concert* of 1975. The last, a three-record set, sold more than a quarter of a million copies, disproving the theory that to play solo piano is to fight a losing commercial battle. The most striking aspect of Jarrett is that he plays with total spontaneity, an attribute frequently alluded to and admired by other pianists. He develops his themes gradually and at length—up to forty-five minutes of playing. As in Cecil Taylor's soloing during the seventies, it becomes clear, when Jarrett plays, that the piano can afford a broader canvas than the thirty-two-bar ballad or the twelve-bar blues.

At the same time other pianists were moving toward a more aggressive, propulsive, and harmonically dense kind of music, a style closer to jazz's African, rather than its European, elements. McCoy Tyner in his *Echoes of a Friend,* recorded in 1973, and Cecil Taylor in his *Silent Tongues,* from 1974, created self-sufficient masterpieces. Their originality is partly the consequence of their explosively percussive attack and articulation. Their hard-hitting but precise technique can be traced back to the more primitive percussive styles of James P. Johnson, Ellington, and Monk. Although they had been important innovators during the fifties and sixties, these pianists returned in more advanced incarnations in the 1970's. Also belonging to this group is Muhal Richard Abrams (1930–), an influential composer among the avant-garde musicians of Chicago. Falling somewhere between James P. Johnson and Cecil Taylor in style (but with a greater economy of notes), Abrams compresses both contemporary and traditional ideas into lean, elegant pieces. After years of obscurity Abrams was encouraged to perform and record in the seventies by the increased level of interest in jazz and in the piano.

The seventies was a golden decade for jazz piano. There were pianists active from virtually every era of the instrument's history, including Eubie Blake, Earl Hines, Dave Brubeck, Oscar Peterson, Red Garland, and Bill Evans. Pianists were increasingly aware of each other and their shared heritage, thanks in part to trade publications like *Down Beat,* the perennial jazz magazine, and *Keyboard,* which began publication in 1975 and whose interviews with major keyboardists helped reveal the strong ties of influence and inspiration among them.

The public's receptivity to jazz piano during the seventies gave several scarcely known pianists the chance they needed. Vincente "Tete" Montoliu, a

Spaniard, blind from birth, had been trained as a classical artist, but devoted himself to jazz after hearing Duke Ellington's music. He studied in Spain with saxophonist Don Byas and worked with American musicians such as saxophonists Roland Kirk and Archie Shepp, when they were on tour in Europe. Montoliu has a command of the piano tradition from Tatum to Cecil Taylor, and he uses rich harmonies and supple, graceful right-hand lines in his improvisation. Joanne Brackeen (1938-) is a self-taught pianist whose training consisted primarily of transcribing jazz piano from records. She grew up in Los Angeles, where she was influenced early in her career by the ideas of Ornette Coleman. In 1959 she worked with Dexter Gordon, Harold Land, and Charles Lloyd. Then, in the sixties, she married saxophonist Charles Brackeen and devoted most of her time to rearing their four children. She returned to full-time playing in 1970 to join Art Blakey's Jazz Messengers, then formed her own trio in 1977 and blossomed into an intense, articulate pianist drawing upon an abundant reservoir of harmonic and modal ideas.

Richie Beirach (1947-) and Jessica Williams (1948-) are two of the individualists whose styles evolved after 1970. A graduate of the Manhattan School of Music, Beirach was thoroughly schooled in classical literature, theory, and composition. A product of the introspective, intellectual piano tradition exemplified by Lennie Tristano, Bill Evans, and Paul Bley, Beirach is a sensitive, subtle player who uses gradually shifting harmonies and tonal variations. Though he can play in a more outgoing, swinging style, his solo album *Hubris,* recorded in 1977, shows a distinct preference for the evenly played left hand of the European tradition. Williams, who studied at the Peabody Conservatory in Baltimore from age nine to seventeen, acquired a commanding technique through her studies with the highly respected piano teacher Richard Aitken. Beginning with Dave Brubeck, Williams incorporated into her training a serious study of jazz pianists from Art Tatum to Cecil Taylor. Williams spent the seventies playing organ and electronic keyboards, flirting with jazz–rock, and soloing along the lines of the open-ended improvising introduced by Corea and Jarrett. But in 1981 Williams proved she had reinterpreted the piano tradition on her own terms in a hard-driving quintet album of original compositions, *Orgonomic Music.* She is a powerful soloist with a crisp, percussive technique and an incisive melodic imagination.

If there is a new strain to be heard in jazz piano during the 1980's, it comes from Anthony Davis (1952-). The son of a professor of English and African studies, Anthony grew up in a university environment, where he had extensive academic training in piano and composition. He sees himself in the tradition of Scott Joplin, Jelly Roll Morton, Duke Ellington, and Thelonious Monk–

men whose primary contributions to jazz were through their work as composers. His music is typically written for piano, violin, cello, tuba, trombone,
saxophones, vibes, and trap drums. His compositions reveal the strong influence of modern European composers and, equally, of the droning and percussive ensembles (or gamelans) of Java and Bali. But on his album *Episteme,* his
most representative work, Davis builds in the opportunity for improvising, for
vocalized intonation of the wind instruments, and for polyrhythmic drumming that, unarguably, swings. While Davis has not yet condensed this synthesis into an organic, unified keyboard idiom, the elements are there, and its
potential exciting to contemplate.

Looking Back

The foregoing survey has presented the jazz piano tradition in broad brush
strokes. It is a map with important landmarks and paths pointed out along the
way but is certainly not intended as a substitute for examining the jazz piano
terrain in its myriad details. Some generalizations, however, can be made about
the population of this territory. First, although jazz pianists are individualists,
they share an underlying heritage, or tradition, and react to, reinterpret, and, in
the case of major artists, build upon their inheritance. Because the pianists
listen to each other so readily, the lines of influence one might draw between
them are not necessarily chronological; indeed, these lines are apt to zigzag and
crisscross, irrespective of style and age-group. Secondly, jazz pianists are eclectic, even more so than other instrumentalists. Because the piano incorporates
rhythm, harmony, and melody, its capacity to adapt to extrinsic musical influences is virtually limitless. Consequently, trends occurring in piano are indica-
tors of what is going on elsewhere in jazz. Thirdly, piano style is intimately
related to keyboard technique, for the simple reason that the instrument's
sound varies dramatically with each pianist's touch. And finally, because it is
such a sensitive, expressive, and capable medium for the improviser, the piano
becomes a different instrument in every jazz pianist's hands. That, perhaps, is
its most intriguing and exciting quality.

PART · TWO

THEODORE
"TEDDY"
WILSON

November 24, 1912— July 31, 1986

Teddy Wilson's contribution to jazz piano has long been a matter of history. Though he was neither as popular nor as flamboyant as some of his colleagues—such as Benny Goodman and Lionel Hampton—Wilson's fleet, complex, and structurally perfect solos broadened and refined the sensibilities of most of the pianists who followed him.

The interview shows Wilson to have a keen historical sense. We had two conversations: one between sets in the basement of a jazz club long since dark—El Matador on Broadway in San Francisco—and the other in Teddy's dressing room during the afternoon sound check for the Concord Jazz Festival. Wilson firmly expressed his musical credo and also made some enlightening observations about the effect of the microphone on his own style and the effect of the wartime cabaret tax on the development of bebop.

Wilson was born in Austin, Texas, but grew up in Tuskegee, Alabama, where his father was a teacher at the Tuskegee Institute. Teddy studied music at Talladega College and in 1929 moved to Detroit, where he toured with territorial bands led by Milton Senior and Speed Webb. Playing in Toledo, Ohio, he heard Art Tatum, who was just developing his awesome harmonic conception there during the early thirties. Wilson's use of tenths in the left hand and his long, flowing, improvised lines had as profound an impact on Tatum as Tatum's harmonic conception had on Wilson.

From 1931 to 1933 Wilson played primarily in Chicago with Erskine Tate, Louis Armstrong, and Jimmy Noone. Wilson's reputation began to spread in 1933, when he joined the Benny Carter band, with which he recorded under the supervision of producer John Hammond. Two years later Hammond teamed Wilson with Benny Goodman and drummer Gene Krupa in a splendid "chamber jazz" trio, which became, in the spring of 1936, the first interracial group to perform in America. Vibist Lionel Hampton was first nationally recognized when he joined the group later that year. It was through the Goodman combos that Wilson's innovation and delicacy added a new dimension to the sound of the piano.

60

From 1935 to 1939 Wilson also led a variety of studio bands for the Brunswick label. These included the great soloists of the Basie and Ellington groups, recruited from the band that happened to be in New York at the time of the recording session. The vocalist on these recordings was often Billie Holiday, with whom Wilson selected and spontaneously arranged songs that later became Billie's greatest hits. In 1939 Wilson formed a permanent group of his own for touring, but he disbanded it within a year.

Wilson spent most of the forties and fifties working for the CBS studios in New York, although he appeared in a Broadway play with Benny Goodman *(The Seven Lively Arts)* and in the film *The Benny Goodman Story* (1956). He also taught piano at the Juilliard School of Music from 1945 to 1952, and he has given private lessons in New York ever since.

Wilson's recent repertoire consists of the popular songs that he recorded in the 1930's, such as "After You've Gone" and "Body and Soul," and a variety of show tunes. He keeps his style meticulously pure and intact, intentionally avoiding its "corruption" by contemporary influences. Wilson has also maintained his lively interest in European classical music, and he spends much of his leisure time augmenting his extensive collection of classical records, which include some rare discs cut on wax prior to the advent of electronic recording. Wilson is a man who keeps the past alive and, so far as jazz piano is concerned, has come to represent it.

Could you describe the beginnings of the Goodman band that made you prominent as a pianist?

Well, [promoter and producer] John Hammond was the mastermind of that whole thing. We were all just free-lancing around New York. He encouraged Goodman to bring me in with [drummer Gene] Krupa as a trio, though not to fire Jess Stacy, who was doing a great job with the big band. Goodman got some opposition from his management, though. They told him he was a promising young clarinetist and he'd ruin his career by bringing me in. The public proved just the opposite. His band was just about international anyway. There were Jewish players, Irish, Italian, southerners, it didn't matter. Goodman picked men on the basis of their music. That was his whole life. It still is. Anyway, the enthusiasm was tremendous. The Benny Goodman Trio was almost like the Beatles became later. People were hysterical. They went wild.

Hammond also set up the sessions with Billie Holiday, didn't he?

Yes. That was for the Brunswick Recording Company. Then they went back to making their bowling balls and sold their properties to Columbia.

What was your impression then of working with Billie Holiday?

I think I might have been more excited about working with [saxophonist] Johnny Hodges. He was an idol of mine, and I think the first records he ever made away from Duke Ellington were in that group. So, to be honest, I was excited about Hodges's alto and Bobby Hackett's cornet. Of course, I was a Billie Holiday fan, too. Ella Fitzgerald, Billie, Beverly White, Mildred Bailey—they were my favorite singers of those days. But I'm more instrumentally oriented. I'd actually rather listen to [saxophonist] Benny Carter than Billie. I liked to hear Ben Webster play his tenor, and Roy Eldridge, trumpet, and [saxophonist] Lester Young—he did an awful lot for that band. See, those records are unique because every one of those men became a household word in the jazz world, though in those days we were all unknown, except for Johnny Hodges with Duke, and Benny Carter, who'd been with the Fletcher Henderson band and a leader himself. Billie was known at a little club in Harlem called Jerry's, but until these records were made, nobody else knew who she was.

Were you excited about her singing?

Oh, sure. I thought she was very original. She was a personal friend, too.

Did you keep up an interest in classical music during this time?

John Hammond played a very important role in that respect. He took me to hear Toscanini. He played records of the Budapest String Quartet for me. That's when I started collecting piano and violin records on my own. I got an offer to perform the Grieg Piano Concerto with the National Symphony in Washington, D.C., if I had it under my fingers. But I didn't feel equipped. I think I got interested in that too late.

Did your classical efforts have a noticeable effect on your jazz?

No. If you can play Chopin, it doesn't help you play jazz. It's as different as day and night. There's nothing in the feeling of nineteenth or even early twentieth-century European music that has the jazz feeling at all.

Having experienced so many eras of jazz, do you have any ideas on what the essentials of good jazz piano are?

Well, there are the traditional disciplines—rhythm, harmony, and melody—that go way back into the history of music. All the great composers mastered them, and they achieved freedom within those disciplines. Harmony moves according to rules; melody has certain characteristics that turn isolated notes—something you'd punch out randomly—into a tune. It's the same way with rhythm. It gives a spark of life to the harmony and melody. Musicians who have become free within those disciplines are the most interesting of all to me.

How do you feel about contemporary jazz players with respect to these disciplines?

I don't get a chance to hear the new players enough to know for sure, but from what I've heard, I get the impression that they're obtaining freedom by throwing some of these disciplines out the window. Twenty years ago [alto saxophonist] Ornette Coleman became of great interest to the jazz world because he threw out the harmonic element. He was performing with drums, two horns, and a bass. There was no chord instrument, no piano or guitar, and he wasn't improvising on well-known tunes. When you're not bound by the discipline of harmony, there's no such thing as a wrong note. That intrigued a lot of players. Now we also have free-form music that takes liberties with the rhythm. What these players play is absolutely unsingable. You certainly wouldn't call it melodic. I enjoy music in which freedom was achieved within these disciplines, and I think the great artists are the ones who have done it.

How did you learn these disciplines?

I had a very fine classical teacher, Richard McLanahan, who discussed them with me. He was very conscientious. He had manuscripts photostated from the British Museum because he wanted to go through all the editions of the great masters. He showed me compositions from the eighteenth and nineteenth centuries that the world has entirely forgotten because they were played on one chord, page after page. Now Beethoven, Mozart, Schumann, Chopin, all the men who've worked within these disciplines, are still played. The one-chord composers are one hundred percent forgotten. They're just as dead as McKinley's funeral, which was a very dead affair. You can't get any deader than McKinley was at his funeral.

Are there any contemporary pianists that you've heard work within these disciplines?

I just heard a very interesting pianist in Europe—Jaki Byard. He does a fascinating history of the jazz piano, from ragtime to stride to Earl Hines, the era I came up in, Art Tatum, and also what's generally in vogue today.

You've often been described as a transitional figure between the Earl Hines style and the bebop era of Bud Powell. Do you think there's some truth to that assessment?

Definitely. My favorites were Waller and Hines. Art Tatum, too, but you can't really place him because he's in a class by himself. Earl Hines would play a trumpet-style piano, using octaves in the right hand. That meant you got much more force than playing melody with one finger at a time. But when I came up, the microphone was being used to amplify the piano, so it wasn't necessary to have all the power that Hines used. This enabled me to do a lot of running in the right hand. I grew up with the rhythm section, so I could do more single-finger playing because of the bass and drums. That inspired me to get into the kind of running thing that a saxophone does, more cascading passages. The trumpet style used octaves because it had to have more punch.

So the miking of the piano liberated me, made it possible to do what I was doing.

How do you attack the task of accompaniment, as opposed to using the piano as the solo instrument?

When I play with a singer, I play an obbligato to the melody, never on the melody. If the singer holds a note, in one of those songs where notes are held, like "All The Things You Are," I'll play some other notes to embroider what she's doing.

Do you tend to embroider above or below the melody?

It's according to taste. It's a last-minute, intuitive judgment.

What about accompaniment with big bands?

Behind horns, I'll chord much more, instead of using the patterns and finger passages I use with a singer. Just rhythmic patterns with chords. Then there's scat singing, which becomes more like horn playing than singing.

Many of your improvisations have an apparent symmetry to them. Are there particular single-finger patterns you have an affection for?

No, I just play it the way I hear it. If it comes out symmetrical, that's better than if it doesn't. When it starts getting symmetrical, the point is being made.

What about harmonic inclinations? Are there certain diatonic scale tones you rely on?

Not really. I use them all, ninths, elevenths, thirteenths, as they occur to me. In a few cases, maybe five percent of my material, I have a set arrangement.

In your trio dates, you seem to group your repertoire by composers, like Duke Ellington, Fats Waller, George Gershwin, and some of the tunes Benny Goodman recorded. Is there any special reason for presenting your material in segments like this?

A lot of those old Benny Goodman Trio numbers are good to play on. There's also an association with that material for me. They're songs I recorded either with Benny or with Billie Holiday, so I've become known in terms of that music. I never used to talk on jobs, but several club owners have asked me to say a few things about the tunes—at least who wrote them—because a lot of people are interested in that. But there are excellent songs to play on, like "Running Wild" and "After You've Gone," and I do them, though I don't have any idea who wrote them.

What have you noticed about the evolution of the role of the jazz pianist?

The piano has always been a prominent instrument in jazz since the ragtime days. All the players were good soloists then, because in the early days of jazz they were playing dance music, not concert music. It didn't become listening music until World War Two, when the tax on dancing ruined the dance business. See, all the big bands of the thirties, Goodman, Tommy and Jimmy Dorsey, Artie Shaw, Charlie Barnet, were jazz-oriented dance bands. When we got into the war, the bottom dropped out because there was a twenty percent tax on every bill at the dance clubs. The musicians had to evolve a way of playing that would draw the customers even though they couldn't dance. That's when they tried to make the harmony more interesting by adding notes to chords that had never been used in them previously. The rhythms were more eccentric, too, and technique developed tremendously. Today you'll hear bass players play with a skill that guitarists wouldn't have imagined back in the thirties, except for maybe Charlie Christian or Django Reinhardt. The technical skill makes for interesting listening music, and it was forced on the musicians by the federal government's tax policy. That was the mainspring of the bebop era.

An economic motivation for bebop?

Right. It developed on Fifty-second Street in New York. They put the tables right up to the bandstand so no one could dance. The musicians had to draw the fans just to listen.

Since you've taught piano, privately and at Juilliard, what type of training do you think a beginning player should follow?

The only thing I've used is ear training and the playing of chords instantaneously in different inversions. Putting your hands right on them. For ear training, I'd play a chord, say, a triad, lower the third, and ask the student what the new chord was. Then I'd add the minor seventh and ask the student what chord I was playing. The student should be able to recognize chords without seeing them played.

What about melodic ear training?

I depended a great deal on two pianos. We'd take turns accompanying each other. I'd play accompaniment and the student would play strictly melody. I got wonderful results with this method. I'd also play recordings of Benny Goodman, Louis Armstrong, [saxophonist] Coleman Hawkins—all one-line players—and the student would start by imitation. I'd write out small sections of the horn improvisations on the blackboard, taking one harmonic situation and writing out exactly what Coleman Hawkins or Charlie Parker or Armstrong played in that situation. They could see what a C chord changing to an F chord inspired Parker or Hawkins or Goodman to do melodically. This also taught the lesson of individuality, how a man can write his name on his music.

What about exercises to improve keyboard facility?

It varies. A friend who studied with me years ago, Dick Hyman, used

Chopin études. Someone else used the Hanon exercises. Jess Stacy did Bach fugues. The closest thing to an exercise I use are trills in various combinations, like 1-3, 2-4, and 3-5, back and forth from one to the other. But I use limbering-up exercises, too, away from the keyboard. Arching the back as much as you can, and then letting it slump. Learning to raise the arm, letting it fall freely. Letting the shoulder go. Letting the wrist, the hand drop freely. This encourages relaxation, so you don't get tired playing. Incidentally, I'd like to give Richard McLanahan credit again. He trained me in this relaxation, rather than a strength-building approach.

I noticed that your posture is erect when you play.

If you sat directly behind me, you'd probably notice that my back moves parallel to the keyboard. I try to stay in line with the keys, whatever part of the keyboard I'm playing in.

What kind of piano do you prefer to play on?

I like the tone of a nine-foot Steinway, or a Yamaha, or a Bosendorfer, or a Bechstein. I can adjust to any of these brands, as long as you're into a size where you have a musical instrument that can be played in public, not just a living room piano. Yamahas generally have a bright tone. They speak out, and give plenty of sound for the amount of work you put into them. The Steinways do, too.

What's your feeling about the electric piano as an alternative or simply on its own merits?

It's like a toy, a hollow caricature of a real piano. No tones or resonances. It's a phony, a pseudophony, which is about as phony as you can get.

As dead as McKinley's funeral?

Right.

Selected Discography

Teddy Wilson: Statements and Improvisations, 1934–42; R005; The Smithsonian Collection.

Teddy Wilson: Giants of Jazz (1933–1976); J-20; Time-Life Records.

Benny Goodman: Carnegie Hall Jazz Concert–1938; CSL-160; Columbia.

And Then They Wrote (ca. 1960); JCS-8238; Columbia.

3 Little Words (1976); CJ-101; Classic Jazz.

MARY
LOU
WILLIAMS

May 8, 1910–May 28, 1981

Mary Lou Williams was an accomplished pianist, arranger, and composer. She was the first woman to make a contribution to jazz as an instrumentalist, rather than as a singer. When I met her, during a ten-day engagement at the Keystone Korner in San Francisco early in 1977, her opinions about contemporary jazz were polemical and controversial. Her condemnations were particularly surprising in view of her own professional history, which had always seemed open to variety and change.

Because Williams did not review her own biography during our interview in her hotel room, it is worth sketching her story to reveal its scope and high points. Growing up in Pittsburgh, she began playing piano at the age of four and was performing in vaudeville at fifteen. The first band she joined was led by saxophonist John Williams, who later became her husband. After that band broke up, Williams worked as a pianist, and often the featured soloist, for bandleader Andy Kirk. They worked mostly in the Kansas City area, where Williams absorbed the highly concentrated style of jazz there: a mixture of blues, boogie-woogie, and swinging rhythms. When Kirk formed the successful band known as "The 12 Clouds of Joy," Williams was the principal arranger from 1931 to 1942. In a musical sense, the band was more hers than his.

When Kirk's band moved to New York in the mid-1930's, Mary Lou Williams began contributing arrangements to the bands of Benny Goodman and Duke Ellington. In 1942 she led a small combo with trumpeter Harold "Shorty" Baker, her second husband. During the forties in New York, Mary Lou became one of the early champions of bebop, and she befriended Thelonious Monk, Dizzy Gillespie, and Bud Powell. The new music influenced her own playing profoundly, although it did not diminish the authenticity with which she played blues and swing-era piano. Williams was remarkably adept at integrating new idioms in her music without dropping the old ones. During this period she also started writing orchestral works, such as "The Zodiac Suite," which was performed by the New York Philharmonic Orchestra in 1946.

68

During the early fifties Williams spent much of her time in Europe performing and recording. Her interests turned toward religion after returning home, and she converted to Catholicism in 1957. She was fairly inactive in jazz for the next few years, devoting herself to church-related work. In the sixties, however, she began composing extended works around religious themes. The most famous of these compositions is "Mary Lou's Mass" (1969), commissioned by the Vatican and later choreographed for the Alvin Ailey dance troupe.

Williams began playing again, thanks to the urging of a young Jesuit priest, Father Peter O'Brien, who became her manager and press agent. She emerged from retirement with a mission, however, that could be neatly summarized by the slogan, "Save Jazz." Her goal was "to cultivate a new era in jazz" that would revive the values of spirituals, ragtime, Kansas City swing, and bebop. "I'm sad in my heart," she told me, "because after Bud Powell and Charlie Parker, they cut off the growth of something beautiful." The villains are commercialism and the avant-garde movement in jazz. Ironically, though, Williams had only recently performed a concert that included duets with Cecil Taylor, perhaps the arch "villain" of the avant-garde.

Mary Lou's own concerts usually began with a demonstration of the history of jazz, which involved her playing in nearly all the important piano styles. When she played "herself," Williams's style was marked by economy of statement, rhythmic power—perhaps a legacy of her origins during the hard-swinging Basie years—and very melodic improvising, bearing the influence of Bud Powell. Williams always played with astonishing modernity and exuberance for a pianist who had already (in her words) "played through all the eras of jazz."

In 1977, shortly after the following interview was taped, Ms. Williams was appointed artist-in-residence at Duke University, where she taught jazz history and directed the jazz orchestra. At least she could rest assured that the young musicians under her guidance were well versed in jazz tradition. Mary Lou remained at Duke University until her death, of cancer, at her home in Durham, North Carolina.

I heard that you never took any formal piano lessons. How did you learn to play the instrument?

This music we're trying to save by getting back into the ears of the public cannot be taught. I'm glad I didn't have any formal training. It's the type of music where you need only a few lessons to help you learn the instrument so you can execute your ideas. The music comes from the mind, the heart, and the fingertips. It comes faster than lightning. The exercises in classical music that they give you in school destroy the natural feelings. When you study too much of the classics, you have a tendency to put runs and fancy things into jazz. But that's wrong. The music is spiritual. It came from spirituals, ragtime, Kansas City swing, and bop, which is when we lost our creative artists. After bop they began going to school. This destroyed that healthy feeling in jazz.

How did you develop a "healthy" feeling for jazz?

When I was fifteen years old, I was tearin' it up in Pittsburgh. I played with a sheet over my head. I played with my elbows, my feet, and I'd play turned around with my back to the piano. I was known as the "little piano girl" on all the talent shows. I was a clown. One day when I came down off the stand, a man thirty-five years old came over to me and said, "I heard you play three good chords. Drop the clowning and stick to them." Today's kids need a shot of the same medicine—and fast. America is losing a great art form.

You just played a concert with Cecil Taylor. Don't you think he's a creative jazz musician who came after bop?

He's very creative and I like a lot of things he does, although some of it I don't care for, personally. But he's from bebop. He's in his mid-forties, and all the beboppers are now in their forties or fifties. But he's not playing jazz. There's no jazz about it at all. It's a feeling that's been lost in the music. Everything now is either technical or electronic, nothing deep and sincere that will touch the hearts of people and make them feel better. All the groups now billed as jazz musicians are really playing rock or avant-garde.

But how did you acquire finger dexterity and develop your ear for music?

I have perfect pitch, which I discovered in the third grade. My teacher didn't have a harp to tune us in, so I raised my hand and said, "I know what key you're singing in." She ran over to test me out on the piano and found out I had perfect pitch. On finger training, you have to sit down and practice passages or take things off records. I used to copy Art Tatum's runs, but that can be like exercises you'd get at school.

If a young pianist isn't going to school, where should he go for exercises? To books?

No, because invariably he'll play those exercises in jazz. It's better for him to write his own exercises. What you're hearing today is those exercise books from pianists who went to school.

Whom did you listen to when you were first learning to play?

Jelly Roll Morton, Earl Hines, J. P. Johnson, Fats Waller, Willie the Lion [Smith]. The right hand didn't mean a thing back then. If you didn't have a strong left hand, you weren't considered a good pianist. The right hand became important around the mid-thirties with Teddy Wilson. The left hand gave you strength and a great beat in your head. You didn't have to stride after that. You could play rhythmic things on top because that beat was embedded in your head. In bebop, the left hand became more similar to the drums in style. The drummer was dropping bombs. That's why they called it bop. He'd go *bop! baba-bop! bop!*

Were there other changes in the right hand you can identify?

If you're modern, you can run any notes on a chord. If the man plays the right bass notes, you could even improvise on bass notes instead of chords.

One style that seems to be new is using tone clusters [groups of adjacent notes that are theoretically undefined], instead of chords, to create mood or special tensions.

That's their way of creating mood. You can create mood with a single note. When I was playing at a café and feeling very nervous, Willie the Lion said to me, "The first note you play creates the mood. Don't be shy. Play that note, get the mood going, hold it, and you've got the audience." It's your touch, your feeling, and the love you're feeding the audience. You can almost feel it yourself.

I noticed that you don't use pedals very often.

Art Tatum taught me how to control the keyboard with my hands. I used to hang out with him in Toledo and Cleveland when he was about eighteen. I'd play at a club while he was resting. When he sat down, I'd sit right next to him, imitate what I heard, and learned a lot of things that way. I don't feel influenced by him because I play my own style. I was even experimenting earlier than that. When I was arranging in the early thirties, I started using the sixth of the chord, and Andy Kirk told me it was against the rules. They only used triads, but we did it because it sounded good. Harmonies were very limited then. It was the beat and the feeling that mattered.

Is there anyone you'd listen to today on piano?

Yes. Who's the fellow who plays like Bobby Timmons did? Oh, yeah, it's Cedar Walton. He's got the feeling I'd listen to.

I know you don't use electronic instruments. Do you think they've been harmful to pianists?

I do use them for writing arrangements. But it's not good for your ears, and it's not good for your soul. Somebody should sit down at the piano instead and get a new thing going like Tatum, Waller, Wilson, Parker, Powell, and Monk. Coltrane had that spiritual feeling, too, but he didn't introduce anything new. He was just a great giant. What you're hearing these days is black magic, exercises, foreign sounds, rock, and free. You're not hearing jazz.

"Free" improvised music is often thought of as jazz, and there have been some new developments, like improvising off tonal centers and modes [scale patterns].

The world is upside down. A lot of that stuff is phony, like plucking on the [piano's] strings. I used to improvise without chords in the thirties in Kansas City, and they called it zombie music. Lester Young and I would go over to a party and they'd say, "Let Lulu play some of that zombie music." On a tape twenty-five years ago I played what music sounds like today. I had a premonition of what it would sound like and played like Cecil Taylor. Melba Liston laughed and laughed. I played it for Dizzy's wife, and she said, "Why don't you call that 'a fungus among us'?" That's where I got the title on my album ["A Fungus Amungus," on *Mary Lou Williams*]. But that cut wasn't as wild as the first tape I made twenty-five years ago.

Do you prefer solo or trio playing?

I prefer trio, if they're together with me. There's some mental telepathy there, and it's more fun. Playing by yourself can sound like intermission piano, if it's not really exciting. There's a problem with bass playing, though. I use two or three different bass players on an album, one for "Gloria" [on *Mary Lou's Mass*], and another one for slower pieces. Bass players are supposed to be able to play blues, bop, and avant-garde. It's impossible. You can't find a man to play all four eras of jazz.

Do you always use a Baldwin piano?

I'd rather use one because it plays all the time. Steinway is too sensitive, and it'll tighten up on you if you pound on it. I prefer the five feet two inches [model] or the five feet seven inches, but I'll play bad pianos, too. Somebody in a class once asked me what I do when I get a terrible piano. I play it. I was trained to do it that way.

Do you always play songs in the same key?

No, it depends what key the last tune was in. I'll always change keys after a song; otherwise, it sounds like you haven't finished the previous song. Most people play "I Can't Get Started" in C. I play it in C sharp. Sometimes a key comes to you all of a sudden while you're playing, and you start preparing for the next tune.

I've heard that you teach.

I teach Saturdays in New York. People don't know how to teach jazz. It's a feeling, and it can't be taught.

Then how do you function as a teacher?

I can't tell you because everybody will start making money off it. Oh, I can tell you this much. I have a way of teaching a student to teach himself. I do a lot of writing for each student, while other teachers are using books. I guess

I'm more of a coach. I helped Hilton Ruiz, who is with Rahsaan [Roland Kirk], by taking him back to Fats Waller for four months.

What's the best thing a pianist can do for himself and for jazz?

Go back to Fats Waller. I'm not telling anyone to play like him, but go back and learn the records. Copy them. That's the metronome. It isn't corny. If you play rock and avant-garde, you're corny for jazz. You're stiff because there's love in the jazz feeling. The avant-garde is cold. I've sent horn players back to Lester Young and Ben Webster to get the feeling. Then let them play what they want. The avant-garde has many frustrated classical pianists, and they'll disappear.

Do you mean that Keith Jarrett and Chick Corea, for example, are not playing good music just because they haven't created a totally different style?

What I should have said is that they are playing good avant-garde. Maybe it's exciting and everything else you like, but . . .

You think it's lost its jazz feeling.

I'd say they lost their feeling – period. Commercial rock and avant-garde are frigid. I'm not putting anyone down personally.

They seem to want to take the jazz tradition in a new direction.

No, they don't. They went to schools of exercise. If we had the records here, I'd prove it to you. You know, some kids have to be taught to play like Bill Evans because they've studied so much they can't play any other way. They can't play with jazz feeling, like [saxophonist] Zoot Sims. He's the greatest of the white players for jazz feeling.

What I've always said about Keith, Chick, and Bill Evans is "Great musician! Great technician!" But they're not what I'm trying to save. Something has to come out of bop that you've never heard in your life before. Spirituals were new. You never heard anything like ragtime before when it was new. These came out of pure suffering of a race of people. Not the suffering of one person, but of a race. You get to Kansas City in the thirties, and you never heard anything like stride before. In the forties bebop was new. See, it's about every ten years. But what you're hearing now is what somebody studied in school. Now I like all those people we were just talking about, but I think even they will admit that they're not playing anything completely new.

I'm looking for a new style in jazz, which will have to be created by someone very young. Charlie Parker was boppin' when he was in knee pants. I heard him with an *oompah, oompah* rhythm section when he was still in high school, and he was already playing bop. There was no doubt. A new music hasn't been created today because today's music is destroying creativity in jazz. I think I could teach anyone to play like the avant-garde people as long as they're not lazy. In the first lesson I give I go into technique. If their wrists are up, I have to bring them down. I have to get them to lay back and relax on each note. They do scales in half steps. But Bud Powell was double-jointed and played like this [with the flat middle section of the fingers]. Art Tatum—you couldn't see his fingers move at all. While the student's doing exercises, I massage the shoulders and tell him, "Relax, I love you, baby." I have to teach them love. The technique alone doesn't mean a thing. We've got to save the jazz heritage. The best way to listen to music is with your eyes closed. See what you feel in your heart. Then you'll know what's happening.

Where do you place yourself in jazz piano history?

I don't place myself. I let others place me, and I just play the piano.

Selected Discography

The Asch Recordings, 1944–47; FA 2966; Folkways.

Zodiac Suite; FA 32844; Folkways.

Mary Lou Presents (1964); FJ 2843; Mary Records.

Embraced: Mary Lou Williams and Cecil Taylor (1977); 2620-108; Pablo.

Solo Recital: Montreux Jazz Festival, 1978; 2308-218; Pablo.

JOHN
LEWIS

May 3, 1920–

Sitting straight-backed, jaw rigid, presiding over the glistening white keyboard of the grand piano, John Lewis clearly brooks no nonsense in his playing, indulges in no improvisational frivolity, and exhibits no breach of discipline nor any phrase that could be construed as formally incorrect. Lewis, of course, can swing, play a soulful blues, and emote through his instrument, but it is the swing and sweat of the concert hall, not of smoke-filled, noisy nightclubs. As music director of the Modern Jazz Quartet from 1951 until 1974, Lewis not only welded four soloists into an unshakable unit but also influenced the presentation of small combo jazz. During the sixties and seventies the MJQ proved that at least certain kinds of jazz could claim a place in the concert hall as rightfully as European classical music.

Lewis was brought up in Albuquerque, New Mexico, and had set his sights on a career in anthropology. However, lack of funding in that field and the influence of drummer Kenny Clarke, whom he played with while in the army, changed his mind. After Lewis had arrived in New York in 1945, he established his reputation as an arranger in Dizzy Gillespie's band, as an accompanist for Charlie Parker, and through his contribution in 1948 and 1949 to Miles Davis's historic *Birth of the Cool* sessions. In the late 1950's, Lewis and his close collaborator Gunther Schuller helped to navigate the uncharted third stream by composing numerous works that borrowed equally from the jazz and European classical traditions. In short, he participated in every movement of importance to modern jazz. Lewis currently teaches at City College of New York and serves as the music director of the Monterey Jazz Festival, a post he has held since 1958.

A description of Lewis's demeanor from Leonard Feather's *Encyclopedia of Jazz* (1960 edition) summarizes the view of many critics: "Completely self-sufficient and self-confident, he knows exactly what he wants from his musicians, his writing, and his career, and he achieves it with an unusual quiet firmness of manner, coupled with modesty and a complete indifference to critical reaction." Above all, Lewis is temperate and disciplined; and these are personal as well as musical traits. The following interview was taped Sunday morning of the Monterey Jazz Festival weekend in the Festival's administrative offices.

When did you start playing piano?

I started when I was seven. Quite a few cousins played, so we played jazz together and had a family band. Then I had a group in the Boy Scouts. I was twelve when I first got paid to play—I got a dollar a night for playing in a little club. But I was also studying written music at the time, the classics. I learned jazz by listening and also through an aunt of mine who went to dances a lot. I heard those bands, too. The thing I didn't like was my private lessons—I hated them. I had them until I went to the war in '42. When I got out in '45, after playing with Kenny Clarke [later the MJQ's first drummer] for two years, I went back to the University of New Mexico, where I took a double major in anthropology and music. Everyone advised me to go to New York because there were no funds for anthropological enterprises. I was much more interested in music anyway, so I went to the Manhattan School of Music. I never was tempted in the direction of concert music, but I still play written music— Chopin, Bach, Beethoven—as much as I can, just for pleasure. Also, I'm a composer, so I'm interested in what they're doing.

What kinds of finger exercises were you doing then?

The usual. Hanon and Czerny.

Ahmad Jamal has said that exercises should be individually tailored to the student's hands and musical needs.

I agree completely, although Hanon and Czerny were great teachers and great pianists. They devised what they thought was valuable for playing the kind of music they played. That was a long time ago, and things have changed. Some revisions could be made.

Which improvisers made an impression on you when you were starting out?

Earl Hines. Several local pianists, because this was before there were many records available. Our principal local pianist, though, was also influenced by Earl Hines. Jay McShann lived in town, too, so that was another influence, and I remember having some lessons from Jay. Then I listened to broadcasts, mainly from the Grand Terrace in Chicago, though there were also some from L.A. There was much more good live jazz on the radio then than there is now. Live musicians were also employed by the radio stations. Remember, there even used to be NBC and CBS symphony orchestras.

When you started playing with Dizzy Gillespie's big band, did you feel a lack of opportunity for personal expression because of the group's size?

I really don't care about that. The thing is to make music; it doesn't matter how it's done, so I just don't care about personal expression. I get marvelous pleasure from hearing wonderfully well-made music, whether I'm the one playing the instrument or not. I'd just as soon not do it; in fact, it's easier.

You'd just as soon listen to records or attend concerts as play music yourself?

If I could listen to all the things I wanted to hear, and I knew there would be a whole lifetime of it, then yes, I wouldn't need to play. I play because I can't hear everything I want to hear unless I do it myself.

How did you get involved with Miles Davis and the Birth of the Cool *sessions, and what was the importance of that music in your estimation?*

Let's see, I went to Europe in 1947 and then went back [again] in '48 and stayed for a while. Miles was writing me letters, telling me that I ought to come back and work with that group of people. I was there when we all used to meet in Gil Evans's little apartment on Fifty-fourth Street. We liked the way Gil arranged, which was the principal attraction for us. Miles wanted me to do something for them that would further the kind of arranging I had done for Dizzy. The whole idea was to try something more sophisticated than just a simple tune and improvising on it. We were a little tired of that routine. I came back from Europe late in 1948, and we [Davis's nonet] had some rehearsals. Whoever had some money would supply what we needed. The arrangers in the band were [saxophonist] Gerry Mulligan, Miles, and myself. Gil and Johnny Carisi arranged but weren't playing in the group. We needed to rehearse a lot because these pieces were difficult. I think we showed you could do more sophisticated things in jazz. That was the influence there.

Was accompanying Charlie Parker an altogether different experience in terms of its demands on your playing?

It was the same thing. I can play only one way. I don't play different from one person to another.

But didn't the unpredictability of Parker's versions of a tune require you to make more spontaneous choices than you did in the Cool *session, where you used arrangements?*

Not for me. In all the years I've written music, there have never been any piano parts, not on anything where I've been the pianist. I invent the piano part each time. For me, improvising is the main attraction, not having to play the same thing every time.

What does stand out in your mind about accompanying Parker?

What stands out in my mind is that everything he played was perfect. Clear as a bell, every note was right, like the best Mozart. You could not do without any of the notes he included. They all made sense together. It was all logical. He was the most logical player we had up until that time.

Did that intimidate you?

No, it was quite an honor though to play with him, because I had great admiration for those records he made in 1945.

Why did he hire you to play on "Parker's Mood" and those other tracks for Savoy?

I really don't know. Maybe Miles said something to him about me. All of us took care of each other then; we were good to each other. Like Dizzy, who was like a father and brother to me when I came to New York. We were all like family.

How did the MJQ start? I've heard quite a few explanations; for example, that the quartet was supposed to give the big band a rest at concerts.

That was it. We were the rhythm section. Ray Brown, a great player in the tradition of Jimmy Blanton and Oscar Pettiford, Kenny Clarke on drums, and Milt Jackson. We were all friends and would even play together when Dizzy's band wasn't working.

At what point did it occur to you to inject more structure in the MJQ's music?

That really was just a continuation of what started back in my first writing for Dizzy's band. Remember that piece "Two Bass Hit"? Well, that didn't get recorded in full because it was too long. We chopped it up. Now, when I look back at the whole thing, I see it had some interesting structure. It was just my way of writing, also in Miles's group.

Have you seen a change in the role of the pianist since the early fifties?

A lot of pianists have become interested in other keyboard instruments because you can fairly easily transfer the same kind of technique. However, a few of them are suddenly getting over that phase because the acoustic piano is a masterpiece of an instrument, while the electrics have many expressive drawbacks. I've tried playing them, and still do occasionally, but they're limited. They're not useful as the foundation instrument. They're more useful for colors and special effects. I used to carry around an electric celeste and harpsichord, and with the MJQ we did some pieces that used prerecorded tapes from the ARP 2600 [synthesizer]. I think synthesizers are capable of more than has been achieved so far in sound quality. They've improved, though, in some respects. Some of them have polyphonic keyboards now.

In addition to playing and writing, you've taught improvisation. What's your approach to teaching it on the piano?

I start students off on three basic forms: the blues, a ballad, and a piece that moves. If pianists are going to play solo, they have to learn the changes, the tune, and a bass line, so I give them a lead sheet which has all these things, including the bass line. You have to have a model to play from and start by imitating.

Lennie Tristano's teaching method involves having the student play the chords to a song alone to get a countermelody going with the left-hand thumb. Is that a technique you'd use?

No, I wouldn't. I had some kids who came from Lennie, and it was a disaster because they couldn't play with a rhythm section this way. The left hand gets in the way if you keep pounding chords out, and I had to get them to stop that. There's one really good teacher in New York–Sanford Gold– who stays pretty much in the East. You might not have heard of him. He hasn't performed in a long time.

Are there jazz pianists you listen to now?

I listen to Art Tatum. Also Hank Jones and Oscar Peterson.

They're all known for their ability to solo. Do you have any plans to perform unaccompanied?

I recorded my first solo album in Japan in January of 1976. It was done for CBS over there, but I don't know if they're planning to distribute it here. In fact, I went to Japan with Hank Jones and Marian McPartland. The three of us played concerts together: solo, duo, and trio. Just pianos.

How did that idea originate?

Marian and I started it by playing a concert at Harvard in Cambridge. We split a program and then played duets. Later at the Smithsonian Institution we added Hank Jones and Teddy Wilson.

There's always been a two-piano tradition in the classics, but it seems pretty rare in improvised music.

My basic two-piano experience was in the classics. But I also listened to Victor Babin and his wife, who were called Bronsky and Babin. They were Russians. They arranged some of their pieces and were tremendous. Actually, I had done this once before when I played a program in Europe with Dave Brubeck, Earl Hines, and Martial Solal. This was in the late sixties. Originally I wasn't comfortable with it, but that's what they wanted me to do, so I gave it a try. Now I like it. Basically I like playing more by myself now because there's so much freedom to move tempos, which you can't do with a group.

Many of the pianists coming up now are moving tempos often. They even stay away from tunes as such. What's your feeling about them?

Well, I have listened to find out what they're doing, and what I've found is that they have one kind of thing going on too long. The element of musical surprise is gone. I still prefer what Hank Jones is doing. You need some cadences or something to make use of this whole two or three hundred years of musical tradition. I don't want just to throw it out. I'm talking about the European musical tradition, harmonically, rhythmically, and instrumentally. How we think about music harmonically certainly comes from Bach and so on. We finally settled on how we were going to use the two great modes, major and minor. Before that, all seven modes were used. Also, we tempered the scale because the untempered scale doesn't work for our ears. You couldn't change keys. The octaves and fifths weren't in tune. Well, you can read up on all of that. Anyway, I'm very grateful to be living at a time when all of that is over with. Of course, they have much different traditions in India and Japan.

Do you consider your music a continuation of Western European music?

No, not a continuation. The special thing that occurred here in the United States was that this type of music [jazz] was borrowed from wherever we had to borrow from. It's an extension of European classical music; African; Latin; maybe that's it. We've tried to use the Indian ideas, too, but I don't think we've succeeded there. I don't think anyone here knows how to do it.

Do you foresee any changes in our harmonic thinking?

I don't think what we have now has been fully exploited. There's lots to get at there.

Did you have a practice routine at school, and do you have one now?

Yes, scales. Learning the pieces in all the keys, even written pieces. We had to do that at school, though I didn't practice that consciously. I was working most nights when I was going to school, so that was enough. Now that I'm not playing so often, I practice pieces, running them through the keys. I'm also trying to solve the solo piano bit. I mean, trying to find a way to give a successful performance alone. I haven't solved it yet. The solo recording I did is partly successful and partly not. You have to pick your tempos correctly, and there is very little leeway in transferring your ideas from a group situation. You have a lot more freedom, but you have to learn how to discipline that freedom, how to use it. I think the successful soloists have been Tatum, Hank Jones, Fats Waller, Pete Johnson, Albert Ammons, Meade Lux Lewis.

But these latter pianists are successful in a very limited style, aren't they?

Not as limited as you might think. You'd be surprised how long you could listen to that music. A lot longer than you could listen to some groups of today, I think.

Why did the MJQ get back together for a Japanese and American tour in 1981? [The MJQ's disbanding was precipitated by Milt Jackson, who felt that the quartet was not making the kind of money that was commensurate with its status in music. Lewis, whose expectations were more modest, is reluctant to reopen this old dispute.] Does this mean the group is being revived as a regular performing unit?

Maybe, but not *too* regular. That Japanese tour was instigated by Jimmy Lyons [producer of the Monterey Jazz Festival], who was asked by the Japanese to see if he could get us for the Japanese version of Monterey. It took about a year to get everyone in the clear. Percy Heath is working with his brother in a successful band, and Milt is always working. We enjoy playing together still, as long as we don't *have to* do it—we're getting older, and it's hard to be out on the road.

Selected Discography

Charlie Parker: The Savoy Recordings (1948); SJL-2201; Savoy/Arista.

Miles Davis: Birth of the Cool (1949); M-11026; Capitol.

Modern Jazz Quartet: Pyramid (1958); SD-1325; Atlantic.

Modern Jazz Quartet: European Concert (1960); SD2-603; Atlantic.

The Best of the Modern Jazz Quartet (1956–1966); SD-1546; Atlantic.

The Modern Jazz Quartet: The Last Concert (1974); SD1-909; Atlantic.

John Lewis & Hank Jones: An Evening with Two Grand Pianos (1979); LD-1079; Little David.

SUN
RA

ca. 1915–

When I interviewed Sun Ra, he was staying at the Bel Air Sands Motel in Los Angeles—a perfectly cylindrical building constructed largely of glass. It towers above a major freeway like some misplaced monolith dropped there by an advanced extraterrestrial civilization. Sun Ra's tenth-floor room, which was strewn with his capes, bizarre headgear, and portable electronic keyboards, provided a view of speeding cars that seemed, from our lofty vantage point, to have diminished to the size of mice. In short, the environment was like an extension of Sun Ra's futuristic consciousness.

Sun Ra's performances are, to say the least, out of the ordinary. The twenty-six members of his Solar Arkestra (also known as the Myth-Science Arkestra) appear onstage in costumes that blend primitivism with futurism. Their leader, no sartorial slouch, wears majestic robes, often topped by a cape, and a bejeweled helmet complete with a flashing blue light. The band starts out by parading around the hall with their instruments chanting, "Space is the place." Their music is "illustrated" periodically by whirling dancers and accentuated by Sun Ra's mischievous keyboard technique, which includes playing one of his electric keyboards behind his back or with the backs of his hands.

Sonny, as he is known to his intimates, generally responds to queries about his background with explanations that he was not born, but arrived from another planet, that he is part of an angel race, and so on—in a perfectly serious manner. But Sun Ra, whose name was once, verifiably, Herman Blount, can also be surprisingly down-to-earth, especially when discussing his recent return to playing solo acoustic piano.

Herman Blount grew up near Birmingham, Alabama, and he led his own band in high school. He attended Alabama A&M University as a music education major. Many of his high school colleagues worked for him during college as well. Blount moved to Chicago, where he went to work at the Club de Lisa as a pianist and arranger for Fletcher Henderson. The influence of Henderson, Don Redman, and Duke Ellington on Sun Ra's arranging and composing for his own big band has been obvious—and readily admitted—throughout his career. At the Club de Lisa, Blount also incorporated singers and dancers in his shows. During the 1950's he formed the First Arkestra in Chicago and lived communally with most of the band members. Some of his principal soloists, like saxophonists John Gilmore, Pat Patrick, and Marshall Allen, have been with him for more than twenty years. Sun Ra's band experimented occasionally with modal compositions and some free and atonal playing during those years. But most of the time Sun Ra followed in the tradition of his major influences, especially Henderson and Redman, by leading a fundamentally swing era band. Sonny and the band spent the sixties in New York, where they performed infrequently but recorded several fine albums for their own label, Saturn Records. The leader's avant-garde explorations and space-age brand of humor continued to develop.

Surprisingly, in 1977 Sun Ra emerged from the Arkestra's theatrical trappings and his own fortress of electronic keyboards to appear onstage alone with an acoustic grand piano: once at an opera house in Venice, Italy, before an audience of 3,000; again on the University of California, Los Angeles (UCLA) campus. His return to the sobering task of playing solo piano was prompted by an incident that he relates as follows: "One night I was riding a streetcar after a concert, and a teenager came up to me and told me he'd been listening to my band. He followed a lot of musicians that came up through my band and went on to form bands of their own. 'But they don't express *you*,' he told me. 'What you should do is come out into the world by yourself. Then they'll understand what you're doing.' " This advice resulted in the solo concerts and two solo LP's for Paul Bley's Improvising Artists, Inc. (IAI) label, *Solo Piano* and *St. Louis Blues*. These contain fairly conservative, gemlike performances that reveal Sun Ra's pianistic influences and his impish sense of humor.

How did the name Sun Ra evolve out of Herman Blount? Sonny sketched the answer for me on a scrap of paper he took from the night table. The only one of his ancestors to play an instrument was his great-grandfather, a violinist, named Alexanra. Separating the syllables, one gets A-le-xan-ra. According to Sonny, the *x* is pronounced like a *z* or *s,* and the word sounds the same regardless of its vowel: "xan," "xen," "xin," "xon," and "xun" all are pronounced *sun*. The *le* of Alexanra worked its way into Sonny's legal name, Le Sony' Ra, which is on his passport. And the *A*? I forgot to pin him down on that. If all this seems confusing, Sonny asks us to remember, instead, that rearranging the letters of "The Ra" yields "Earth."

When did you play your first instrument?

At about ten or eleven years old. I came home from school one day, and there was a piano waiting for me. It was a gift from my mother for what they call a birthday, or arrival day. I had never taken any lessons, but I sat down and played a few songs on it that I had heard elsewhere. A friend of mine, William Gray, who played the violin, used to bring me music, even the classics, to see if there was anything I couldn't read. He never did find anything. It was the mystery of the family. How could I do that? Well, my sister started piano lessons, and I read through all her books, too. The only regular musical training I had was at college. They told me I should take standard courses so it would be acknowledged that I had studied music. I began to work with Mrs. Willa Randolph, who was a pianist and used to write articles for *Etude* magazine. She became like a private tutor to me. It was a teachers' training type of major, so I had to study a little bit of everything. The composers I studied were Chopin, Rachmaninoff, Scriabin, Schoenberg, Shostakovich, the whole gamut. I think I studied everything at that school except farming.

Why do you think you could read music without any training?

It was a gift. I was also surrounded by music as a child. I used to listen to Fletcher Henderson, Bessie Smith, Ethel Waters, all the jazz greats. Those were the records my family had. Duke Ellington was another one. I came across his records when I was fourteen. Later, playing for Fletcher's band made me very happy because it was my favorite band for its discipline, its togetherness, and a particular kind of swing that no one else has been able to capture. He was an unselfish man, too. Helped a lot of people to get somewhere.

When did you begin writing arrangements for Henderson's band?

He was playing in a club [in Chicago] where I was playing on the band's off nights. I used to work with the producer of their shows, like I would arrange the music to the choreography. I'd been doing this for two or three years. Sometimes I'd write the outline for the music, and Fletcher would fill in the score for his band. That's what we were used to. But he also played for people to dance between the shows. The club did both types of music. Fletcher once asked me to do some arrangements outright for the band, but I told him if I brought in what I had, no one would be able to read them anyway. The boys thought that was crazy because they'd been reading Fletcher's arrangements easy, so how could they not be able to read mine? He called a special rehearsal, and I brought in two charts: "Dear Old Southland" and a ballad, called "I Should Care." What happened? The notes were there, but they couldn't play them right. They couldn't read them. After three hours Fletcher gave up. It was a different kind of syncopation, and they didn't have it. That's been true through the years. Not everyone can read my music. Every note has to be played a certain way, and if you don't have that nuance, it won't sound right. There are about a thousand ways to play a single note.

You're referring to attack or articulation?

Right. You've got to hit it right, or the next note you play won't connect. The funny thing about it is that the public can tell. Even though they aren't musicians, the listeners can tell if something isn't right. We played a concert in Philadelphia, and a friend of mine told me afterward that for a split second he heard something like a big wall of darkness or confusion. It was a note played by someone in the band. But then the band made like a big vacuum cleaner and drew the note inside them and got rid of it. "What was it?" he asked me. "I'm not a musician, but I heard that sound. And everything else was perfect." Well, it wasn't that the note was wrong; it's that it wasn't hit right. That's the problem of reading my music.

Do you require a similar articulation when you play solo piano?

First, I have to say that the piano has to be the right kind of piano. The piano on that solo album [*Solo Piano,* on IAI] was a fine one, but it wasn't the right piano for me. I know of a better one in New York. The piano has to be able to express any kind of feeling at all, and not every piano can do this. Some are too polished; some are too rough; some are too loose; some are too tight. I have what you'd call a tension touch that I use to test the instrument. The piano's right when I can hit the keys with ten fingers, press them all the way down, and you don't hear a sound.

But if you press a key down slowly, you'll just hear the felt hitting. Right?

I can hit them hard, and you don't hear a sound. It's mysterious. I can't explain it either. It's even more of a mystery with ten fingers because every finger has a different pressure, according to size and weight. Yet every finger applies exactly the same pressure when I do this. There's no way to practice this. You just have to be able to do it. And every piano is made differently, so you have to know the individual instrument. I just got a piano at home after trying out all the pianos in a music store. It's a Chickering upright. It's my favorite piano. I've also heard a Chickering baby grand I like. The bell has to be in the upper register; down in the bass you've got to have the thunder. It really has to express every kind of feeling.

I was just listening to my recording of "Take the A Train" [*Live at Montreux,* on Inner City], and the piano sounded like someone in a steel mill hitting up against a piece of iron. I wanted to make the piano sound like a train.

Can you tell me more about your solo playing, especially how you feel now that you're playing without the Arkestra?

Actually there were two earlier solo albums on Saturn, but I'm not surprised you don't know about them because of our distribution problem.

[These are *Monorails and Satellites, Vols. I and II,* on Saturn.] I ultimately felt all right about the IAI album because I was able to coordinate myself to the piano. Each of the songs went out in another direction; each one was played to another dimension. That's one good thing that album had. See, the piano is a work of art, too, and it has to be able to reach out to vastness.

Whom were you influenced by on piano, especially solo?

Well, I listened to Fats Waller a lot, but I don't try to play like him because he plays a stride bass, which is not what I'm into. Actually now and then I find myself playing a stride bass without really thinking about it. Sometimes a song calls for it. One critic described what I was doing as "atonal stride." That's not bad. I think Duke Ellington went in a new direction as a pianist in the latter part of his career. Of course, he always said he wasn't a pianist, but he was magnificent. I listened to him on piano because it takes a lot of years to get the brilliance and spirit he had. It doesn't just come automatically. I think it comes down to having a spiritual element that makes the song come alive. The pianist feels it as alive.

The pianist has to be a careful artist. It's like a painter trying to duplicate the work of an old master. He must get every detail and every fine line. Of course, a true artist wouldn't want to duplicate someone else's work, but he would be capable of it.

Does this mean, as Plato said, that art begins with imitation?

No. It begins with discipline. At least mine does. Everything else in life has to be put aside. Get into the note. That's the reason I could read the first time I saw music. I had given myself over to the music. I listened closely to everything I heard. It happened in reverse with me. I could hear, so I could read. By the time I was fifteen I could write anything I heard off a record. A trumpet player, Bill Martin, who was with Count Basie, told me what keys all the instruments were in. I told him I had never done any transposing, and he said it didn't matter, I could do it anyway. So I could, because I didn't know I wasn't supposed to be able to. I listened. I obeyed my teachers. You might call it faith. That was my discipline.

Why did you start playing so many other keyboards?

Because a lot of people had been stealing my ideas. I had to keep doing new things. When the first Wurlitzer came out in the early sixties, I got one and made a record called *Jazz by Sun Ra* [on Transition, currently *Sun Song* on Delmark]. Once I was playing downstairs at Birdland, and Ahmad Jamal was playing upstairs at the Persian Lounge. He'd always be in the phone booth or somewhere listening to me play. He did some things that made him a million-aire [judging by my interview with Jamal, this seems to be a gross exaggeration], but those things he did were essentially what I was doing. The song that skyrocketed him to fame was "Poinciana," which I was doing at the time. He also used Vernel Fournier on drums, who I was using at the time. He did "But Not for Me," and I have an old tape of me doing that song, and it's pretty close to what he was doing. I decided people weren't really going to know where all this music was coming from, so to keep one step ahead, I went to electronic instruments.

I liked the Wurlitzer because it had a tender, lyrical kind of sound because of the reeds they had on it. It had the sound of a guitar or a lute to me. The Rhodes sounds more like vibes, but it has a beautiful sound in a different way. Its keys seem to be heavier [slower to respond] than the Wurlitzer. I got a small Wurlitzer organ after the piano.

Come to think of it, I actually played electronic instruments before they had those keyboards. I got a Solovox, which you attached to your piano, and it allowed you to play one note at a time through it. It sort of simulated violins. Stuff Smith and I did some duets with it. One of the records, "Deep Purple," is on Inner City. Just piano, violin, and Solovox.

After the Wurlitzer I got a Claveline, which is made in France. It has a very clear voice, and I used it on the *Magic City* album [on Saturn]. After that came three different models of the Farfisa organ. Then a Gibson Kalamazoo organ and two types of Yamaha organ. There was also a Baroque, which was made in England, supposedly financed by the Beatles. It's the heaviest instrument I've come across, too heavy to travel with. It has the sound of a piano, vibraharp, and special *wah-wah* effects. Then I got a Rocksichord made by RMI, and it sounds so much like a piano you can hardly tell the difference. In Italy last winter I was searching the music stores and picked up a Crumar Mainman, which is like a piano, organ, clavichord, cello, violin, and brass instruments. But it's not a synthesizer. It's just got all these effects. The only synthesizer I've used has been a Moog, which was drawn up with special schematics for me. It was one of the first Mini-Moogs.

I've been able to express more depth and vastness with electronic keyboards. The instruments become like a laboratory where something is created once but may never be repeated. In fact, that happens on the piano sometimes. The moment is the thing. Everything changes according to where the sun is, the stars are, the moon, how many people are in the room—there's a delicate tension that exists when you play an instrument. If there are one hundred people in the room, and one of them leaves, I'll be changed. The music will change. This happens without my being aware of it. You see, I'm dealing with feelings, nerve energies. The music can touch the unknown part of a person. It can awaken part of him that we're not able to talk about. Music is a special language.

Do you enjoy electronic keyboards as much as playing the piano?

I enjoy them, and it protects me from other piano players' stealing my stuff. As soon as I make some money, I'll go back to playing nothing but piano.

Why did you start using dancers with the Arkestra?

There comes a point where musicians, being limited by man-made instruments, can't bend to a certain thing you want to express. The dancers know how to bend, so they can express music the band can't. The dancers become a note by the way they stand or move, and the people can feel it. The dancers have to move according to the movement of the band, and the band moves according to the way I play, which is never the same way twice. They've been trained [the musicians] to play in my style. They know to play in D while I'm in E flat. They play in 4/4 while I play in 3/4. Other musicians are just beginning to talk about this [polytonality and polyrhythms], but my musicians have been trained to do this for several years now.

Were you happy with the way the band played on Saturday Night Live? *Were you surprised to be on the show?*

I had told the band two years ago that they should get ready for TV, that the creator of the universe was going to intervene and that's probably the only way we'd ever get on TV. Nothing artistic or creative gets on TV in America. I had a date to play solo piano in San Francisco at the same time, but some friends stepped in and made the choice for me. They said it was better to be heard by all the people of America. More people have heard us all over the world than at home.

The band sounded good. They told us we had to play six numbers in six minutes. That was astounding. I told the band to telescope the music down and make a miniproduction of the whole repertoire. That's where the discipline comes in. They sounded good. The brilliance came out. We did "The Sound Mirror": "Behold the sound mirror/a mirror of the sound of you/the you you never allowed to become a reality. . . . Love dwells on the other side of the boundary of the last possibility." Did you ever hear anything so abstract on TV in America?

The song is true, though. There's no love on this planet. It dwells elsewhere, but it's our last hope to survive.

Do you have other philosophical observations about living here and how it affects your music?

The planet Earth is an isolated planet. It's beautiful but isolated. It's a place of freedom—and that's what freedom really is: being isolated. Everyone wants to become part of the freedom plane—free from being a part of the universe. That's the only kind of freedom they can think of. It's a petty kind of freedom, dangerous and destructive, not life-giving. It's like stocking up food in your house and believing that you are self-sufficient. Eventually the resources are going to disappear. And on this planet they're getting low right now.

We can't remain isolated. It's better to expand and become part of the universe. The universe is big enough to give everyone a planet, and that could be done by the artists, innovators, and pioneers. But unfortunately they are being held back. Creativity is limited by all this talk of equality. The pioneers are brought down to the level of the people who are not creative. That's what equality does: It penalizes those who are superior in some way, those who could become the teachers and rulers of people. The true leaders, the creative people, are at the mercy of the people who don't know any better. For example, what happened to the people who were trying to develop solar energy? They were stopped by the business and political people.

Do you think the artists should be in control of world affairs?

Not necessarily. I'm thinking of music, and I know musicians can't work alone. They have to have a leader, a director. They're working on an art form that's expansive and universal. It's too big out there. Everyone needs someone as a guide. Some people are controlled by forces on other planes. I am, so I'm not really free.

Do you think your music achieves a universal dimension? How can you tell if it does?

You know the drummer Sonny Murray? He once told me my music had hooked up with the universe—like making a long-distance telephone call. It happened at an outdoor New York City concert, where I used a hundred-piece orchestra. It was sort of cosmic coordination—I have a song by that name, too. When you hook up with the universe, you're in tune with everything. You can express everything, too. Anyone who is listening to it can become part of it. They can be coordinated with the universe and know there is something out there besides the Earth.

How would you like other people to listen to, or evaluate, your music?

My music is not about understanding; it's about feelings. People sometimes judge my music by its intelligence or dexterity, but that's not what I'm dealing with. I'm only dealing with feelings.

Selected Discography

Atlantis (1960); AS-9239; Impulse.*
The Heliocentric Worlds of Sun Ra (1966); 1017; ESP.*
Sun Ra: Solo Piano, Vol. 1 (1977); 37.38.50; Improvising Artists, Inc.
Live at Montreux (1976, with Arkestra); IC-1039; Inner City.
St. Louis Blues: Solo Piano (1977); 37.38.58; Improvising Artists, Inc.

GEORGE
SHEARING

August 13, 1919–

George Shearing likes to make it clear that he is not a jazz pianist, but a pianist who plays jazz; nor is he a blind pianist, but a pianist who happens to be blind. My first meeting with Shearing acquainted me with a small fraction of his extensive classical repertoire, some of which was learned by ear, the rest from Braille editions. Sitting in the sunny upstairs music room of his San Francisco home, I was treated to an excerpt of Mozart's Double Piano Concerto in E flat (K. 365) performed by George and his wife, Ellie. Shearing plays with about a dozen symphony orchestras around the country, and he is particularly fond of Bach, Mozart, and Delius.

Though classically trained, George is a natural improviser. He began playing at age three, when he would pick out tunes that he heard on his family's radio. In the interview that follows, George narrates the development of his career and of the famous George Shearing Quintet, one of the first small jazz groups to achieve popularity with the general public. Shearing's appeal comes from his soft touch, graceful melodies, and the distinctive harmonies constructed out of the locked-hands style of playing chords (which Shearing explains in some detail). He is known, too, as the composer of one of the classics of modern jazz, "Lullaby of Birdland."

Shearing and I talked at length in his living room, where he illustrated his comments with snatches of classical compositions or facile improvisations. Right away the conversation turned to his favorite kinds of pianos, the Baldwin, German Steinways, and the Bösendorfer. He compared distinguishing a good instrument from a mediocre one to "knowing the difference between properly brewed and instant coffee." Shearing is known for his urbane, graceful manner and rather sardonic wit, the latter epitomized by his response to a TV talk-show host who asked him if he had been blind all his life. "Not yet," George replied. Shearing is a broadly educated man, and he enjoys conversation, choosing his words with evident pleasure, as the interview below reveals.

Aside from a piano's somewhat intangible "personality," what objective qualities do you look for in an instrument?

A certain mellowness of tone and sustaining power. This is what's great about the Baldwin SD-10. The decay, the fading out of a note, is very slow, so the melody lasts. You'd particularly notice it in playing the slow movement of a Mozart concerto. I know that because I've been performing K. 488, K. 459, and K. 466 [No. 23 in A, No. 19 in F, and No. 20 in D Minor, respectively] pretty regularly. In fact, I recently had the pleasure of playing with Clara Siegel, a wonderful pianist and piano coach from Chicago.

Are there Braille editions of all the classical pieces in your repertoire?

In most cases, yes, though I don't think there's a Braille version of the Double Concerto. Clara taped it for me, and I learned it from the tape. I don't advocate this, by the way, for every blind player because you have to have a very discerning ear. I advocate using Braille music, and I use it myself so I can keep in touch with the theoretical aspects of the music, the phrase marks, and the fingering. Of course, there are some composers who are less exacting than Mozart. Then a tape wouldn't be as difficult to learn from. If you have a good ear, it's certainly faster than Braille.

Are there pieces by other composers that you're working on now?

I've started to learn the Poulenc Harpsichord Concerto, and I'm doing the Bach Concerto No. 3 [in D] and Gershwin's Concerto in F. I think the Gershwin is a marvelous piece, and Oscar Levant is definitive on it for my taste.

Levant does Gershwin's Three Preludes *beautifully.*

Yes. I have those in Braille, too. There's quite an extensive library of music available in Braille. *The Well-Tempered Clavier,* Chopin's preludes and waltzes, Bach's *English Suites* and *French Suites.* It's practically endless.

Is it true that your only formal training was four years of classical piano at the Lindon Lodge School in England?

Yes. I had classical piano and theory as well, but only from age twelve to age sixteen. That's why it's so important for me to learn concerti from Braille—to keep up with my theory.

What motivated you toward jazz?

I suppose it was this natural gift, an aptitude for improvisation. You see, in terms of forming hand shapes, hitting chords, and hearing inner voicings, I never had any difficulty. That came immediately. So to start with, you have an ability to break the rules, and if you want to refine yourself, you go on to find out what those rules are. The two elements you need are uninhibited creativity and the ability to refine it by understanding the rules of classical music. This is why I've always advocated a concurrent study of classical and jazz. You've got to learn the rules and break them in such a way that you exercise good taste.

When John Coltrane reached for notes that weren't on the instrument, the rule seemed to be: Come as close as you can to achieving the impossible. Of course, it might have seemed that way to me because I didn't know what he was driving at. If I condemned it, I'd be confirming George Bernard Shaw's adage that we're always down on the things we're not up on. But one example I can talk about more readily is the Gerry Mulligan Quartet. He had two-part inventions and fuguelike things going with [trumpeter] Chet Baker or maybe [trombonist] Bob Brookmeyer, and everything was in order. When he broke the rules, he knew what he was doing. Ravel didn't adhere to the rules of baroque music, but the rules are broken in the best of taste. And again, before Bach, resolutions were always on open fifths. The major third was considered dissonant in those days. So in a way, Bach himself was breaking the rules.

You seem to rely readily on the concept of good taste. What, exactly, do you mean by it?

For me, something is in good taste if I can accept it, understand it, and judge it as valuable property. Ravel disguises his breaking of the rules so beautifully that you're not aware of the blatant consecutive fifths and all the other thou-shalt-nots of the early composers. You know, I think we tend to say, "It's bad," rather than, "I don't like it."

What was the impetus for your coming over here?

I met some wonderful musicians before and during the war—Mel Powell, Peanuts Hucko, Glenn Miller, Fats Waller, and Coleman Hawkins. They all said, "Man, you've got to come to the States. You'll kill 'em!" So I expected to slay everyone when I got here, because I could play in the style of Art Tatum, Teddy Wilson, Fats Waller, and Bob Zurke. Well, the people started to say, "Oh, that's nice, what else can you do?" My wife at the time was kind of annoyed and she'd say, "What do you want him to do, stand on his head?" Of course, what they were saying in effect was: "How can we differentiate him from the pianists we've already got over here?" It wasn't until I played with the quintet that I could establish my own style and musical identity.

The piano, like any other instrument, needs a performer with an identity. My identity came from two sources: the block chords of the Glenn Miller saxophone section and the block chords of Milt Buckner, the pianist with Lionel Hampton's band of the forties. In fact, to my mind, Milt Buckner is the inventor of the locked-hands style, not me. What I did was to take it from Buckner's blues context and use it as a vehicle for tunes.

Can you define the locked-hands style?

A four-note chord in the right hand with the left hand doubling the little-finger melody played in the right hand, the whole structure occurring within one octave. In the quintet I added the guitar playing the melody in the lower register and the vibes playing the melody in the upper register. That's the theory behind our sound. This isn't necessarily pianistic, relative to the way the piano has been used. But my solo [unaccompanied] playing is still basically Tatum. I have two prime requirements for soloing: well-ordered inner voicings and bass lines, and tone production, getting every note in the chord out with a little extra pronunciation of the cantabile melody, so it can be heard slightly above the rest of the sound.

Were there pianists other than Tatum who influenced your solo style?

Tatum had such a strong influence on me that I felt he was the complete solo pianist. Now that doesn't mean that Bill Evans is not complete playing solo. But by comparison with the strong rhythmic satisfaction of Tatum's stride playing, Evans's beat is more implied, which adds looseness to it. With Tatum, there's no question where the music is at. It's like the difference between a Buddy Rich-type drummer and a Paul Motian-type drummer. Motian is implied. Now I don't know if I'd want to hear Buddy Rich with Bill Evans—it would probably bog Evans down. But put it this way: I never liked to hear anybody with Art Tatum. That's how complete I felt he was. It would be like adding a third voice to a Bach two-part invention or like putting sugar on something that already has its own sweetness. You know, gilding the lily.

There's a lot of bebop in your right-hand lines. Did you listen to Bud Powell?

Absolutely, lots of Powell. But one of my strongest influences when I first got here was Hank Jones, whom I'll still go a long way to hear. I think he's one of the most underrated pianists in the business. He has a beautiful, deep sound, clarity, and a sense of economy. Impeccable taste.

Did [critic] Leonard Feather suggest the instrumentation of the quintet?

Yes, he did. I had a trio with Denzil Best on drums and John Levy on bass. We were playing a little club, I think it was the Clique Club [which later became Birdland], and the manager came up to me and said, "I have a chance to get Buddy DeFranco. Would you mind?" Well, I'd only been in America a year and would I mind working with the world's greatest clarinetist! So we called the group the Shearing-DeFranco or DeFranco-Shearing Quartet, depending on which wife you spoke to. Well, Buddy was involved with Capitol, and I was negotiating with MGM, so our careers could not go in tandem. We split up that group around the end of 1948. At that point, Leonard said to me, "You've heard [guitarist] Chuck Wayne and [vibraphonist] Marjorie Hyams with their groups. Why don't we put them together with your trio?" That was the birth of the quintet in 1949.

How soon did the quintet's sound depend upon the locked-hands style?

Right away. I had heard Milt Buckner playing that way as early as 1945. It was a big factor in our success.

What prompted you to replace Marjorie Hyams with Cal Tjader?

Well, she wanted to stay in town. Most musicians get tired of working for someone else and drawing a salary and traveling. Majorie stayed in Chicago and married a banker. I hired Cal after hearing him with Dave Brubeck's band.

What did you think of Dave's playing back then, before his quartet had been formed?

I heard him play while I was in Hollywood, and I heard him record solo. Dave could show restraint as well as that emotional release that usually accompanies the last chorus of his solos. Being an impressionist and a rather gentle player myself, I must say I preferred the restraint to the tremendous release at the end.

The early trios with Dave, Cal, and Ron Crotty involved some doubling of the melody line between vibes and piano. Was that what made Cal's playing appealing to you?

I think Cal appealed to me as a natural-born musician and rhythmic genius. He loved those Latin rhythms. For a while I had Cal on vibes and timbales, Armando Peraza on congas, and Al McKibbon playing as fine a Latin bass as anyone ever has. Cal and Al were really into that stuff, and that band of "restless natives" generated a lot of excitement.

Do you take some credit for stimulating the interest in Latin jazz during the 1950's?

I hope we can. At the peak of the Latin Quintet recordings, we were as authentic as any Latin rhythm section, and we were listening to Machito and Tito Puente in New York. If I ever reassembled the quintet [which Shearing disbanded in 1978], it would be to get back into some of that Latin stuff. But I wouldn't use an ersatz rhythm section. It would have to be the real thing.

Of all your employees, like Gary Burton, Joe Pass, Toots Thielemans, and the others, does anyone stand out in your mind as inspiring to work with?

I love Gary Burton's musical mind so much I fought with the record company to get them to let me record an album composed and arranged by him [*Out of the Woods*, on Capitol]. We used the quintet with a woodwind quartet. They wouldn't have known how to face me if that record had taken off, but it didn't take off. It just held its own. Gary and I also did a two-piano piece on it, partly written and partly improvised. I had to sit down with a tape recorder and learn all of his music carefully because it's very original and not easy at all.

Gary plays piano?

Oh, boy, does Gary play piano!

What's the story behind the writing of "Lullaby of Birdland"?

The owners of Birdland asked me to come up with a composition that they could use as a theme song for their radio show. I wrote that thing over a steak at my dining-room table when I lived in New Jersey in 1952. I didn't use the piano at all. Somebody came over later, and I dictated the music so it could be written down. I've gone back to that butcher, but I can't seem to get that steak again. The strange ending to that story is that I sold my house in 1961 to an attorney. He came to see me when I was appearing in New York in 1976. "Do you remember me?" he asked me. "I eat my dinner every night at the table where you wrote 'Lullaby of Birdland.' " I said, "I'm glad you stopped by because I've got a gig for you." I had him negotiate the apartment in New York that we're living in now. So "Lullaby of Birdland" prevails.

What's your feeling about the free playing of pianists like Chick Corea and Keith Jarrett?

To be honest, I'm a tune- and song-oriented player—and cantabile-oriented. Now I loved Corea's "Windows" and "Spain." But I think there are times when these players feel a bit bored with what they might consider the plebeian approach of their earlier work. This is too bad, because their earlier work was, perhaps, more grounded. They're at an unpredictable stage where they're given to experimentation, which is why I prefer their earlier work. Yet they're both masters of the instrument, and of composition, so they're marvelous in that sense.

You've been using some double-octave figures recently.

That's an old Phineas Newborn trick. I don't use them nearly as frequently as I do single-finger lines or block chords. I think of double octaves as another color. I do whatever I can for color in a small group like piano and bass.

What technical exercises do you recommend to improve finger dexterity?

Braille music is so tedious and takes so long to learn that I've seldom indulged in much literature on technique alone. Of course, there are the Cramer and Czerny studies, but I think if you go through the Bach *Inventions* and *The Well-Tempered Clavier* and a lot of Chopin and Mozart, you'll have a pretty well-rounded technique.

You've expressed a belief in a strong connection between jazz and European classical music. Yet jazz is often thought of historically as black American music.

To be inhibited by a historical view of jazz is to limit your approach to the music as an art. Yes, it is largely black American in concept. But if we were to take, for example, the twelfth fugue from *Book II* of *The Well-Tempered Clavier* and extract some of the somberness with which it was written: [Shearing goes to the piano and plays the melody alone—it sounds like a bebop line]. No one can tell me that's not jazz just because it doesn't have this. [He adds blues chords beneath the line.]

What's your feeling about electric keyboards? Have you ever used one?

Once, in a concert I did with Ray Charles. I think if you want to make a small band sound like a big band, electric instruments are a cheap and fairly effective way of doing it. But every time I hear a guy like Bill Evans use an electric keyboard, well, for the time he's using it he has lost all of his individual pianistic personality—which in his case is considerable. The marvelous sustaining quality he has, the way he makes a note last, can be achieved only on an acoustic piano. The electric strips a man of his individuality, his tone production, and his pianistic approach.

Is there any player who you think excels the others on the contemporary scene?

I think Dave McKenna is the best pianist playing right now. His lines flow like mad, he doesn't suffer from playing solo, and he's the most complete. While Oscar Peterson is absolutely astounding and has more technique than the rest of us put together . . . well, there are some who take a little more time to smell the rose, if you know what I mean.

I've always admired McKenna's momentum, when he gets that single-note bass line going.

That's right, it's just incredible.

What is McKenna a product of, historically speaking?

Somewhere between swing and bebop and even a little Dixieland at times. He's so individual, it's hard to say. He and Bill Evans and Erroll Garner—they're all originals.

I hear in McKenna some of what Tristano was doing in the fifties, especially the single lines in contrary motion.

Yes, except he's more conventional than Lennie. He won't play those odd phrases, like Lennie used to group notes into phrases of five or nine. When McKenna plays a fast line, I hear a fluid tenor player like Stan Getz, that kind of linear construction. I've recently taped a McKenna album from the early fifties. I hope you're going to include all this about him in the [published] interview because he's been unfairly neglected, while people like Oscar and me have received more than our share of mention.

Absolutely. While we're on the subject, whom do you hear in your own playing, and where do you place yourself in the history of jazz piano?

Well, locked hands is what the public thinks of George Shearing.

Strangely enough, I don't use that much of it anymore. The reason that the George Shearing Quintet broke up is that I got tired of limiting myself to the narrow box that obedience to my identity required. Historically locked hands is the culmination of Milt Buckner applied to ballads as well as blues. Anyway, I got tired of that after twenty-nine years and decided to drop that part of my identity.

To me, the gentle touch and single-note melodic lines will always remain, whether I do an album with arranger Robert Farnon, which I just did for MPS, or an album with guitarist Jim Hall, which I just did for Concord Jazz. The dismissal of the quintet will allow me to address myself to the proposition of being a pianist, rather than a bandleader resting on his laurels. So I can't answer your question too specifically because I don't want to limit myself. If I sat down with the Basie band, by the way, I'd play Basie, not Shearing, because Shearing is not appropriate to the Basie band. There are too few pianists who have enough flexibility to adhere to their surroundings. When you play Bach, you don't use a Chopin trill; you use a baroque trill. I suppose I'm too elusive now to define myself historically.

Selected Discography

George Shearing: The Early Years, Vol. II (1948, pre quintet); FS-236; Everest.

So Rare (1949, quintet); SJL-1117; Savoy/Arista.

Shearing Touch (1960, with strings); SM-1472; Capitol.

Latin Escapade (ca. 1962); SM-11454; Capitol.

My Ship (1974, solo); 20-22369-8; MPS/BASF.*

Blues Alley Jazz: George Shearing/Brian Torff (1979); CJ-110; Concord Jazz.

George Shearing/Jim Hall (1981); CJ-177; Concord Jazz.

DAVE
BRUBECK

December 6, 1920–

For many years Dave Brubeck was virtually a household name, thanks to his quartet, which was one of the flagships of jazz almost from its beginning in 1952 through 1967, when Dave disbanded the group to concentrate on composing. The quartet featured Paul Desmond on alto sax and included Eugene Wright on bass and, from 1956, Joe Morello on drums. Brubeck himself signified vastly different values for each of his different types of audiences. To the college crowd, which constituted the majority of the quartet's fans during its early years, Brubeck personified modern jazz, for bebop had not yet filtered "up" into white middle-class America. To the critics and musicians, most of whom were based in or near New York, Brubeck was a West Coast, or cool, musician or a "classical pianist" who had turned his attention to jazz. Of course, he does not fit neatly into any of these categories. Brubeck, in fact, *never* played European classical piano music. He recounts his career and development in the interview that follows, dispelling this and some of the other myths about his music.

There are two simple truths to keep in mind when Brubeck the pianist is assessed. First, he was a unique stylist, especially for the fifties and early sixties, because he favored complex harmony over complex melody. He was not a nimble-fingered athlete of the piano like Tatum, Powell, Peterson, and most others of that era. Rather than improvise a graceful, melodic line, Brubeck used rhythmic interplay with the bass and drums and his ever-spreading, steadily thickening blockbuster chords to express emotion. Secondly, Brubeck approached the piano as a composer, applying the theory of polytonality to improvising at the keyboard. That was evident in his experimental writing for the octet he organized in San Francisco in 1946 and in his early trios with Cal Tjader on vibes (or drums) and Ron Crotty on bass. Although the trio played mostly standards, Brubeck had more or less recomposed them. Later the quartet's *Time Out* and *Time Further Out* albums, which included the famous "Take Five" and other originals in odd time signatures, provide further examples of Dave's conceptualizing. In addition to his harmonic originality, his rhythmic vigor, and the quartet's unmistakable sound, Brubeck's music has always been guided by an informed intellectual purpose.

During the eighties Dave Brubeck continues to tour, with a new quartet comprised of his son Chris on bass or trombone, Jerry Bergonzi on tenor sax, and Randy Jones on drums. He also performs his own lengthy scores with symphony orchestras around the country. When I met him in June 1982, he was about to rehearse a local orchestra in his seventy-minute *The Light in the Wilderness* for an evening concert at the Paul Masson Winery in Saratoga, California. We met in the dining room of the winery's "château," which overlooks much of the Santa Clara Valley. Over lunch, with Chris and Dave's wife, Iola, we talked about Dave's youth in Concord and around Oakland, both located about fifty miles north. (The Brubecks have since moved to a ranch in rural Connecticut.) After lunch Dave and I sat outside, where we talked in the shade of a small oak grove in sight of the vineyards sloping down into the valley. Now white-haired and distinguished at sixty-two, Brubeck was relaxed and nostalgic as he reminisced.

I know you came from a musical family. Is that what got you involved with the piano?

Oh, yes. My mother was a pianist and a piano teacher. When I was born, she was practicing all the time, as she was with her first two sons. Howard [a composer] is four years older than I, and Harry [a music teacher] is eleven years older. She believed in prenatal influence, so she practiced through all her pregnancies. When we were born, we were all put near the piano to listen to her practicing. I heard Chopin, Liszt, Mozart, and Bach from infancy. When I was about five years old, my mother went to Europe to study with one of the best piano teachers in the world at that time, Tobias Matthay. My mother also studied with Dame Myra Hess. One day at a lesson in London my mother was staring out the window at a young family walking by. Myra Hess asked my mother, "Are you married?"

"Yes."

"Do you have children?"

"Yes, I have three sons."

So she said to my mother, "If I were you, I'd go home to my children. That's what would be most important to me." Maybe she had no children of her own, I'm not sure. But my mother came home after that; she had been gone six months.

When I was eleven, we moved from Concord, California, to Ione, where my father managed a forty-five-thousand-acre ranch. I was raised there until I went to the College of the Pacific at seventeen. I wasn't planning to be a musician during that time because my father wanted me to be a cattleman. I didn't practice much. I wasn't a good student anyway because I had a lot of trouble with my eyes. One eye was crossed, pulled all the way over to the side. I wore glasses from the age of two, and this problem discouraged me from reading music. My mother didn't know I couldn't read while she was teaching me. I could play whatever she put in front of me because I had heard it so often from her or her other students. But I couldn't get too far, and I missed out on a very good education. I use only one eye most of the time now, although they don't look crossed anymore.

I went through the College of the Pacific as a music major [1938–42] without being able to read music, until a little bit at the end. Strangely enough, I could write music down, and that helped me to read gradually. It took me a long time to admit to this problem because I thought it would disgrace my mother, and my whole family, if people knew I couldn't read music. I never played classical piano. My subjects were composition, theory, ear training, and piano in the last year; that's when I couldn't hide the problem any longer. There are a lot of us who are that way, although the public doesn't realize it. Erroll Garner is another one who couldn't read a note.

But he advertised the fact; it was part of his publicity strategy.

Later, yes, but I think that was his manager's idea. Early on he didn't tell too many people. Basie learned to read at a very late age, and I'll bet he's not a very good reader today. I read now, but badly. I've known some fantastic composers and arrangers who couldn't read; it would surprise you.

For example?

Well, let me emphasize that this is only my *opinion:* Being around Duke Ellington, I'd say we had some very similar problems. I did record dates with him—I remember one with the Cincinnati Symphony—and I noticed he always had to go back to the beginning of a section. The conductor would call a bar line, and he could have started right in the middle if he had been reading, but he went to the beginning, which made me think he had it memorized. That is my speculation anyway.

How did you get around this problem when you studied with Darius Milhaud?

Milhaud knew I couldn't read, and I studied composing with him: fugue, counterpoint, orchestration, but not piano. People seem to think I'm a classical pianist and composer who turned to jazz. It's not true; there's no truth to it at all.

How did you play what you wrote for him?

He always found that amusing, because I could only play things close to what I wrote. The theme and the bar lines came out right, but there were a lot of things happening at the piano that were not on paper. He thought it was funny.

Aside from composing, did you feel that your studies with Milhaud influenced you as a pianist?

The important influences on my playing were Milhaud, Duke Ellington, and Art Tatum. When I studied with Milhaud, I was interested in polytonality and polyrhythms. Milhaud was the world's expert on that, in my opinion. He was also the first to use jazz in the classical idiom when he wrote *The Creation of the World* [1923]. This was before [Ernst] Krenek and [George] Gershwin used jazz in compositions. So Milhaud had a tolerance for me, more than our homegrown American teachers might have. Milhaud also believed I'd be a composer, and when your teacher believes you can succeed, that's the greatest thing a teacher can give you. Milhaud told me I would compose, but in my own way. He said he couldn't give me a European background because it was too late for me to acquire it.

I studied with Milhaud at Mills College [in Oakland] from 1946 to about 1949 on the GI Bill. I had served in the army from 1942 to '46, and I played a lot during those years. I was in the army band, and then I was flown over to Europe with the infantry, and I formed a band over there that played for the troops. I never considered myself anything but a jazz musician for all those years, ever since college.

What were the influences of Tatum and Ellington on your playing?

Actually the first guy I liked, before Tatum, was Teddy Wilson. Louis Armstrong's pianist also recorded with his own trio, and I listened to his playing carefully. That was Billy Kyle, an early influence on me, and I got to play with him and Armstrong on an album called *The Real Ambassadors* [on CBS]. That was a thrill for me because I admired him for so long. With Teddy Wilson it was the single-note lines that I liked so much. But I never played like him or anyone that was influencing me. I went out of my way not to sound like them. If you do that, people think of you as an imitation. Today I'm more liable to sound like those pianists than I did when they were influencing my playing.

Duke Ellington influenced me through his band. His band was an extension of his piano playing. There was this guy accompanying Sarah Vaughan in about 1948–Jimmy Jones–and I once asked him, "How do you do so much harmonically? What are you listening to?" His answer was: "The Duke Ellington Orchestra." I was talking to Sarah about Jimmy Jones just a couple of weeks ago, and she told me Jimmy didn't, couldn't solo like most piano players. He could only play chords. He didn't like to solo. Harmonically, though, he was one of the greatest players I ever heard. Did you ever hear him?

Never.

Really? You know, that happens so often. One of the guys who influenced Paul Desmond was Pete Brown. When someone asks me who influenced Paul to play sax the way he did, I say Pete Brown. Invariably the person says, "Who? Never heard of him." I think he was with Ellington. I don't know too much about him, as a matter of fact, but Paul used to talk about him all the time.

Do you ever go back and listen to your early trio recordings with Cal Tjader (on drums and vibes) and Ron Crotty (on bass)? There was a two-record set of those sessions reissued on Fantasy recently.

Yes, I had to go back and listen to them for that reissue. There was a lot going on there. I never really locked in and polished up any one of the things I was doing. As far as being judged as a pianist is concerned, you're better off to lock into something and polish it up. That's something I always thought I'd do when I was fifty. Now I'm sixty, and I'm still thinking maybe I'll start to polish something up. Maybe I'll never do it, though. I was just listening to myself on a videotape of a concert at the winery last year—it's going to be on television—and I realized that whatever I did last year, I'll never do those things again. So how can you polish anything if you do that? The great technique that a jazz musician should have is to play something you never played before and to make it happen. But that's a problem if you're being judged as a pianist.

But the public judges you on emotional content, I think. It's the musicians and critics who think technically.

Yes, that's right. But for this honesty of approach, you're going to pay a lot of dues, especially to the critics and musicians. It's putting the cart before the horse to get everything clean and perfect like classical music. Of course, I'm guilty of that in my taste. I love Tatum, but he polished and polished. You can hear him doing "Tiger Rag" in 1938, and he'll still be doing that "Tiger Rag" on a recording from the 1950's. Yet he didn't need to. That's what's so funny.

Critics used to describe you as "heavy-handed." How did you, or do you, react to that kind of criticism?

With amazement. I was a light-handed player on the *Storyville* album [on Fantasy]. The next night I might be very heavy. You know the piano was originally called *piano e forte*—soft and loud. I believe in using the full range of dynamics that the piano has to offer. That's what it is to play emotionally, reacting to what's going on around you. If you're with a heavy drummer, you've got to play heavier. On those early Fantasys, I was doing what I should have been. Those first four songs ["Blue Moon," "Indiana," "Tea for Two," and "Laura"] were done in one take. With the three-minute limit, you had to go in there knowing what you wanted to do. Later on, when we got into the LP's, you could approach recording differently.

What kind of impact did Paul Desmond have on your playing, or vice versa?

He and I approached ballads the same way, emotionally and in terms of developing the melodic line. Paul took a part of me and developed it more than I had on my own, but he got his approach, or at least he told me he did, from what I was doing. There are so few guys that can play with the purity Paul had, but when I hear them, like [trumpeter] Art Farmer, people who can develop a theme, and not play a million notes, but rather choice notes, I think, we were right. These are the guys who knock me out. Almost anybody can go play an Art Farmer or Paul Desmond chorus again, but you can't play a Charlie Parker chorus unless you really work at it. But you know that Paul was picking these notes with a great combination of intellect and concern for the purity of his sound and that he wasn't out to dazzle anyone. You can almost write down what Paul played, and it holds up. You see, I like Parker very much, but can you imagine Paul's mind going as fast as Parker's, but only to play one note where Parker would play sixteen? But there is the same conviction and choice, the same perfection and commitment to playing.

When Joe Morello joined your group in 1956, did he have the same kind of impact on your playing? Did he help bring out anything in particular as Paul did?

Joe Dodge [Brubeck's previous drummer] and Joe Morello have completely different approaches, both valid. As I've often done in my career, when I get a new guy in the band, I switch to what he's involved in instead of making him adjust entirely to me. That way the new players will stay interested in your group, and they'll continue to develop. I could tell that Morello wasn't going to come in and just be a timekeeper. He obviously could play those time signatures that I wanted to get into ever since the days of the octet. I hadn't had a drummer who could do that since Cal Tjader. The octet, for example, recorded "What Is This Thing Called Love?" and the bridge was in seven [7/4 meter]. That was a 1946 arrangement, and [clarinetist] Bill Smith was writing things in five and other odd meters. So this was something I'd been into for a long time, not always in jazz, but it had been an interest. Even with Joe Dodge, we did "I'm in a Dancing Mood," which has some strange utilization of two-, three-, and four-metered bars. I've always counted "Singing in the Rain" in 6/4 time.

Speaking of compositions, two of my favorites of yours are "The Duke" and "In Your Own Sweet Way." Are there any stories behind those pieces?

"In Your Own Sweet Way" was the first original that I'd written in years. It was about '52 or '53. We had just done a concert in upstate New York, and back at the hotel Paul said, "We really need some original material," because we'd been doing practically all standards. "We better find somebody to write some," Paul said. I looked at him and said, "You got to be kidding. I'm a composer. I can write two originals in a half hour." So I sat down and wrote "In Your Own Sweet Way" and a piece called "The Waltz" in thirty minutes just to show him. Paul titled "In Your Own Sweet Way." He really liked it. I don't think either of us liked "The Waltz."

"The Duke" I wrote while taking my son Chris, now our bass player, to nursery school. I was driving through Oakland in the car and wrote it in my head. When I got home, I wrote it down. Originally it was going to be called "The Duke Meets Darius Milhaud," but that was too long. The first eight bars of that piece go through all twelve tones in the bass, which I didn't realize until I was told by a musicologist. It just keeps moving and hits everything. The bridge is polytonal, which is the Milhaud part. The first eight bars also remind me of some things Duke did with [bassist] Jimmy Blanton.

What about Paul Desmond's piece "Take Five"?

That was written in '59, when we were getting ready for the *Time Out* album. I told the guys the album should include unusual time signatures. Joe Morello had been messing around with a 5/4 beat when he was warming up, and Paul was always intrigued by it. So I said, "You guys write the one in five/four because I know you've been fooling around with it." Paul came to rehearsal with two themes, but he said he hadn't gotten anything on paper. I had him play the two themes, and right away I said, "You've got a tune right there. Use the second theme for the bridge." That's how it happened. My wife and I wrote lyrics for it later. Suddenly it's being sung a lot, like by Al Jarreau. Carmen McRae was the first singer to record it. It's hard to believe that "Take Five" was something the average musician could not play. Now any studio guys could probably play it without any problem. High school kids don't even think twice about it now. At the time the public was more ready for that than the musicians.

Why did the quartet break up in '67?

I was ready for a change. I gave the guys a year's notice. Everybody knew about it, but a lot of people thought it was a rumor until it happened. Paul and I kept playing together on and off during that period. I wanted to write and be home more. Fortunately Paul and I also got back together for a reunion in 1976, our twenty-fifth reunion. Paul played the last concert of his life with my sons and me at Avery Fisher Hall in New York City. He was on tour with us. He had to cancel a lot because he was so ill. He had to choose very carefully whatever he played because he had cancer in his lungs and couldn't really hold a note. He had to breathe two or three times in passages he used to play without a breath. Sometimes he'd look over at me, and I could see the corners of his mouth in the embouchure turn into a smile. Like he was saying, "Hey, let me breathe." He was amazing. Through this terrible illness he never complained.

When you say you wanted to write more, are you referring to note-for-note composing?

Yes, we've just been performing *The Light in the Wilderness* with the Seattle Symphony. It's seventy minutes long and [written] for symphony orchestra, chorus, and soloists. That's what I was working on in '67 and '68, when the quartet broke up. There are five more of those rather large works, and in my part, I'm free to improvise on the themes. Of course, I've learned to read my own writing by now, and other people's if it's not too complicated, but I don't always have to write out my own parts. All these works are recorded, except the *Easter Cantata.*

Why the religious themes? Have you become more religious personally?

Well, the Old Testament and the New Testament speak so well to so many of today's problems. One section which is overwhelmingly relevant to today says, "Love your enemies/Do good to those who hate you." If we don't figure out how to interpret that sentence and live by it, the world's through. It's even more important today than when Christ said it two thousand years ago and when Buddha said it six hundred years before that, "The crowning enlightenment is to love your enemy." That's the most relevant sentence ever spoken to keep our world from being blown up. The Bible, to me, is inspired writing and speaks to today.

Your music has been described as West Coast or cool jazz. What do those terms mean to you? Are they accurate?

No, West Coast jazz is just the sound of guys who played on the West Coast, if it means anything. If there was a distinctive sound, maybe it had something to do with our isolation. The label "cool" was stuck on us, but when I listen to "Look for the Silver Lining" and "This Can't Be Love," which were taken off radio broadcasts in the early fifties, those are the antithesis of what cool jazz is supposed to be. The quartet might have sounded cool on ballads, but we didn't play ballads all night. Another thing that has bothered me is that people said the octet was a copy of Miles Davis's band in New

York, the one with Gerry Mulligan and Lee Konitz [which recorded *Birth of the Cool*]. But we got started in 1946, before Miles, and there were no records for us to listen to anyway until 1949. We couldn't have heard them.

Lennie Tristano was another allegedly cool pianist in those years. Were you influenced by him?

I deliberately didn't listen to Lennie because at that point in my life I didn't want to be influenced. Especially by him because I knew we had a similar approach in that we were both experimental in rhythm and harmony. He also worked with alto players like Lee [Konitz] and Warne Marsh, and I was already working with Paul during the octet days.

Are you playing solo piano these days, or are you confining the piano to the new quartet and the orchestral contexts?

I enjoy playing solo at home more than in performance. I'll do a little in the midst of performing, but I can't just walk out cold and start soloing. That's one reason I admire Peterson and Tatum so much, because they can do that.

There are pianists now who do that very well, Keith Jarrett, for example.

Yes, he's great. What Keith has done is, in a lot of ways, what people should be shooting for. As Cal Tjader said before our first recording session, "Let's not have a lot of preconceived ideas ahead of time." For Keith to go out there and play spontaneously, well, he's making a strong statement by doing that. I once recorded a tune called "In Search of a Theme" for Columbia on a solo album, and I really was in search of a theme. Tristano was into that, too.

It seems to me the mind just falls into ordering things in a familiar way, and it would be almost impossible to break those patterns in a sustained performance. Do you think Keith really can play without using any ideas or patterns that are familiar to him?

I don't know. If you try to find this solo album I did for Columbia, you'll see I talk about different approaches to piano playing in the liner notes. The summation is this: You can play piano so that the music is memorized, and you might be a pretty good pianist. Or you can play from a bag of tricks, where you coast between certain progressions by using a familiar trick or phrase, a run, a turnaround, or something you know will get you by. There you're in and out of creativity. The third way is where you're creative and don't play anything you've played before. That's where I think more pianists should strive to be. They'd be closer to what jazz is all about.

In this third approach, you're not going to be as clean, as perfect, or swing as much, except one or two nights a year, when you'll be out of your wig and your technique will be able to support anything you can think of. If you play in approaches one and two, you'll be limited to those areas. If you strive for creativity, which no one can really explain, there's a world of possibilities. If you really think you're a jazz pianist, you should leave some room for true creativity. That means you leave room to be bad. Trade some of that [perfection] for some greatness. We're not getting enough of that these days.

Selected Discography

Early Fantasies (1948–53); 80-5547; Book-of-the-Month Records.

All-Time Greatest Hits (1956–65); PG-32761; Columbia.

Brubeck and Desmond: Duets (1975); 703; A & M Horizon.

The Dave Brubeck Quartet: Paper Moon (1982); CJ-178; Concord Jazz.

AHMAD
JAMAL

July 2, 1930–

A man of dignified dress and manner, Ahmad Jamal appears to be as meticulous and disciplined as his music. His piano playing gained him a select following of musicians in the early fifties in Chicago, but he was virtually unknown by the public until 1958, when he recorded *At the Pershing* (on Chess) with bassist Israel Crosby and drummer Vernel Fournier. Jamal's light touch and carefully planned trio arrangements showed the power that could be achieved with only a few well-placed notes. With his crisp, precise attack, he builds a solo dramatically, as can few other pianists using the same, spare ingredients.

Jamal's penchant for understatement influenced many musicians, among them Miles Davis. Jamal is best known for his treatments of "But Not for Me," "Surrey with the Fringe on Top," "Poinciana," and his own composition, "Ahmad's Rhumba." This last piece was recorded in 1956 in a big band version by Miles Davis and Gil Evans, who built their orchestrations from Jamal's piano score. Quite often Jamal's interpretation of a composition sounds definitive, for reasons he explains below. An example is the simple folk melody "Billy Boy," which Red Garland popularized in 1956, following Jamal's conception of the song faithfully.

In 1959 Jamal disbanded his trio in order to make a pilgrimage to the holy places of Islam. After returning to the States later that year, he opened the Alhambra in Chicago, a "dry" nightclub which folded the following year. Dissatisfied with the musician's erratic life-style, Jamal virtually retired from music, except for sporadic recording, from 1962 to 1965. He then regrouped with Jamil Nasser on bass and Frank Gant on drums, recording for Impulse from 1969 to 1973. In 1974 Jamal became Twentieth Century-Fox's only jazz artist, and his recorded playing changed noticeably. Unfortunately he often submerged the piano within string and horn sections or depersonalized his playing by using an electric piano, essentially undermining the selectiveness he had exhibited in his trio work. But Jamal did continue to perform in night-clubs, where his playing displayed more favorable divergences from his earlier style. In short, the "space" (though that is a misnomer, according to Jamal) that had been a constant feature of his style was suddenly filled in by harmonic changes. That stylistic evolution, as Jamal explains below, is the result of greater self-assurance.

What was the first music you played on the piano?

I was playing Lizst études in competition when I was eleven years old. So if I was doing that at eleven—and they were finger breakers—then I started very, very young: at three. Then I played everything that appealed to me, whether it was "Christopher Columbus" [by Razaf and Berry, a swing tune popular in the thirties] or my own arias. I began studying at seven with the founder of the first black opera company in America, Mary Caldwell Dawson. I also studied with fledgling and aspiring musicians around Pittsburgh, and we never had that separation of classical and so-called jazz music. It was music, either good or bad. If we wanted to play Duke Ellington, we did. We considered Art Tatum a study, just like Bach or Beethoven. Look at some early Tatum books [transcriptions], which were fairly accurate—they demand the same concentration as the three B's. I began to study everything I could get my hands on until I was seventeen. Unfortunately I left on a professional job right after high school, so my training ended there. I never got to college because I had to support a family—I began to pursue the music from a make-a-living-or-perish point of view. But I did have good teachers when I was very young.

What technical exercises have you found valid?

I accept the rule of thumb that many of the things we did—Hanon, Czerny, and so on—were central. However, I also think there's a lack of new material, new directions, and new approaches to the basics. Everyone's physical structure varies; no two hands are the same. A runner like Jesse Owens is different from the runners of today. If we go back to the time of Mozart or Bach, there's an even greater span. I'd like to have my own approach to technical exercises based on my own thinking and physical structure. I wish I had thought of this earlier, instead of pursuing the same timeworn exercises. I think the things I studied were and are valid to a degree; they're just not exhaustive.

Some of your left-hand chording is very much in the style of Erroll Garner. Was he an early influence on you?

Erroll happens to be a milestone in pianistics. There are several: Art Tatum, Nat Cole, Teddy Wilson. I'm talking about contemporary American music, the only art form that has had its development in America. Remember, the art form that's unique to this country is not the classics, but our so-called jazz. So anyone that has never been influenced by Erroll has not been in our field. Erroll was an orchestra within himself. He always played that way. I'd say he's from the impressionistic school and of the rank of Ravel or Debussy. Any stylist has to have influence, and in his case, it's his two-handed approach to the piano.

That list omits Earl Hines, who was an early influence on a lot of pianists.

I wouldn't rank Earl in the same category as Tatum or Garner. Hines was associated with big bands, not trios, which require the piano as the focal point at all times. I'm not taking anything away from Earl Hines, who has been rediscovered of late, but I don't think we're talking about the same sort of pianist. Like Duke Ellington: I think we listen to Duke as a whole musician, not as a pianist. We listen to his composing, his structures, his harmonies, and his great leadership abilities. Not like we listened to Art Tatum or Teddy Wilson. Then you're talking about total piano. Now I don't like to say that I'm influenced by anyone but Ahmad Jamal, because my influence comes from within, not from without. But everyone has to start out by emulating. You have to be careful whom you emulate to achieve your goal.

How did the Ahmad Jamal Trio get started?

We were originally the Four Strings, which was Ray Crawford on guitar, Tommy Sewell on bass, and Joe Kennedy, violin. Joe left, and for a while we stayed the Three Strings. In the early trio days the things that Ray did on the frets of his guitar were wonderful. Ray was the first to bring in that percussive sound you hear [in guitarists] today. If you go back to our early records like "Billy Boy" and "Will You Still Be Mine?" you'll hear a man playing conga, only it isn't a conga, but Ray hitting the frets of his guitar. This was taken up later by Barney Kessel and Herb Ellis [when they played in the Oscar Peterson Trio].

Wasn't it unusual to have a trio without a drummer?

Nat "King" Cole's was the classic cohesive trio that everyone patterned themselves after at that time [around 1949]. Nat was a fabulous pianist, and he worked with just bass and guitar. Listen to those things he did with Lester Young and his own trio. They were masterpieces. Subtlety was the trademark of that instrumentation. It was quite a challenge, especially to play some of those big rooms without a drummer. I played with that group [the Ahmad Jamal Trio] from about 1951 to '57. In 1957 I got into drums with a remarkable drummer, Vernel Fournier. That group made some monstrous headlines with Vernel and Israel Crosby on bass.

What accounts for the sudden recognition that band received? Was it solely on account of that live recording At the Pershing?

From my point of view, it wasn't sudden recognition. I had been recording for years, and in Chicago I became an artist-in-residence at the Embers during the mid-fifties. That's a great opportunity for any musician. Everybody came to see us, musicians, singers like Billie Holiday and Sammy Davis, Jr. We were publicized only by word of mouth, which is the best publicity you can get. Another thing that made all that happen was the album, one of the most perfect albums ever made in the history of American classical music, which is what I prefer to call it [jazz].

The record came about after [Chicago deejay] Sid McCoy and I decided it would be great to do a remote recording from the Pershing. We influenced Leonard Chess to carry it through. Sid, by the way, is now the voice on some very big commercials made in Los Angeles. It was the spontaneity, that wonderful element that [producer] Norman Granz used to capture on record, that made it successful. It hadn't been done in so long we resurrected it. We picked eight out of forty-three recorded tracks for the album, and that's being very selective. All the ingredients were there, even a wonderful engineer, Mal Chisholm. Everything was right. Our concepts were strong, too. Vernel Fournier grew up in that marvelous New Orleans environment, so he had marching bands, funeral processions, and all that great stuff in his background. He had the greatest brush work in the world. Israel Crosby was marvelous, too.

Speaking of your concepts, Miles Davis said in the mid-fifties that you were his inspiration. What do you make of that, and have you ever discussed that issue with Miles?

Not really. "New Rhumba" and "Medley" were transcribed note for note by Gil Evans for Miles's big band album *Miles Plus Nineteen* [also called *Miles Ahead*, on Columbia]. He just orchestrated things I had done early in my career. I was delighted. We needed that kind of support at the time Miles came along and paid us that compliment.

Why do you think your piano playing was so easily adapted to a big band score?

Because I've been trained to think orchestrally. That's the difference between the sound we get in our trio and some other bands. Thankfully, my three pieces sometimes give the illusion that they are six or seven pieces. We've become one instrument. Having been influenced in my childhood by the bands of Duke Ellington, Earl Hines, and Count Basie, and having stayed up late at the Savoy in Pittsburgh to hear those big bands, and playing with big bands, well, that's what happens. I don't think in single lines. I think in big band concepts.

By contrast, one of the things you've been known for is space, openness, and lightness in your music. Isn't that the antithesis of the orchestral approach?

No, it's not openness; it's discipline. Some people call it space, true. But I call it discipline.

How does your orchestral thinking get transferred to the keyboard? Do you write out your voicings [chord positions], bass lines, and so on?

Yes, contrary to what people have said, most of the things we do are written. Of course, I don't write the improvisational sections, but the songs we do are structured on paper.

Can you give me an example of how you start out with some new material? What did you do with "But Not for Me" on At the Pershing?

Well, that was about twenty-four years ago, so I honestly don't remember whether I just wrote out the chord changes in symbols or if I did something more. You know, there were other things that we definitely did *not* write out. When players have been together for a long time, you can do things that sound written even if they're not. Ballads, especially. I don't write out ballads unless for some reason the band can't hear where I'm going with the chords. I prefer the players to feel what I'm doing on a ballad. Otherwise, whatever we do is carefully planned and thought out.

When you're structuring a piece of music for the piano, are there any general rules that you follow?

Writing music is very difficult. When you reach a certain level, like in journalism or whatever you do, the work begins to dictate itself, as you must know. The most difficult thing is getting started. I don't push it. That's one rule. I won't sit down and force myself to think of something. Another thing I do is [write] the piano score first. When the piano part is written down, I'll set down a bass line, which is usually parallel to mine.

You mean your bass notes coincide with the bassist's?

Oh, yes. There are exceptions to that. Sometimes I'll give the bass the bottom [root tone] and I'll play the subordinate tones. If I'm working with a quintet, I'll extract from the piano score what I want for the trumpet and sax, too. I use close harmonies, very close. I also use what I'd call sensible and meaningful directions in the music, based on my experience of what works. I like strong rhythmic ideas, too. I guess that sums it up.

There are a lot of pedal tones, and superimposed chords in your playing.

That's one of the things that identify the Jamal approach to composition. I like pedal point and was influenced by it very early in life, and I like the superimposition of tones because I'm from the impressionistic school. Some of it came from my classical sources—I leaned heavily toward Ravel. He's one of my favorite composers.

Sometimes there's a large separation in your music between what's going on in the treble register and bass register on the keyboard? Do you think that's what people might mean by "space"? There are also times when you don't play at all.

Well, people have to call it something, but I still call it discipline. Philosophically I felt there are times when I should just lay out because I didn't think it was necessary for me to play.

For economy of expression?

You could call it that. But I'll still call it discipline. There might not be the same kind of discipline in my playing these days because I'm trying to achieve different things. Now I'm looking for consistency of performance as opposed to achievement. The ultimate goal of any performer has to be to play at a high level night after night.

I'm glad you brought that up. Your playing seems much fuller and busier now. Though I hate to use the word, there's not as much of what everyone called space as there used to be. I was planning to ask you about that.

When I was young, I was trying to achieve something—recognition, not necessarily from other people, but from myself. I was trying to gain confidence. When you have more confidence, the ideas flow more easily. That's what the difference in my playing is now. It's more fluidity, fluency. You have a greater flow of ideas when you have more confidence. I'd say my playing is fuller now, broader, and more percussive.

Where do you see yourself in the jazz piano tradition?

I don't see myself in that way, certainly not following the tradition of any other jazz pianists. I came through three different eras. I was a boy when Ellington and Hines were at their peaks. I was a young man when the Gillespie-Charlie Parker era came in, and I was quite an adult with the advent of electronics. This is also true of Thad Jones, Miles Davis, Mel Lewis, Clark Terry, and Quincy Jones. These guys have spanned the eras, and they're still around. Right now I see myself as a product of these different eras. And being fortunate enough to have that broad background, I'm just following my own individual ideas and experiences.

Selected Discography

Live: At the Pershing (1958); 628; Argo/Cadet.*

Tranquility (1968); AS 9238; Impulse.

At the Top: Poinciana Revisited (1969); A-9176; Impulse.

Jamal Plays Jamal (1974); T-459; 20th Century Records.

Ahmad Jamal Live At Bubba's (1981); WWLP-21021; Who's Who in Jazz.

HORACE
SILVER

September 2, 1928–

For more than a quarter century Horace Silver has led his own quintets in an extroverted, driving, and blues-based modern jazz style that historians refer to as hard bop. Silver's music is thought of as East Coast because most of the musicians who played it lived and worked there. East Coast jazz had qualities that seem to contrast with the more disciplined West Coast and cool styles. As noted in Part One, Silver's influence began to be felt in the mid-1950's, when he played in a group with Art Blakey that later became the Jazz Messengers.

In 1956 Silver formed his own band with Art Farmer on trumpet and Hank Mobley on tenor sax. Subsequent editions of the Horace Silver Quintet were famous for their exciting trumpet/sax front lines, such as Blue Mitchell/ Junior Cook, Freddie Hubbard/Wayne Shorter, Woody Shaw/Joe Henderson, Randy Brecker/Mike Brecker, and Tom Harrell/Bob Berg. Horace himself was celebrated for his catchy, singable compositions like "Señor Blues," "Sister Sadie," "Blowin' the Blues Away," and "Song for My Father." Silver's ability to ignite other soloists with staccato, rhythmic accompanying chords is legendary. His bluesy and melodic solos revealed, at a time when the long, tortuous improvised line prevailed, the power of simplicity. To a greater extent than his peers, Silver's improvisations have the economy of expression and balance of composed melodies.

I met Horace Silver at the Sam Wong Hotel bordering Chinatown. His room was austere, lacking even a telephone, but the decor was somewhat enlivened by a vegetable juicer and an impressive lineup of vitamin pills on the dresser. When Horace was in his thirties, he cured an arthritic right hand with a regimen of physical therapy and a diet to which he still adheres faithfully. In his fifties, Horace is slim, energetic, and bright-eyed. Keeping fit is necessary for his physical style of playing. When Horace digs in up-tempo, he curves his torso over the keyboard, his shoulders sway like a cat ready to pounce, and he seems to attack each note with his whole body. His technique would give a classical teacher nightmares, but it enables him to swing with the precision of a tightly wound metronome. Like his hotel room, Silver's soloing is simple, angular, and Spartan. At the top of his hierarchy of values is what he calls "in-depthness" or "simplicity coupled with profundity." It is perhaps this quality that makes both his soloing and compositions easily grasped yet durable.

Another word that captures the feeling of Silver's music is "funky." Reared on the linear sophistication of Charlie Parker, Dizzy Gillespie, and Bud Powell, Silver simplified and "bluesified" these influences in his own music. Introducing a driving and sometimes "Latin" rhythm behind his melodies, Silver's sound used to be called soul jazz, before "soul" became associated more strictly with rhythm and blues. In fact, Herbie Hancock had recently referred to Silver's work as "some of the earliest funky music," and the first thing on my mind was to find out what this quality meant to Horace himself.

What does the word "funky" mean to you?

"Funky" means "earthy, blues-based." It may not be blues itself, but it has that down-home feel to it. Playing funky has nothing to do with style; it's an approach to playing. For instance, Herbie Hancock and I have different styles, but we both play funky. "Soul" is the same, basically, but there's an added dimension of feeling and spirit to soul—an in-depthness. A soulful player might be funky or he might not be.

How does the directness of your approach relate to the complexities of bebop?

I've found in composing that being simple and profound—having in-depthness in your music—is the most difficult thing to do. Anybody can write a whole lot of notes, which may or may not say something. Bebop was a good example. From what I've heard, the way bebop got started was in small dives where guys would bug the musicians to let them sit in. The musicians were trying to keep these sad musicians off the stand, so guys like Dizzy or Bird or Monk started writing these complicated lines, so nobody else could play them. That way these sad musicians couldn't be dragging the session. But why make it complicated for the musicians to play? Why make it difficult for the listeners to hear? The hardest thing is to make it simple. What separates the men from the boys is whether your simple lines have profundity in them—whether there's longevity there or whether they're trite.

What kind of background did you have?

I studied, but not as long as I should have. My uncle's girl friend was a piano teacher, and that's where I started. But after I took a half dozen lessons from her, she and my uncle broke up, so that was that. Then I studied for a year with another woman who was giving group lessons. I didn't learn much, but it only cost fifty cents a lesson, which was great for me because I came from a poor family. My third teacher was a classically trained organist at one of the white churches in town [Norwalk, Connecticut]. His name was Professor William Scofield. Actually I consider him my only teacher, though I did get bored with classical music. It just wasn't what I wanted to do. He realized I had natural ability, and he wanted me to go to the conservatory, so he was going to get some rich white folks to sponsor me. But I really didn't want to get hung up in that classical thing–though now I wish I had studied with him a little longer, for purely technical reasons.

Do you feel limited technically?

No. I'm not the technician others may be, but my technique is completely adequate for my style. I can play what I hear, and that's all that's necessary. I don't hear all that activity all over the piano, like an Art Tatum. If I wanted to play that way, I'd have to practice, but that's not the way I hear music.

Do you practice a lot?

I practice, but not regularly. When I'm home, most of my time is devoted to composing. Occasionally, if my chops are down, I'll do some whole-tone scales or something from an exercise book, but my chops are usually up because I play so much. I'd recommend practice for anyone who's not out there playing every night.

What did you do for harmony and ear training and who were your influences?

I got a harmony book from a music store and studied basic root positions. An older musician in Norwalk showed me how to embellish chords. Then, having a good ear, I used to take those Charlie Parker, Bud Powell, and [saxophonist] Dexter Gordon records on Savoy and put them on an old windup machine and slow the speed down. That would put everything in another key, but I'd hear the chords that way and pick them out note by note. I was playing augmented ninths, flatted ninths, elevenths, diminished chords, and so on without having any idea what they were called. The very first tune I learned was "What Is This Thing Called Love?" I'll never forget it because it took me about five minutes to find C7 in root position. Later on, from Teddy Wilson records, I learned how to play tenths and open the voicing up.

How about melodic ear training?

I used to play a lot of Bud Powell solos off the record, and when I played tenor, I practiced with Lester Young records every day. In fact, I'd go out on gigs and play parts of his solos. In a sense, I'm self-taught; I applied myself. But my teachers were all these great guys on records.

How do you approach accompaniment?

I think a piano player has to like to comp in order to do it well. If you're preoccupied with soloing, if you're just sitting up there halfway feeding the horns, waiting for your turn to solo, you won't be a good comper. You have to enjoy it as much as you enjoy soloing. I love the feeling I get when the rhythm section is really hitting it together. We can make the horn players better, and I don't give a damn how good they are. If we're goosing them in the ass, and the shit is really happening, the piano's digging in, they're sitting there in the palms of our hands. We've got to raise our hands and uplift them to the sky. See, the music's got to float. If we let them go, they'll drop. I've never been one to lay back during horn solos. You shouldn't play with a band if you do that. You ought to play solo or with a trio.

Your playing has evolved since you were with the Stan Getz group in the early fifties.

It's true. I hadn't completely formulated my style at that point. I was very heavily influenced by Bud Powell and Thelonious Monk, and on those Getz records I was also very nervous, a young kid from Connecticut thrust into the studio with all those great names. I started thinking about where I was and who I was with. Being young, I lacked self-confidence, so I got shaky. After I left Getz and stayed in New York for a year, I did a record date with [saxophonist] Lou Donaldson for Blue Note, and I was a little more relaxed. When I listened to those tapes, I heard something in there that was definitely Horace Silver. I didn't know what it was exactly, but I knew that no one else was playing that way, so I decided to work on it. I took my record player and records, packed them up in the closet, and played no records for a long time. I didn't want to be influenced by anybody. I just practiced.

What was it that you recognized as "you" on those early recordings?

It's an intangible thing. I can't even tell you today in verbal terms. I can't put my style into words. Maybe somebody else could, though I might or might not agree with what they came up with.

When did you first get a chance to record your own material?

I was supposed to be on Donaldson's second recording session, but three days before, Alfred Lion called to tell me Lou couldn't make it, and he invited me to do a trio session for them. It was pretty short notice, but I realized it was a once-in-a-lifetime opportunity. Fortunately I had a backlog of compositions to draw on, so I didn't have to do any writing. All I had to do was write out some bass parts for Curly Russell and get my own chops together. [This session was eventually released on *Horace Silver* (Blue Note). It features drummer Art Blakey and conga player Sabu Martinez.]

How did you meet Art Blakey and begin playing with the Jazz Messengers?

I was playing a gig in some club—well, it was a dive really—in New Jersey. We played for a floor show, but our tenor player was working with Art Blakey and the nine-piece band that he had then. I believe that was also called the Messengers. Blakey's piano player was goofing off and not showing up for rehearsals and so on, so the tenor player on our gig brought me over to audition for Art. I got the job, but that band was very short-lived. We could hardly get arrested with that band, let alone find work. We played some dances around Harlem, once a week at the most. The next thing that came along was Art getting a couple of weeks at Birdland. He had been hearing about [trumpeter] Clifford Brown. You know, there were rumors then about this cat in Delaware who played so great. Art just dug him out of there and brought him to New York. Art, Clifford, Lou Donaldson, Curly Russell on bass, and myself—we made that gig in Birdland, and that was how the record *A Night at Birdland* happened.

We played two weeks in New York, a week in Philadelphia, and that was it for that band. We couldn't get no work, man. None. Clifford went with [drummer] Max Roach. About a year later [1955], Art got a band that lasted, which was the Jazz Messengers, including me, Kenny Dorham, Hank Mobley, and Doug Watkins on bass. That group was together for a year, playing the circuit, New York, Boston, Philly, Washington, and so on. We never made it out to the West Coast. We made the records from the Café Bohemia with that group.

Had you ever played with a drummer as powerful as Blakey?

Never. I never worked with one as powerful since either! Well, that's not to say I haven't had strong drummers in my band—like Billy Cobham, Roy Brooks, Louis Hayes. But Art is one of a kind.

How did his playing affect you as a pianist?

It made me much stronger as a rhythm player, especially comping, backing up a soloist. There's another thing Art instilled in me as a player—and not by talking to me but by example! Art never lets up. I've seen him go days without sleep, come down with a bad cold, and no matter what, every time the man goes up on the bandstand, he puts fire to the music and there's no letting up. That rubbed off on me.

Why did you leave that band?

I don't care to go into the reasons why I left because it's personal. It had nothing to do with Art or any person in the band. There weren't any personality clashes. Just personal.

How did your own group get started?

It happened a few months later. I had intended to take a rest and then get a job with another band. But my record "Señor Blues" came out, and it was doing quite well in Philadelphia. This guy asked me to come down and play, but I told him, "I don't have no band, I just made a record, that's all." He said, "Put one together and come down for a week. Let's see what happens." It worked out pretty well. I had Art Taylor on drums, although he only worked that week; then Louis Hayes replaced him. There was Doug Watkins, Art Farmer on trumpet, and Hank Mobley. The "Señor Blues" band was the same, except Donald Byrd replaced Art on trumpet. That happened because Blue Note and Prestige were always feuding with each other, and I guess Bob Weinstock [owner of Prestige] wouldn't let Art record for Alfred Lion [owner of Blue Note]. So here I had a record date and couldn't use my trumpet player. Fortunately Donald Byrd was studying then at the Manhattan School of Music and made the gig.

You've been quoted as saying, "I didn't want to become too pianistic in my approach to the instrument." Is that true?

Yeah, it's true. My influences in music were not all pianists. Of course, I played sax at one time, and I'm in love with [saxophonist] Lester Young. I idolize him. And I've always dug Dizzy, Miles, [saxophonists] Coleman Hawkins, Sonny Rollins, Charlie Parker, so many horn players. So I asked myself, "Why does a pianist have to approach the piano pianistically?" There's nothing wrong with approaching it pianistically, of course. It *is* a piano. Anyway, I love to be different. I might do something just because it's the opposite of what everybody else is doing. Monk doesn't approach the piano in an entirely pianistic way, but he gets some beautiful things out of it, unique things that pianistic players like Oscar Peterson wouldn't even dream of. Look at what Milt Jackson did for the vibes. Until he came along, all the vibes players, except maybe Lionel Hampton, sounded alike. They'd been getting the same tonal quality because they used the same approach. When Milt came along, he realized you could slow down the motor and get a vibrato out of the instrument. That's one of the things, aside from his mastery of the instrument, that gave him a unique sound.

Melodically, then, there's an element of horn playing in your approach. But your accompaniment style seems highly percussive.

It's true in a sense, though I don't consciously think about it in that way. I'm very involved with rhythm, and that's an important part of jazz to me. I like to play around with rhythmic patterns when I'm comping behind horns. I suppose I do have some percussive attack on the piano, but the way I look at it, I'm just trying to be myself and hope to be original.

Do you still feel the need to avoid the influence of other musicians?

Oh, no. I listen to everybody. I always have my radio tuned to [jazz station] KBCA [now KKGO] in Los Angeles. My ears are open to all of it, but when I'm playing, my ears are shut to everyone but me. In your formative years the influences you're absorbing possess you, which is okay when you're young and trying to get it together. But there comes a time when you have to find your own direction. I did that a long time ago, so I don't have to throw my record player in the closet anymore. I can listen to anyone now, and even get ideas from them, without being influenced by them or falling back on them. When you become creative in music—or maybe in anything—the only thing you fall back on for inspiration is the Creator. You do get something from divine sources. Ultimately everybody does. It's just that as a creative musician, you're getting it directly and not through another person who's an "influence."

Are you being metaphorical when you say the source of music is the Creator, or do you mean it literally?

It's a fact of life. Even when I was copying other musicians, trying to learn from their styles—they were possessing me, in a sense—the divine force was coming through them on a higher level than I was able to attain. I was getting the inspiration *through* them. Now I can get it more directly, from the main source.

The late saxophonist Cannonball Adderley once said he felt like a "vehicle of musical expression," that the music was passing through him.

He's right. The drummer Billy Higgins was quoted as saying, "Music doesn't come from you, it comes through you." That's very profound. Anybody who's trying to create has got to have help. Sometimes when I sit at the piano trying to compose, I feel like a stranger to the instrument. I have no ideas; my mind draws a blank. I wonder if I'm the same man who has written all these other compositions because just then I'm empty. So where does it all come from? I can sit for days without an idea, but if I keep at it and tell myself to get off my ass, it's as if somebody *knows* I'm trying to write a song and comes over to whisper something in my ear. Suddenly, BAM! The shit just flows. Most of my compositions come at one sitting. Being theoretical, when you sit at the piano you concentrate on the spot on your forehead that represents the third eye. But when the idea hits you, it doesn't hit the third eye. It hits you on the back of your head, the medulla oblongata, or on the top of your head, where the pineal gland is supposed to be. I've thought about this a lot. Maybe a yogi could explain it. I don't know how to explain it, but I know how I feel when I'm writing.

Do you use the piano to compose?

Usually, although I once wrote a tune in Boston on a paper bath mat. That was "You Gotta Take a Little Love." "Psychedelic Sally" came to me in a hotel room somewhere. Those cassette players are invaluable, too. In Detroit once I sang a tune onto a tape and then worked it out on the piano when I got down to the club.

What has your experience been with electric keyboards?

I've done three recordings, a series called *The United States of Mind* [Vol. 3, Blue Note, is still in print], with vocals, on which I played the RMI. They're fine recordings, but they seem to have got lost in the shuffle because people are still asking me when I'm going to record on electric. I enjoyed the electric for that particular work because of the musical contexts. There's a variety of moods—gospel, Latin, rock, straight-ahead jazz, blues. I was searching for one instrument that could handle all of them. I didn't want to use the Rhodes piano because I'm tired of the sound. Everybody uses it to death. It does have more of a piano action than the RMI, though. The RMI action is more like an organ. It doesn't respond very fast, and you have to hold the key down a long time to hold the note out, so you have to play fairly simply. It has a sustain pedal, but it doesn't sustain very long. What I liked about it was the stops and the variety of sounds you can get by mixing the stops. The one stop on the RMI that I didn't like was the piano stop. It just didn't sound like a piano. I loved the combination of lute and harpsichord, though. I also put a *wah-wah* on it. When it comes to acoustic instruments, I prefer a Steinway. That's the Cadillac of the piano world. I'll take a Baldwin as a second, though.

Your album Silver 'n Brass *is a departure from the quintet format. How do you feel about that album and the large ensemble context?*

We laid down the quintet tracks first and then overdubbed the brass. Wade Marcus orchestrated the brass, and I think there's a hairline difference between orchestration and arranging. I arranged the tunes, in a sense, because the harmonies were taken directly from my piano voicings. Wade and I sat down with the tapes, and I'd show him the notes I was using in my comps. Then he'd write it out for the brass, putting everything in the right place. He did a beautiful job. Several musicians told me they went out and bought that album, and when that happens, it's rare. It is a fine recording, and I'm not just saying that because it's mine.

Except for those first trio sessions for Blue Note, you haven't made any albums which actually featured the piano, such as an unaccompanied piano album. Do you think of yourself as an ensemble pianist?

It's just that as a composer, I don't get complete satisfaction out of playing my compositions in trio form. I've been told I have the ability to make two horns sound a lot bigger than two instruments. I try to get that big sound by fooling around with the harmonies, because I've got only five pieces to work with. I get a charge out of hearing the band play my stuff, and it sounds empty to me in a trio, even though I can play all the same notes on the piano.

Do you consider yourself primarily a composer or a pianist?

I feel like both. I hope I'll always do both. I was once asked which I'd choose if somebody were to put a gun to my head and tell me I could only be one or the other. I'd have to choose composing in that case, because there's something I receive when I write music, when that tune comes, that rejuvenates my whole system.

Selected Discography

The Trio Sides (1952–68); LA474-H2; Blue Note.

Miles Davis: Tune Up (1954); P-24077; Prestige.

Horace Silver (1959–66); LA402-H2; Blue Note.

Art Blakey: A Night at Birdland (1954); BLP-1521/BST-81521; Blue Note.

Blowin' the Blues Away (1959); BLP-4017/BST-84017; Blue Note.

Doin' the Thing (1961); BLP-4076/BST-84076; Blue Note.

OSCAR PETERSON

August 15, 1925–

Mₒᵣₑ than any other pianist, Oscar Peterson has inherited the harmonic conception and awesome technique of Art Tatum, his mentor and early idol. The most abundantly recorded pianist in jazz, Peterson performs for live audiences only with the assurance of a tightly controlled setting. For a time he would appear in nightclubs only on the condition that no drinks would be served, nor cash registers used, while he played. I remember him playing a tender ballad in a now-dark Boston club called Lennie's on the Turnpike when a customer at the bar began whistling along with the melody. Oscar stopped abruptly, took the mike, and snapped at the audience, "Whoever's whistling has the worst taste in the world!" He walked offstage and imposed an unscheduled thirty-minute intermission.

But Peterson's regal manner disappears offstage. When we first met, which was in his suite at the Fairmont Hotel at the crest of San Francisco's fashionable Nob Hill, we discussed baseball, Oscar's children, his grandchildren, and his native Canada before I realized that we would never get around to the subject of Oscar Peterson unless I brought it up.

Peterson came to the States from Canada in 1949, thanks to a happy coincidence that brought him to the attention of impresario Norman Granz, who has managed Oscar's career ever since. Peterson's style is basically an amalgam of swing and bebop. There are critics who downgrade the effect of his glorious technical command of the keyboard, accusing him of an overly mechanized style and of indulging in virtuosity for its own sake. True, Peterson can be showy and rococo; but more often than not, his technique operates in the service of his art. I have heard him solo using a stride technique or a walking-bass line in the left hand. The music gathers momentum until the piano itself seems to be strutting across the stage; Oscar's husky, Buddha-like body works and sweats to put the instrument through its paces; and so I have trouble condemning Peterson as a mechanistic player. It is the spirit, more than physical dexterity, that drives him.

Peterson has been a nearly ubiquitous accompanist and collaborator, especially for the many legendary figures whose concerts and records were produced by Granz. Some of his best work in this role has been done with saxophonist Lester Young, Ella Fitzgerald and Louis Armstrong, trumpeter Roy Eldridge, vibist Milt Jackson, and Dizzy Gillespie. He is particularly well matched with guitarist Joe Pass, whose technical dexterity and style of harmonic development match Oscar's own. Amazingly, Peterson has had arthritis in his hands since high school. He said that the condition is a familial tendency, that it sometimes causes him pain when he plays and occasionally requires him to cancel a performance.

Peterson's virtuosity—his speed, articulation, and endurance—inspires and intimidates other pianists. His dexterity also enlivens his style, for Oscar has never varied the premises he inherited during the early 1950's from Tatum and Powell. Fortunately, though, his technique enables him to vary infinitely the way he implements those assumptions. And of course, he can always turn on the steam.

What were your very first experiences with the piano?

My first experiences were of not wanting to play it because I was interested in trumpet. In fact, I played trumpet in a small family orchestra, but after spending almost a year in the hospital with tuberculosis, I was advised by the doctor to give up wind instruments. I continued on piano, which I had begun along with the trumpet, though mainly at my father's insistence. The piano didn't start to appeal to me until my older brother Fred got into jazz, or whatever jazz was then, playing "Golden Slippers" or something like that. What I went through as a student was probably what everyone else grooming himself for the classical field goes through—Czerny, Hanon, Dohnanyi. All of these things just serve to broaden digital control. It was something I wanted to get behind me as quickly as possible.

How long did it take you to get it behind you?

Do you ever, really? You like to tell yourself so, I guess. Probably I started feeling comfortable around the age of sixteen or seventeen. That's when I started feeling that I could transmit to the keyboard most of what I conjured up mentally. Prior to that it was a scuffle. I'd be thinking something and then run into a snag on executing it. That used to bug me.

What were your early practice routines?

I'd start out in the morning with scales, exercises, and whatever classical pieces I was working on. After a break I'd come back and do voicings; I'd challenge the voicings I'd been using and try to move them around in tempo without losing the harmonic content.

I also practiced time by playing against myself and letting the left hand take a loose, undulating time shape while making the right hand stay completely in time. Then I'd reverse the process, keeping the left hand rigid and making the right hand stretch and contract. You know, practicing that way takes the urgency out of getting from Point A to Point B in a solo. It gives you the confidence to renegotiate a line while you're playing it. It gives you a respect for different shapes.

You must have been practicing the piano all day.

About eighteen hours a day. I got into that when I decided I really wanted to play. It was during high school, just before I got my first group together. I figured I'd have to get myself together first because there'd be enough questions in a group context. I couldn't afford to have any questions about my end of things. I'd practice from nine in the morning to lunch and from after lunch to seven in the evening. Then I'd go from supper until my mother pulled me off the instrument or raised hell.

After all that exacting practice how did you feel when you hit an occasional wrong note?

It didn't bother me too much. My classical teacher used to tell me, "If you make a mistake, don't stop. Make it part of what you're playing as much as possible. Don't chop up your playing by correcting things, even when you're playing for yourself. It's a bad habit, and it will make you a sporadic player." One thing I try to convey to my students when I'm teaching is the relativity of notes. From a melodic standpoint there are wrong notes. But from a creative standpoint there are no wrong notes because every note can be related to a chord. Every note can be made part of your line, depending on how fast you can integrate it into your schematic arrangement. Of course, if you're playing the national anthem and you miss the melody or hit a major chord wrong without its being a revision of the chord, then you've made a mistake. Playing on a theme, however, is a different kind of thing. I think this idea is the basis of a lot of the avant-garde music today, although I don't believe in making it quite as easy as they do. But there's truth to the idea that you shouldn't be thrown by a note.

It sounds as if you're more interested in the effect of the phrase than in each note within the phrase.

That's right. I'm an admirer of the beautiful long line which starts out and then reaches a point of definition. If you reach a point of definition, it validates all the other aspects of the line. I think we went through a period of short-phrase artists. I won't derogate them or get into names, but the hesitation and the short five-note phrase are not my bag. It makes me nervous to listen to it. I'm an advocate of the long line, but it's got to mean something.

Here's a list of long-line players: Art Tatum, Bud Powell, [saxophonist] Charlie Parker, [trumpeter] Dizzy Gillespie, [saxophonist] Eric Dolphy. Would you add to the list?

I'd add Hank Jones, Cedar Walton, and Bill Evans. Let me draw an analogy. I don't think you should speak until you have your sentence together in your mind. It's easier to listen to someone who knows what he wants to say than a person who stops, starts, picks up another idea, continues, and winds up with a series of chopped-up phrases. Well, to each his own.

What do you remember most about the pianists who were influences on you?

I remember one story about Nat Cole, who I think was one of the deepest time players ever. Ray [Brown] once told me he was with Dizzy's big band and they were playing the Los Angeles Coliseum. Nat's trio was on the bill, too, and Ray said the trio wasted them just because of the time factor. We've experienced that; when my trio's at its deepest point, when we get that far down into the time, we make it hard for a bigger band to operate. It swings that hard. That was the biggest influence Nat had on me: making time pop. When I play with Dizzy, Ray, Zoot [Sims, saxophonist], Clark [Terry, trumpeter], or [guitarist] Joe Pass, they're all aware that when I'm in the section, I deal with time, nothing else. For a rhythm section to give what it has to give, you have to deal that heavily with time. In fact, I'd recommend using time to combat these complaints you sometimes hear of stale playing. I'm a waltz freak personally. If you feel that a piece is getting stale, put it into 3/4 time. Generally I don't go past the 3/4 because many of the other signatures, like 9/8, have been overdone, and I think you inevitably come back to a 3/4 or 4/4 feeling anyway. From a listener's point of view, how far is 6/8 from 3/4?

Who influenced you in your appreciation of the long line we were discussing?

There's Teddy Wilson. From Teddy I got the beautiful long line, the interconnecting runs that tie together the harmonic movements in a ballad, the impeccable good taste of the right touch, and the idea of how to make a piano speak. I got that from Hank Jones, too.

When I asked about people who have influenced you, I was hoping for some stories about Art Tatum. He's a legend, but unfortunately very few of us had the pleasure of hearing him in person.

Do you know the story of when I first heard him? When I was getting into the jazz thing—or thought I was—as a kid, my father thought I was a little heavy about my capabilities, so he played me Art's recording of "Tiger Rag." First of all, I swore it was two people playing. When I finally admitted to myself that it was one man, I gave up the piano for a month. I figured it was hopeless to practice. My mother and friends of mine persuaded me to get back to it, but I've had the greatest respect for Art from then on.

How did you first meet Tatum?

In the early fifties, I was playing with the trio in Washington, D.C., at a club called Louis and Alex's. I used to kid Ray [Brown] about [bassist] Oscar Pettiford. We'd be playing and I'd say, "Watch it now, Oscar Pettiford's out there!" He'd say, "Hell with him. I'm going to stomp him." He'd do the same to me about Art Tatum because we both had tremendous love and respect for these men. On the third night of the gig we were playing "Airmail Special," and Ray said, "Watch it, Art's out there." "Hell with him," I said. "He's got to contend with me." See, he'd pulled that a dozen times, and I would always go into my heavy routine. "No, this time he's *really* out there," Ray insisted. "Look over at the bar." There he was! I closed up the tune immediately and took it out. The set was over. I froze. Ray took me over to meet him, and I still remember what Art said: "Brown, you brought me one of those sleepers, huh?" He told us to come by this after-hours joint and he'd see what he could do with me. I was totally frightened of this man and his tremendous talent. It's like a lion; you're scared to death, but it's such a beautiful animal, you want to come up close and hear it roar.

Did you make it over to this club?

Yes, we went to the club, and Art told me to play. "No way," I told him. "Forget it." So Art told me this story about a guy he knew down in New Orleans. All he knew how to play was one chorus of the blues, and if you asked him to play some more, he'd repeat that same chorus over again. Art said he'd give anything to be able to play that chorus of the blues the way that old man played it. The message was clear: Everyone had something to say. Well, I got up to the piano and played what I'd call two of the neatest choruses of "Tea for Two" you've ever heard. That was all I could do. Then Art played, and it fractured me. I had nightmares of keyboards that night.

Did you and Tatum see each other much after that?

Yes, Art and I became great friends, but I had this phobia about him, and it lasted a long time. I simply couldn't play when he was in the room. One day he took me aside and said, "You can't afford this. You have too much going for you. If you have to hate me when I walk into the room, I don't care. I want you to play." I don't know how it happened exactly, but one night at the Old Tiffany in Los Angeles, I was into a good set when I heard Art's voice from the audience saying, "Lighten up, Oscar Peterson." I knew it was Art, but it didn't bother me. I got deeper into the music instead, and I knew I was over it. Both Art and my father died within a week of each other, and I realized in one week I lost two of the best friends I had. That's been the Art Tatum thing with me.

After all these years, can you tell me what got you started, what got your career off the ground?

It was Norman Granz, Jazz at the Philharmonic, and the concert at Carnegie Hall in 1949. Actually the first time Norman heard me was on a recording, under protest at the time, on RCA. I was playing boogie-woogie, and he detested it. The next time he was finishing up a promotional trip to Montreal and taking a cab to the airport. I was on the radio. He thought it was a recording, but it was a live broadcast from the Alberta Lounge. The cabdriver straightened him out on that point. The cab turned around and came down to the Alberta.

You owe it all to a hip cabby?

It hatched the beginnings.

Let's talk about the Oscar Peterson trios. Why did you start out with bass and guitar? Was the Tatum trio with Slam Stewart on bass and Tiny Grimes on guitar your model?

No. Of course, I heard that group, but they didn't do the kind of complex arrangements we did. The reason for the trio originally was that I wanted to write some things with contravening lines, something fuller than you could get with a bass. I used Barney Kessel for his obvious capabilities on the instrument. [The Peterson Trio with bass and guitar began in about 1952 and lasted through 1959. Irving Ashby was the first guitarist but was soon replaced by Kessel. Kessel was replaced by Herb Ellis in 1954.] The music was written very tightly, although we didn't want to lose the spontaneity in the improvising because you don't have jazz without that. I kept a firm hand on what was going on and didn't let anyone else write for the group. I didn't want them to change what we were doing.

Why did you replace your guitarist with drummer Ed Thigpen in 1959?

I must admit part of the reason was an ego trip for me. There was a lot of talk about my virtuosity on the instrument, and some people were saying, "Oh, he can play that way with a guitar because it's got that light, fast sound, but he couldn't pull off those lines with a drummer burnin' up back there." I wanted to prove it could be done. We chose Ed Thigpen because of his brushwork and sensitivity in general. I came across him in Japan, where he was stationed in the army. When he got out, we were ready for a drummer.

Your next steady partner was Niels-Henning Orsted-Pedersen, whom I first heard on a record he made when he was fifteen years old and backing Bud Powell at a Copenhagen club. How did you meet him?

I first heard him in Paris, in Montmartre. At the time we had George Mraz in the group. Later on we had a tour booked in Czechoslovakia, where George is from, but because of the way he left the country, which wasn't under the best of circumstances, he couldn't go back. We couldn't find any other bassists who wanted to make the trip except for Niels. I guess he was feeling a little suicidal. I was pretty rough on him and pulled out some arrangements without telling him. Niels is like having another soloist in the band.

I'd be interested in your reaction to something LeRoi Jones [Imamu Amiri Baraka] wrote about you in his book Black Music: *"I want to explain technical so as not to be confused with people who think that Thelonious Monk is 'a fine pianist, but limited technically.' But by technical I mean more specifically being able to use what important ideas are contained in the residue of history. . . . Knowing how to play an instrument is the barest superficiality if one is thinking of becoming a musician. It is the ideas that one utilizes instinctively that determine the degree of profundity any artist reaches. . . . (And it is exactly because someone like Oscar Peterson has instinctive profundity that technique is glibness. That he can play the piano rather handily just makes him easier to identify. There is no serious instinct working at all.) . . . Technique is inseparable from what is finally played as content." What's your impression of his idea that technique and content are separate?*

My first impression is that he doesn't play.

What he'd realize is that technique *is* separated from playing. Thelonious Monk *is* limited technically. But let's not put Thelonious down. You can say that about me, too. I can think of a whole lot of things that I'm not technically capable of playing. Otherwise, what does the phrase "playing over his head" mean?

I'll tell you what I think technique is, and since I'm a player I think it has a little more validity.

Technique is something you use to make your ideas listenable. You learn to play the instrument so you have a musical vocabulary, and you practice to get your technique to the point you need to express yourself, depending on how heavy your ideas are.

Louis Armstrong is an example of a man who developed a technique of playing to the point he needed to pursue his ideas. If he had wanted to go further technically, he might have gotten into Dizzy's bag. He was capable of it. Roy Eldridge has fantastic technique on the instrument. But there's a case of using just what you need and no more. Roy's a very simple person. He's a very direct person. Now you'd never hear a simple solo from me; you'd never hear simple solos from Bill Evans or Hank Jones or McCoy.

But you would hear simple solos from Monk.

Monk is a very harmonic player, and that requires a special type of technique. As a linear player, well, I don't think Monk is a linear player. Usually someone who's not a linear player is hamstrung, so they don't come up with that [linear solos].

Do you think it's fair to say some techniques are better than others? Or is technique a relative concept? Does its value depend on what you use it for?

It's a selfish, relative concept. Selfish, because you use it only for what you want. When I teach, I teach technique because like raising kids, you want to give them the broadest scope possible so they can face whatever they come up against. The funny thing about technique is this: It's not a matter of technique; it's *time*. I'm talking about playing jazz rhythmically. You have an idea, and it's confined to a certain period in a piece on an overlay of harmonic carpeting. You have to get from here to there in whatever time you're allotted with whatever ideas you have.

I could have five guys sit down and play a line, and you'll get five versions of it. You won't like all five, but it's not because some guys missed it or couldn't play it. It's because rhythmically, jazzwise, it didn't happen. That gets into interpretation and articulation. It goes beyond the digital facility one has on the keyboard. I know pianists who have ten times the technique I have–I won't call any names, though–but they can't make it happen. Rhythmically and creatively they don't have that thing, whatever that *thing* is.

Can we get into some explicitly technical questions? For example, in your concert last night, were you trying to create countermelodies in the left-hand chord voicings?

No, it wasn't a matter of countermelodies. It was a matter of comping as if I were playing for a soloist, comping without having the voicings break down. I didn't want to sound like I just came up with a chord to get myself out of a situation or to get myself to the next chord. Voicing is putting something down for your right hand to play off of. See, you really play off your left hand. Most players think of themselves as playing off the right hand because there's so much activity there. What's really happening is that the right hand is determined, although that's probably too strong a word, by the left-hand formation. The left hand can add tonal validity, too, by augmenting with clusters what the right hand is playing. But it's the left hand that starts the line off and determines its basic movement.

In other words, the harmonic structure determines the melodic content?

Yes, I believe it does. It's also true that the left hand punctuates the line.

Do you recommend practicing voicings in all the keys?

By all means. I used to do that. Things take on a different shape in a different way. It's not a matter of easy or hard keys. They just have different shapes because the fingering is different.

What other piano exercises did you do?

After the movement of the voicings, I'd go to the right-hand lines alone. I'd try to play the melody with real feeling, as if I were playing a horn, pedaling and controlling the touch so it wouldn't sound staccato. Then I'd duplicate the right-hand linear playing in the left hand. I figured I'd develop a lot of control that way. Sometimes I'd play fours with myself to give the left hand more dexterity. ["Playing fours" involves trading four-bar improvisations between players or, in Peterson's context, between hands.] That comes in handy after you finish a right-hand line and you want to move down to a different pedal tone. You're not relegated to simply hitting it. You can move down or up, tying things together, walking.

Do you finger the octaves in a parallel way?

No, because they're played by two different hands. Each hand is constructed differently, and you'll never make them play the same way. My theory is to have the phrase under your hand with whatever it takes to do that. If you find yourself reaching awkwardly, you know that for your hands there's bad fingering there somewhere. At this point the fingerings just fall under the hand for me. Each finds its own. If you think of the whole phrase you want to play, you shouldn't have to think about fingering at all. It should be that well integrated from your mind through your heart and soul to your hands. You shouldn't have to ask yourself whether to cross over or not. The conception and the physical transmitting of it should merge.

You've used walking tenths in the left hand to great effect in much of your playing. Since your hands are so large, you can play them fluidly with alternating 1–4 and 1–5 fingering. Do you have any advice for pianists who don't have the reach to play them smoothly?

There is a way to convey the same musical picture if you can't reach that in the left hand. It's not a deception, but it's a way of establishing the theme in the listener's mind. Just play the walking tenths with two hands at different times during a tune and people will swear they're present all the time. Of course, you can't do that when you're way up in the treble register, but you can stop everything else and let the tenths walk. I've done that, too. Once you've established the theme, the listener hears it through the piece.

Your arpeggios are very fluid as well. Do you have any tips here?

Most people tend to accent every fourth note, although exercise books never denote accents. Students interpret them that way, though, and their teachers seem to accept it. I don't. If you play me an arpeggio, I want to hear it up and down with no accents and no divisions. A way to practice this is to intersperse scales and arpeggios. Go up with an arpeggio and come down with a scale, and then vice versa. Retain the same feeling in each.

You seem to use the soft pedal as a rhythmic device, especially during stride playing.

I employ the soft pedal to tie a lot of things together, especially rhythmically. I use it on descending tenths or stride jumps to get more of a smooth, undulating effect than sharp breaks every time you hit a bass note.

Do you feel that some of the outstanding young jazz multikeyboardists have damaged their piano technique by playing electronic instruments?

Without getting into names, I heard two pianists who have been using the electric piano recently, and it does take a toll when they switch back to acoustic. Their fluidity has been lost, not just technically but in terms of sound. That answered some questions for me. It's easier to go from acoustic to electric than from electric back again to acoustic. They're going to have to work to get their touch back. This is not to say that the electric doesn't have validity in certain contexts, though. I have to add this about the Rhodes: It's beautiful for certain types of things. I wrote for a TV series called *Crunch,* and played the Rhodes for the two initial shows. For some reason, it was never released, but you might see it some night on a late-night special. I also did an album with Basie on which we both play electric piano. It sounds fantastic. Also, Gary Gross, a dear friend of mine, must be one of the great keyboard players in the world. We teach together occasionally, and when I have him play the electric, I listen to him with the greatest respect in the world. He's that talented.

To take up another recent development in jazz, are you drawn to modal, or tonality-based playing as an alternative to playing on the chord changes?

I'm a product of my own procedures. Tonalities affect me in a different way from the way they affect someone who's exposed to them in a different musical time period. Chick [Corea] and players like him came in when the tonality thing was very big and important. It's a different era.

Would you say the era began *after Coltrane?*

After Coltrane, Ornette, Eric Dolphy, too. And certainly Cecil Taylor. I'm an extension of the things I've been involved with over the years. My roots go back to people like Coleman Hawkins, harmonically speaking, certainly Art

Tatum, which you can hear, and Hank Jones, too. I approach solo playing from that angle.

I don't have anything derogatory to say about any of the solo playing I've heard from, say, Keith [Jarrett], because I enjoy it. It's a different scan of the piano. Pianistically I *feel* differently about it. I feel a deeper approach is required from the standpoint of accompaniment of one's self within the harmonic structure. Having been furnished a background by other instruments, like bass and guitar, I have a natural, innate desire to supply that type of [harmonic] feeling in my playing.

That is, to express your ideas within a framework of changes within a key or keys?
Right.

Are there other pianists you listen to? Evidently you've heard Keith and Chick.
Well, I spend a lot of time listening to recordings, like Herbie Hancock's.
Hancock of the sixties?

All of Herbie Hancock. I have a feeling about Herbie. Although he's into another sphere right now, when you talk about soloists among the current pianists, he's the guy I'd vote for as the best among the younger pianists. That is, he *could* play the best solo piano. I think he has the most equipment and the most creative incentive.

You don't mean electronic equipment, do you?

No, I really mean musical equipment–and not just technique. I mean inventiveness. I sense in the span of Herbie's playing that he'll eventually get into it. Let's be realistic. What he's done musically speaks for itself, and now he's following a particular direction that's brought him into the public eye. But none of us are irrevocably set in one groove. Though I think Herbie has the best mind around in terms of the younger pianists, I don't always agree with the means he uses to project these ideas. [In 1982, five years after this interview was taped, Peterson and Hancock began performing as a piano duo.]

Is there anyone else you especially admire?

If I had to choose the best all-around pianist of anyone who's followed me chronologically, unequivocally–were he able to do it and hadn't had the mishaps he has had–undoubtedly I would say Phineas Newborn, Jr. As Art Tatum said to me, "After me, you're next." That's how I feel about Phineas. He definitely had it, and when he decided to blossom, that would be it. If I had to choose after Phineas, I'd say Herbie, and after Herbie, Keith Jarrett.

Has playing solo opened up any new possibilities?

In one aspect. I use certain harmonic movements with modulating root tones while I'm playing the melody, which I couldn't do with the trio. The bass player would always wonder where we were going. Another thing that my solo playing has brought out more predominantly is those double-handed bass lines. They stand out a little better now. I use them to connect very harmonic parts of a piece to other segments of it.

You think of these double-octave lines as transitions?

Right. It's the most direct playing possible. It's barren, as if the piece had been stripped down to a line. Phineas was using this quite a bit. Subconsciously I guess I dropped a lot of the double-octave things for a while because I didn't want any controversy over who started what.

What albums do you think should appear in a selected discography of your recording?

I'd have to cite *The Trio* album in Chicago (on Verve) and the new Pablo album called *The Trio*. The *Night Train* album because we accomplished what we wanted to in terms of feeling. I'd cite the *West Side Story* album because it was a departure in terms of material from what the trio was doing at the time. Then there was *My Favorite Instrument,* the first solo album I did for MPS.

Are there albums you're dissatisfied with?

I won't be coy with you. In all the years I've been with Norman Granz, I've always had the option to kill something if I didn't like it.

I wanted to ask you about West Side Story *and the other show music albums because many people consider it a commercial departure and criticized it on those grounds.*

To the contrary, that album is one of the biggest challenges I've taken on musically. I said no to the idea at first for the exact reason you're citing. I didn't want to get into the Showtime U.S.A. bit. But as I listened to the *West Side Story* score over and over, I realized it represented a new challenge. It was one of the roughest projects we tackled, and it came off differently from the other show albums.

Leonard Bernstein's compositions impressed you?

That's right. I don't consider him to be the same type of jazz writer as Benny Golson or Duke Ellington. I don't think we have anything in the jazz world comparable to that, structurally speaking.

I've never considered Bernstein a jazz writer at all. I've always thought of those compositions as show tunes.

I feel they have a jazz context.

You have a reputation for being skeptical of the seriousness of jazz audiences.

Well, I really started to take aversion to one aspect of the jazz world, and that was the general conception that if you come into a club, you don't necessarily have to pay attention. Occasionally, when people are noisy, I'll turn to them in anger and say, "Would you act this way at a classical concert?" It would seem like a form of snobbishness on my part, but I don't think there's any need for different outlooks toward the different forms of music. It doesn't matter whether you're going to hear jazz or [violinist] David Oistrakh at Lincoln Center.

Selected Discography

In Concert (1950–56, with Ray Brown, Herb Ellis, and Barney Kessel); 2683-063; Verve (England).

Lester Young: Pres and Teddy and Oscar (1952); VE2-2502; Verve.

Dizzy Gillespie/Stan Getz (1953); VE2-2521; Verve.

West Side Story (1962, with Ray Brown, Ed Thigpen); UMV-2068; Verve.

The Sound of the Trio (ca. 1963); UMV-2078; Verve.

My Favorite Instrument (1969, solo); 7069; Pausa.

The History of an Artist (1972–74); 2625-702; Pablo.

The Paris Concert (1978, with Joe Pass, Niels-Henning Orsted-Pedersen); 2620-112; Pablo.

WILLIAM "RED" GARLAND

May, 13, 1923— April 23, 1984

Red Garland made his comeback performance at the Keystone Korner in San Francisco in 1978. It was the first time he had played outside his hometown of Dallas in fifteen years. Backstage he chain-smoked Lucky Strikes and traded stories with drummer Philly Joe Jones. They had last worked together in the magnificent Miles Davis Quintet of 1954-58, the band that included John Coltrane and, sometimes, Cannonball Adderley on saxophones. On the Davis album *Milestones,* Red's version of "Billy Boy," with Jones and Paul Chambers on bass, was a classic illustration of the perfectly structured solo, the superb interplay of the trio, and Garland's powerful use of block chords. But Red was regrettably not in such good form at the Keystone, where he was accompanied by Philly Joe and Ron Carter on bass. His playing was, by his own description, "uneven." "I freeze occasionally, and nothing comes out," he admitted. There were ample passages, however, that demonstrated the Bud Powell-influenced melodic improvising and the deep-grooved rhythmic force that had made Red prominent during the fifties.

In 1959 Garland formed his own trio, attempting to take advantage of the notoriety he had received with Davis. But jazz was entering its stormiest decade, and Red was not enough of a businessman to weather it. He remembers feeling "disappointed because all the clubs were closing and none of the musicians were working." There were those who made adjustments, or somehow made ends meet, or just plain stuck it out. Garland, however, returned to Dallas, where he lived in his father's house. Reluctant to talk about his long "hibernation," he briefly spoke of watching a lot of television and playing rarely at some local clubs.

In 1978, coaxed out of his virtual retirement by producer Orrin Keepnews, Garland emerged to record for the recently established Galaxy label, which specializes in the hard bop style. Having recorded under Keepnews's guidance during the 1950's for the Riverside label, Garland knew he had a producer who understood him. "But three albums of material in one session damn near killed me," he added. Though customarily reticent, once Garland resigned himself to the interview ahead, he turned out to be cheerful and talkative. He enjoys reminiscing and readily narrated his autobiography, which included one of the most intriguing stories I had ever heard about John Coltrane.

When did you begin playing piano?

I didn't begin on piano. In fact, I never played the piano until I was in the army. You couldn't call me a child prodigy. I started on clarinet because my father wanted me to. It was his idea. He loved Benny Goodman, so he wanted me to play the clarinet. The truth is I've always wanted to play trumpet. At least I did then. At the dances we used to go to as kids, the brass section seemed to have the most fun. They'd sit there with the trumpets across their laps, clapping to the music.

I took up the piano when I ran across Lee Barnes, a pianist in the army band. He started teaching me how to play, and I soon grew to love it. He inspired me. Nobody had to tell me to practice because I was playing piano all day. Lee even wrote out exercises for me. When I left the army, I bought an exercise book by Theodore Presser, and that was a great help to me.

In 1945 I played my first gig on piano. It was with a tenor player, Bill Blocker, who had a quartet in Fort Worth, Texas. We played mostly in the dance halls. During those years I was listening to Count Basie. He was my first favorite. He didn't have a lot of technique, but I thought he was very tasty. I started to copy him for a while. Then I began to copy Nat "King" Cole, who was more of a pianist than most people know. He was tasty, too, and he didn't have a bad technique. Then [trumpeter Oran] Hot Lips Page came to town with his band. We used to call him just Lips. Anyway, his piano player got fired while the band was down in Texas. I think it might have been because of drunkenness. Then Buster Smith, the alto saxophonist, came to my house at four o'clock in the morning to tell me to hurry and get dressed because Lips wanted me to go with him. I told him, no, I wasn't ready. I wasn't good enough yet. But they talked me into it anyway, and we toured all the way across the country into New York City.

When I got to New York, I ran into the tenor player Eddie "Lockjaw" Davis, and I asked him where all the good piano players were. He told me Bud Powell was about the baddest cat in town. "Who's Bud Powell?" I asked him. "Don't worry, you're going to find out," he told me. Well, one night I was working at Minton's with Max Roach, and I looked over toward the door, and in walked Bud. I could hardly play because of everything I had heard about him. I froze. Bud came over and started forcing me off the bench. "Let me play," he kept saying to me. "Let me play." Max was yelling to me, "No! Get him away. Keep him away from the piano." Max was afraid he was crazy or something and was going to ruin the gig. I got up anyway. I figured if Bud wanted to play that bad, I wasn't going to stand in his way. Well, he sat down at the piano and scared me to death—he played so much piano! I told Max, "I quit! Give him the job!" See, Bud took my cool.

But a few days later I went over to Bud's house, and he showed me some things. In fact, I came back day after day to learn from him, and we became buddies. He was really friendly to me and the greatest influence on me of any pianist, except for Art Tatum. I still don't believe Art Tatum was real.

There was a club named Luckey's [Rendezvous], owned by Luckey Roberts, and it was just for piano players—no bass or drums allowed. There's where we'd separate the men from the boys, when you can't lean on the bass or drums. Art Tatum was a frequent visitor there, and I'd stand over his shoulder to watch what he was doing. One night he stood behind me as I was playing. "You're forcing," he told me. "You're forcing. Don't play the piano. Let the piano play itself." I was tight, so he gave me that piece of advice, and I've always remembered it. He gave me some arpeggios to work on, too, and I'm still working on them.

Then I was working in a small club in Boston with Coleman Hawkins when Miles [Davis] came in to hear me. He told me during the intermission that he wanted to get a group together with me on piano, Philly Joe, Curly Russell on bass, and Sonny Rollins on tenor. Two weeks later I heard Sonny couldn't get released from his rehabilitation program, so I left town for Philadelphia. A while later I got a telegram from Miles asking me if I knew anyone in Philadelphia who could play tenor sax. I told him I knew a cat named John Coltrane, and Miles asked me, "Can he play?" and I told him, "Sure he can."

John and I met Miles in Baltimore. Meanwhile, Miles had found a kid out of Detroit, named Paul Chambers, and he played bass for us. Philly Joe was still on drums. We had never played together until the night of our first gig, so we got together about five in the afternoon and jammed. From the opening tune we clicked. We just clicked right away, and that was that. We stayed together from '55 to January 1959. I did a few trio gigs by myself and then went home, like I told you.

I noticed at the club last night that you seemed most comfortable playing the blues. Do you feel looser playing blues?

Not necessarily, but people are more receptive to the blues. There are clichés that get the people going, that get a good response. I guess I use the blues as a crutch. When the house is getting cold, play some blues and you can bring it back to life.

What other repertoire do you depend on?

Show tunes. I have to play tunes I like if I want to express myself, and I do like show tunes: Broadway shows; musicals; themes from the movies. I used to listen to the radio all day long to get to know the show tunes. Right now I'm starting to listen to records again, mostly Bud Powell and Charlie Parker.

You don't seem to play many tunes composed by the musicians you like. Why is that?

The other night I played "Daahoud" by Clifford Brown. If you play a lot of the jazz tunes—figures, we used to call them—people won't dig it. They won't listen. At least that's what I'm afraid of, but maybe I'm wrong, and I ought to play more jazz tunes.

Are you confident of your playing right now?

No, not yet. It's going to take a few more jobs before it comes back. The ideas are there, but technically I'm not making them. I'm not thinking with my hands. I don't have the feel back.

I noticed you traded fours and eights with Philly Joe quite often. Was that designed to give you a rest or to show off Philly Joe?

Both. It was a rest for me, but it also gets a dialogue going up there which makes things more interesting.

Did you ever experiment with the electric piano?

The owner of a small club I played in down in Texas went downtown and bought me a Fender Rhodes to use at the club. But I kept turning away from it to play the acoustic. Finally, the owner asked, "After all I spent on that piano, are you just going to let it sit there?" Well, I played it for him, but I didn't like it. It's too metallic for me. I love hearing other people play it, like Chick or Herbie, but it's not for me.

What do you think of jazz/rock or fusion music? Do you like it?

Sometimes, except that it always sounds like it was played on one chord. It doesn't move around enough for me harmonically.

Coltrane used to play on one chord, too.

I know, and I got down on him about it. I'll tell you a story that's never been printed before. One night I went down to the club where Coltrane was playing, and he came down off the bandstand and said, "Red, let's go over to the side bar and have a cheap one." You could get a cheaper drink at the side bar. So we sat down, and the first thing I said to him was this: "Trane, do you dig what you're doing? Do you have faith in it?" See, this new style of playing he was into wasn't the John William I knew. So he laughed and dropped his head like a shy kid, and he said, "Yeah, sort of. But I got myself out here, and now if I turned back and started playing the way I used to play, people would think I was a phony. I'd lay a lot of the cats right out because they've been following me." I said, "Then you don't really have faith in what you're doing." And he looked at me and said, "Sort of . . . sort of." Anyway, I didn't dig Trane's music after that because he was just running up and down the horn, and it didn't mean anything to me.

How do you feel about what Miles Davis has done since you last played with him?
That's not for me either.

What don't you like about albums like Bitches Brew *or* Live/Evil?
Everything! I liked the swinging Miles, but he's left my style and gone off into something else.

How do you plan to get your piano technique back?
I'll go back home and start practicing scales again. I always practice them with traditional fingerings, but when I play a job, I just use whatever works. Sometimes I find I don't even know how I fingered a passage. All I know is that it came out right.

Do you try to get a countermelody going in the left hand when you play, or do you emphasize a bass line?
It varies. Usually I leave the bass line to the bass player. Sometimes I just use a tonic and a fifth, which is what Bud Powell did. Otherwise, I'll go to chords, especially ninths, raised ninths, and thirteenths, and if I can get a countermelody happening, that's even better. It's a good idea to play something warm in the melody and clash it with a raised ninth in the left hand. Sometimes I'll even use inside voicings to get a special effect, a clash of sounds, or something unusual. If somebody asked me to describe what I was playing, I'd have to say I just push down on the notes. Another harmony I like is a raised ninth in the left hand with a diminished in the right hand. I did that on a record date, and [saxophonist] Jimmy Heath said, "Hold that! Stop right there." And he wrote it down. If he didn't stop me, I still wouldn't know what I was playing.

Was the Galaxy record date difficult for you in terms of repertoire? Three albums is a lot of songs.
When I first walked into the studio, I couldn't think of any tunes at all. I sat down and started writing down all the names of tunes I could think of. I think we even did that college tune "The Whiffenpoof Song" on one cut.

Has Philly Joe's playing changed since you last worked with him?

No, he just got better. He told me he had some new things for me, and then he started doing some drum rolls in a backwards direction. Yeah, he's improved.

How do you like the new Yamaha pianos? I guess you had one at the club and at the Fantasy Records studio.

They're very nice. The action is easy, which is good for me because I don't like to fight the piano. At home I have a little Baldwin spinet, which actually belongs to my aunt. I'm thinking of buying it from her. The truth is that I'd rather play on a Steinway, even though the action is a little stiff. The tone is beautiful, and to me it's still the king of pianos.

It's good to know you're playing again. How does it feel?

Well, thank you. That feels good. It's put some sense into me to play again. I thought jazz was all finished, but now I see there are still people who love jazz.

More people than ever, I think.

Yeah, I'm finding that out. And I'll stay out here as long as the reception stays as beautiful as it's been at the Keystone. I guess if that changed, I'd go back into my shell and hide and just tell myself, "Later . . . later."

Selected Discography

Miles Davis: Workin' and Steamin' (1955); P-24034; Prestige.

Miles Davis: Round About Midnight (1956); PC 8649; Columbia.

Miles Davis: Milestones (1958); PC 9428; Columbia.

The Red Garland Quintet (1957, with John Coltrane); PR-24023; Prestige.

Red Garland: Saying Something (1957–61); P-24090; Prestige.

Crossings (1977); GXY-5106; Galaxy.

Red Alert (1977); GXY-5109; Galaxy.

JIMMY
ROWLES

August 19, 1918–

Jimmy Rowles has a low profile and—as far as the general public is concerned—his talents have been largely ignored. Among musicians it is a different story. Rowles's touch, taste, and harmonic imagination make him an ideal accompanist, and he has been highly valued in that role by a succession of demanding employers: Peggy Lee, Billie Holiday, Ella Fitzgerald, Sarah Vaughan, and Carmen McRae. Saxophonist Stan Getz tried to rescue him from obscurity by producing a Rowles album for Columbia *(The Peacocks)*, and bassist Ray Brown did the same for Rowles on the Concord Jazz label, accompanying him on an LP of piano/bass duets *(Jimmy Rowles)*.

Rowles attended Gonzaga University in his home town of Spokane, Washington. His first important jobs, in the early 1940's, were with bands led by saxophonists Ben Webster and Lester Young. Apart from accompanying singers, Rowles also worked over the years as a pianist for Benny Goodman, Woody Herman, Chet Baker, Benny Carter, Charlie Parker, and Zoot Sims. During the 1970's he lived in Los Angeles and worked regularly for the Hollywood studios. Despite his reputation as a musician's musician, his apparent lack of interest in promoting his own career has left him a virtual unknown. But he has much to say about the immensely important role of the piano in accompaniment.

The following interview was taped after the Concord Jazz recording session produced by Ray Brown. Explaining that he dislikes the studio atmosphere, Rowles had the lights turned down, lit a cigarette, and sipped at a vodka Collins, which he nursed along throughout the session. He was self-critical of his playing and requested numerous retakes of several pieces. Before recording "Rosalie," he remarked, "I've got to throw my left hand to hit those bass notes, and I don't know how many takes that's going to take." Eventually Ray Brown insisted that Rowles keep one heavily striding version, commenting, "Nobody plays piano like this anymore." For the last cut of the session Jimmy played a solo called "Looking Back," which is essentially what I asked him to do for me.

What was your early background on the piano?

I used to listen to my mother, who could play by ear, and I imitated her and started playing by ear myself. My sister had a boyfriend who had a real Earl Hines feel to his playing, and he taught me the first song I ever learned to play, "Saint Louis Blues." I did a little studying with a private teacher, but it didn't work out too well, since what I really wanted to be was a tennis player. I probably had a couple of private teachers I quit on. What changed me was listening to Guy Lombardo's pianist. In fact, I liked his whole orchestra. I was the guy who wouldn't even listen to Benny Goodman. After hearing something I liked on piano, I started looking for a teacher in my hometown and eventually found a guy named Norm Thue. He had me go through all the chords and the keys, throw my hand to the bass notes, and practice a stride that was built on tenths, not single notes.

The next step was while I was studying at Gonzaga, where I met Don Brown, a Blackfoot Indian and a real genius. He forced me to listen to Teddy Wilson, and I resisted at first because I thought I knew what I wanted. But after about four bars I said to myself, "That's it! That's the way I want to play piano!" So I started studying him—and I'll never leave him entirely—and then I went on to discover Art Tatum, Fats Waller, and Earl Hines. This was around 1936, and I also began to listen to horn players like Chu Berry, Roy Eldridge, and Ben Webster, the [Jimmy] Lunceford band, Ellington, Andy Kirk. I guess of all those I was closest to Ben Webster, who became like a father to me, musically and personally.

Your playing—the harmonies and understatement—has such a modern feeling to it I'm surprised to hear you mention influences from another era.

Well, I have had some more modern favorites, too. Red Garland, Wynton Kelly, Tommy Flanagan, and Hank Jones. But still, I'm not in the Herbie Hancock/Chick Corea bag. It's great stuff—for them—but that trend isn't my thing.

I've noticed a strong sense of bass line in your playing. Your bass-line melodies really sing out.

Yeah, I focus on that quite a bit. When I studied with Norm, he stressed the fact that all chords start from the bass note. Not necessarily the tonic of the chord, but the bottom note and the notes that lead to it. They're essential. If you've got the right bass note down there, you can fool around all you want on top of it. But if your bass note's wrong, the chord isn't going to sound right no matter what you do.

In analyzing a tune, do you work on the bass line separately from the rest of the music?

Sure. I figure out the bass line even before I work on the melody. Sometimes I'll mess around with a countermelody in the thumb of the left hand, but I don't take that as seriously as getting a good bass line down there. With everything else, I honestly mess around and hope everything comes out right.

It sounds as if you're using a lot of flat-ninth intervals for right-hand dissonances. Where does that come from?

That's Ravel. He's my man, but I like a lot of those cats. Debussy, Scriabin, Prokofiev, Rachmaninoff, Erik Satie, Villa-Lobos. I really love that stuff. You know, you can get tired of listening to jazz because every so often you crave something really deep. Stan Getz wouldn't have had a theme song if it weren't for Ravel. But I have to admit: Everything is relative. I went up to this old-timer in Spokane—he was playing in one of the bars—and I asked him what he thought of Art Tatum. He said, "Oh, well, he's got his style, I got mine." I loved that answer.

When did you first start playing professionally?

It was college bands at first and some small groups in Spokane, but I used to hang around the after-hours joints and play with all the black cats, which is where I got my first real jazz experience. Not long afterward I went to Los Angeles just to see what would happen, and I ended up with Lester Young. It was quite a group. Big Joe Turner was singing the blues; Ray Bryant was dancing; Billie Holiday came out to sing with us. Eventually Billie and I got very close and worked well together over a period of years. I've always liked lyrics, been sensitive to them, and making albums with her was the time I really learned how to accompany. But I also learned a lot from working with Peggy Lee and Ella [Fitzgerald]. Practice makes perfect. Ellis Larkins in New York is a great accompanist, and you could take a real lesson by paying him some attention.

Can you tell me more about the singers you've worked with?

When I got out of the army after the war, that's when I started working regularly with Billie. We had hit it off when I was with Lester Young's and Lee's band [Lee Young, a drummer, was Lester's brother] Billie was making some records and asked for me. The recording group also had Benny Carter, "Sweets" [trumpeter Harry Edison], and Ben Webster. It was wonderful working for Billie. The sessions were smooth, and she seemed happy. I never had any problems with her. After Billie, I went on the road with Evelyn Knight, Vic Damone, and Peggy Lee.

Was Peggy Lee a jazz singer? Some people say she was, but I've always had ambivalent feelings about her.

She had jazz feeling, but she wasn't an improviser. She did swing; she was sort of a rhythmic singer. I was with her about five years. For many years afterward I worked in the staff orchestra at NBC. That lasted through most of the sixties. Some of the interesting people I worked for were Andy Williams and Henry Mancini. I think I was with Mancini on and off for seventeen years.

Then I worked for Carmen McRae and Sarah Vaughan, who was the greatest of all the female musicians. She did the arrangements and everything else. She was sort of the Art Tatum of singing, and she has an impeccable ear. She's also a good pianist. She can sit down and just "noodle" and it'll scare you. I wish she'd play more often. I also worked for Ella for two years, but there's no comparison to Sarah in musicianship. In terms of range, no one can touch her [Sarah].

Now Billie Holiday was a completely different kind of singer. She didn't have a voice, really; she had a sound. It was a very natural sound like Louis Armstrong's, but it wasn't a singing voice. Sarah's sound is cultivated, almost classical. In terms of feeling, phrasing, and sound, Sarah and Billie are in different worlds. They only have one thing in common—they're both perfectionists. That was the basic similarity, but Billie was never the accomplished musician Sarah is.

Well, what can you say about a method for accompanying singers?

I'd say there are two rules. Anticipation of the singer is one of them. The other is subduing yourself. If you don't subdue yourself, the listener is going to get confused because the piano part will be competing for the listener's attention. That's the worst thing that can happen. What you're doing is weaving carpets for the singer to stand on, and maybe you do little things that fit into the open spots. Don't play too much, don't play too loud, and don't play the melody. Now some of this is going to depend on who the singer is. For Sarah Vaughan, you could play World War Four on the piano, and she'd still be right in there. Carmen [McRae] is that way, too. But there are some singers—and I won't mention any names—who want you to play the melody so they know where they're supposed to be. But that's just a special case.

How did you learn to accompany yourself? Is it different?

Actually I wish I could accompany myself better, and it is different. I started singing just for the fun of it in the army; but when I was working for Peggy Lee, she liked my singing, and she used to make me sing. Some people actually liked it. As far as I can tell, I sound like old Gravel Gertie. What I keep in mind, most of all, is the interpretation of the lyrics. When you're singing a song, you're telling a story. I can't stand a singer who listens to the sound of his own voice and doesn't show any sign that he knows what he's singing about. I'd rather hear Louis Armstrong. I'll bet he never thought about his voice for a minute.

Another feature of your music seems to be space. There are a lot of silences, a sparseness.

Good, I'm glad. I don't like to kill the keyboard.

You might be considered the opposite of an Oscar Peterson.

Well, let's be honest. I don't have his chops. But even if I did, I'd still be myself. I like to take things a little easier, although I admire Oscar's playing a great deal.

How did you acquire finger dexterity?

I used to own a windup phonograph, and I'd slow it down so I could really hear the runs of the other pianists. Then I'd transcribe the solos and imitate them note for note. Teddy Wilson was a favorite, and I did a few of Art's solos. I knew I was in trouble when I got to Fats Waller because he could think in two directions. His left hand was saying one thing, and in his right hand, he'd be fooling around with another thought.

Do you have any exercises now for your fingers or hands?

I often bend my fingers back at the bottom joint, although I never crack my knuckles. I know a lot of guys who do, but I avoid it. When I'm playing, I often lower my hand, just let it hang and then shake it around, loosen it up and get the circulation going. You should also try to remember that the source of tension is in the back of the neck, so keep your shoulders relaxed and generally try to keep cool and loose.

Do you have any reflections on your recording career?

I was never too happy with it, as far as my personal music goes. The first recording I cared for at all was done in the late fifties with Henry Mancini and Neal Hefti. Mancini likes to keep his music fairly simple, but we did the score for a picture called *Harlow,* and on the piece "Girl Talk" Henry gave me sixteen whole bars with strings. That was actually satisfying.

How do you choose your repertoire?

I like to do a song that I can camouflage. I like to give it a fresh interpretation and present my own feelings about it. Ray [Brown] and I just did "Like Someone in Love" as a stride thing. During an opening set at a gig in New York, where I do most of my playing, I did "Sophisticated Lady" as a bossa nova. Sometimes I'll throw in some Rimsky-Korsakov or do "Yesterdays" as a bolero. If I can play the song differently, I'll do it. I also dig up tunes out of the past that no one else knows about.

I noticed you don't play the blues as such, but there's a lot of bluesy feeling in your standards.

I get that from Erroll Garner, who was one of my favorite pianists and people.

Have you worked on any electronic keyboards? How do you feel about them?

Well, I've been forced to use the novachord and the Fender Rhodes. In fact, I made a whole album on the Rhodes with Barney Kessel. I don't mind them all that much, but I'd sure rather play a beautiful Steinway B, like the one I just recorded on. You see, as a studio musician in Los Angeles, which was my gig when I used the electronic equipment, you can't put any feeling into the music, anyway, unless you happen to dig what the session leader is doing. With an electronic keyboard it makes matters a little bit worse because you have to deal with the mechanical nature of the instrument, too. The best feature of an acoustic piano is that you can really express yourself on it.

As Stan Getz says in his liner notes about you, your name isn't exactly a household word. How do you feel about your career now?

I like the musicians I'm playing with. I like what's going on in my head. And I think people are getting more receptive to the kind of music I play, so I'd have to say everything is getting better. I only hope it continues.

Selected Discography

Billie Holiday: Stormy Blues (1955); VE2-2515; Verve.

Ray Brown & Jimmy Rowles: As Good as It Gets (1979); CJ-66; Concord Jazz.

Ray Brown & Jimmy Rowles: "Tasty" (1979); CJ-122; Concord Jazz.

Jimmy Rowles Plays Duke Ellington and Billy Strayhorn (1981, solo); FC-37639; Columbia.

Music's the Only Thing That's on My Mind (with George Mraz, bass; 1981); 7009; Progressive.

PAUL
BLEY

November 10, 1932–

Canadian-born pianist Paul Bley is adventurous and enterprising. While still in his teens, he organized a fund-raising concert in Montreal, brought Charlie Parker up from New York as the main attraction, and accompanied the master saxophonist on piano. Bley soon made his first record with Art Blakey and bassist Charles Mingus, who had heard him perform while Paul was studying at Juilliard in New York. In 1958, having moved to Los Angeles with composer Carla Bley, then his wife, Paul had the audacity to hire Ornette Coleman and Don Cherry to work with his own band at the Hillcrest Club, at a time when these iconoclastic horn players were being booted off every bandstand in town. As Bley explains ahead, Coleman's "microtonal" approach to improvising struck most listeners at that time as simply out of tune.

After returning to New York in 1959, Paul worked again with Mingus and with Sonny Rollins before leading his own trio, which included Paul Motian on drums and either Steve Swallow or Gary Peacock on bass. Paul's group had a subtle but detectable influence on Keith Jarrett and probably other pianists for reasons Paul discusses in the interview below. When electronic instruments became more portable, Bley and vocalist Annette Peacock presented what was reportedly the world's first synthesizer concert—in New York's Philharmonic Hall in 1969. Six years later Bley and a new partner, visual artist Carol Goss, founded Improvising Artists, Incorporated (IAI), a record label that has produced about twenty high-quality LP's and two dozen (unreleased) videotapes and distributes albums by an impressive roster of musicians, including Bley himself, Dave Holland, Gary Peacock, Ran Blake, Sun Ra, Sam Rivers, and Jaco Pastorius.

Bley can be moody and brooding at the keyboard. But he can also play bright, well-defined lines that turn sharp, clean corners without warning. Artistically he is full of surprises, and that is part of the total image he likes to project. He is a lanky, cordial man with a resonant voice and a penchant for smoking a pipe, which he will even light up between tunes onstage. Paul

Bley's robust entrepreneurial spirit is in striking contrast to his professorial persona and art-for-art's-sake dimensions. "Everyone wants to paint, write, or play an instrument," Bley once told me. "The difference between the amateur and the professional is that the professional can survive the corruption of the marketplace."

The interview that follows reflects both Bley's interest in the pragmatics of success and his artistic insight.

How did you begin playing piano, and how did you start out in music?

The first question any musician has to answer for himself is this: Is my aspiration to become the greatest living player on that instrument or not? If his answer is no, he's wasting his time. And this probably rules out ninety percent of the aspirants because very few people will cop to that goal.

Is there a "greatest" player? Who was greater in 1955, Art Tatum, Bud Powell, or Thelonious Monk?

Okay, the half dozen greatest.

Who are the greatest players today?

Everybody knows who the greatest are. That question doesn't need answering. It's those people you're considering when you ask the question. If they're near the word "great," then they are great.

Do you recommend formal study of the piano or learning on the job?

Everybody knows how to study music. Books are full of it. Magazines are full of it. I will not tell anybody how to study the instrument. All I can say is, choose what you want to do. If it's your aim to play in Carnegie Hall, go to New York and live near Fifty-seventh Street.

Aren't there technical problems that come up in the act of playing, physical problems which have keyboard solutions? How did you learn to play in this sense?

I hired Charlie Parker to play with me, and I did that by learning to make transactions early. I was sixteen. He was in a basement in New York. I lived in a suburb of Montreal. So I got on a plane, went to New York, took him by the hand, and led him to Montreal. It was a geographic problem. Quite frankly, the only way to be good is to play with people four times better than you. If you're going to ask them to engage in a transaction with you where they have to suffer your performance, you'd better have a pretty strong reason for asking.

As a teenager, what was it like accompanying Charlie Parker? What were your impressions of him?

Being a teenager, I was struck by how paternal he was. I was adopted, my parents were already divorced, so I appreciated someone being paternal with me. It might have seemed I was taking care of him, though. I raised the money for the concert, flew down to New York, and brought him back for the job. Accompanying him was a shock because of the volume. He played about three times louder than I had ever heard anyone play. You can't tell how loud he played from listening to the recordings.

Another pianist had that experience the first time he accompanied a really good saxophonist—Sonny Rollins. I can't remember who the pianist was, but he told me he could hardly hear himself because Rollins had such a loud, powerful sound.

I can tell you a story about that. One night at the Open Door [in New York], Rollins was working with Art Blakey and a bassist as a trio. Blakey's forte, as you know, was playing thirty choruses, each one louder than the next. Rollins knew this and started climbing slowly with Blakey until they got to the top of Art's volume. Then Sonny climbed about twenty more choruses volumewise.

Any more recollections of Bird?

Another problem was that Bird was always several bars ahead of you. When you were in the middle of a chorus, he was always starting the next section.

Harmonically? How is that possible?

Well, anticipating. Melodically leading. He'd be starting the turnaround for the last eight bars while you were still finishing the bridge. It was a kind of race between Parker and the other instruments to see who could get to the next section first. The tempo was an obvious problem, too, because he could play so fast.

How did you wind up working with Ornette Coleman at the Hillcrest? Did he offend the audience to the extent that legend claims?

I had the Hillcrest job first for my trio with [bassist] Charlie Haden and [drummer] Billy Higgins. We were very well liked there. Billy brought in Ornette and Don Cherry. Carla and I liked them very much, right away. I remember that we went out into the parking lot after the first set and asked ourselves, "Well, what are we going to do?" We wanted to hire them, but we thought if we did, we'd lose our year-and-a-half-long job. So we hired them, and we lost the job.

Ornette had some very interesting ideas that we all loved. For example, you didn't have to play tunes the same way each time. That was new then. Tunes could be rerhythmized; there was no end to the ways you could play a phrase. You could make sixteenth notes into half notes and vice versa.

The audience was so shocked by the band that they left the club. But they loved the club, too, so they stayed outside and waited. If you drove down

Washington Boulevard, you could tell when our band was playing because the street was full of people.

How long did you last on that basis?

Two or three weeks.

Wasn't there flexibility in other musicians during the late fifties, like Charles Mingus? There were meter changes and even atonality in some of his pieces?

Mingus's real flexibility was in timbre. He wanted the horns to growl and moan, à la Duke Ellington. But Mingus didn't rerhythmize, for example. When he did a song on different recording sessions, it was basically the same song.

Did Ornette tell you at some point that he wasn't going to use a pianist anymore?

No, the job was over, the band broke up, and we had no more work. After working with Ornette, I made it a point to sit in with every band in Los Angeles, and I got offered every job in Los Angeles.

Why, if Coleman's style was so shocking and unpopular?

Because people couldn't interpret or appreciate what he was doing due to the microtonality [playing pitches between the legitimate "notes" on the instrument] of his horn.

Which you can't duplicate on the piano, unless you played in the cracks between the keys.

Right, so it was easier for people to appreciate that flexibility when they heard it in simplified form, without microtones. They were aware of the fact that there was something there they didn't know about, which is generally the way I've gotten my jobs with other bands.

So what did you do with all those job offers?

The result of getting offered every job in Los Angeles was that Carla and I decided to go to New York and sit in with every band there. On the way back we stopped at the Lenox School of Music in Massachusetts just in time for the last concert on the very last night of the session. Everybody was in the audience. Ornette, Don, John Lewis, Gunther Schuller, George Russell, and when we walked in, Ran Blake was playing. What happened was that I got to sit in and play the last tune of the night, a blues. I got about two years' worth of work out of that tune. Another result of that night was that Ran invited me out to Bard College, where he was a student, and that's where I met Steve Swallow.

I wanted to ask you about your trios during the sixties, with Steve and later Gary Peacock on bass and Paul Motian on drums. Why did that group turn out so well for you? I think it influenced a lot of people.

Steve and I worked for two years as a duo. I wasn't that concerned about drummers because drummers really didn't contribute that much until they gave up [keeping] time. Bass players gave up time much earlier. When you talk about bassists like Charles Mingus and Steve Swallow, you're talking about bass players that perform a rhythmic function. But when you talk about Scottie LaFaro and Gary Peacock, it gets a little more interesting. You're talking about bass players literally playing a linear, melodic part. When I played with Scottie in California, I put him in front of us on the bandstand. That was quite startling to the audience.

I was reading an article about [ECM Records producer] Manfred Eicher, who intimated that your album Footloose *[on BYG] was an influence on Keith Jarrett. So I listened to it again, and I could really hear that kind of bluesy Americana Jarrett sometimes uses in your tunes "Syndrome" and "King Korn." Do you think that music influenced Jarrett?*

Well, I consider that a compliment. But it's not difficult to understand what happened. Before "Syndrome" there were no recordings of piano where the tempo was constant but the harmony was up for grabs—as a procedural matter. Obviously anything that followed that recording would have only that as a reference. Things like that had been done on a horn, but people didn't expect that kind of flexibility from the piano. You know, I made a practice of never making records of things I knew how to play, but only of recording things I hadn't yet worked out, the point being that the recording can serve as a learning tool for me. I've never done anything long enough to popularize it. With that methodology, I've spawned a lot of spin-off bands, spin-off players, and influences. Keith isn't the first and won't be the last.

Doesn't that kind of movable identity make it hard to develop your career? It seems the public would find it hard to know who you are or what you do. Has that made things difficult for you professionally?

Definitely, absolutely. But in the end you're left with your playing, not your public. An artist has to choose his terms, and my terms are that the next record won't sound like the last record. My audience likes that and the fact that when I play in person, each piece won't sound like the last piece. Ultimately I think one's style—in quotes—does come clear, but it comes over a longer period of time, not by repeating albums.

Where do you see your style historically? Do you have a vocabulary to describe yourself, the kinds of terms that are generally applied to jazz piano—stride, bebop, tonality-based playing, impressionism, or something along those lines?

Well, look at the end of that road for a keyboard player. These styles you named lead up to purely atonal and electronic music.

What makes you say that?

These are the end points of acoustic music in terms of complexity. That
was the case in classical music, where you have romanticism, impressionism,
and atonalism following in cycles of thirty, or fifty, years. At the end of that,
pure acoustic music ceases to be as meaningful. Now how do you retain the
jazz flavor when you're dealing with atonal music? By being a jazz musician, I
guess. The whole point of all of this is to play without any givens, without any
compositions.

You see that as the goal of the jazz keyboardist?

Absolutely. It's a quantum leap forward. You're telling human beings that
they can trust their intuitions to create forms, rather than need forms in which
to create intuitions.

*Back to Keith Jarrett, that's exactly what he claims to be doing. Do you think
that's what he's doing?*

That's between a musician and himself. The audience won't always know.
The musician may even prefer to make it sound as if he did have a composition.

*Some jazz composers like to work with form itself. Will that become obsolete in
your opinion?*

No, but there's not that much difference. The improviser works with
forms that may sound as if they had been planned. They'll wind up with just
as much form because the brain just refuses to go into a random mode. You
have to organize. Improvising is also a good exercise to push yourself and your
mind to its limits. Then, when you come back to more traditional material,
you can inject things that make it a richer experience.

*I was recently talking with Jaki Byard, who is probably at the opposite end of the
spectrum from you. He starts and ends with established forms, and he keeps to them
pretty rigorously.*

Jaki has a wonderful opportunity to preserve the heritage intact, so to
speak. He can play the piano the way people have for the last forty years, and
he gets very close to how it was actually done. To throw that heritage out the
window in order to play "free" would be wasteful. Better for a younger person
to go forward. Let an older person play what he knows best. I've played five
genres of music, and I guess I'm trying to make it six.

Are you trying to preserve these genres in what you do?

I'm trying to preserve the jazz element in quite random material, whether
it's atonal or electronic. I'm trying to find out what *is* the jazz element. How
do we differ from Karlheinz Stockhausen?

American musicians have proved two things. First, if you're going on a
trip, you don't necessarily need a map. Second, this music could only have

been made here. For one reason, academia is much stronger in Europe than it is in America. It was because Buddy Bolden didn't know there was an extra octave on the trumpet that we extended the range of the trumpet. We're talking about a lot of personal work, rather than taught, or learned, work. We strike out for unknown territory. That's what improvising is all about. If the territory is known, it's not that interesting. That's my bias.

What are you doing with electronic keyboards at this point [1982]?

I'm preparing a polyphonic synthesizer album right now, using the Fair Light digital synthesizer. You enter information with a light pen. I'll also be playing twenty-eight solo piano concerts this year. These endeavors are related. They feed each other. [A note of] electronic music can sustain indefinitely, but [a note of] acoustic music decays very quickly, even if it's well recorded. After getting used to being able to sustain, I became interested in what's left in the sound after the attack in acoustic music. I started making piano music with long decays so you could hear the overtones [for example, *Open to Love;* and *Alone Again,* on IAI]. That was a result of electronic music. Electronics has slowed me down. There was a time in my life when I was trying to play faster than I was capable of.

What are you doing now with Improvising Artists, Incorporated?

Videotapes. That illustrates my credo of getting involved in what I don't understand yet. Videotape is an expensive hobby. The money from my performances has been financing the record company and the videotapes. We have about thirty tapes, each one done differently, by the way, but they're not released yet. I'm not sure people are ready for what we have. One interesting thing that's come out of this is how the medium affects what you play. On a seventy-eight rpm record in the big band era, when the trumpeter had to solo on the bridge, he had to do it all in eight bars. But in the last thirty years or so the length that's required of improvisers has increased. You now have up to a twenty-four-minute LP side, a one-hour disc side, and up to an eight-hour videocassette side. Next time you speak to Jaki Byard, ask him if, when he goes to the date and finds out that he has to play for eight hours, that will affect what and how he plays. These are the things that keep me amused.

Selected Discography

Live at the Hillcrest (1958, with Ornette Coleman); IC-1007; Inner City.
Footloose (1963); 529-114; BYG.*

Virtuosi (1967, with Gary Peacock, Barry Altschul); 37.38.44; Improvising Artists, Inc. (IAI).

Paul Bley & Scorpio (1972, synthesizers); MSP-9046; Milestone.

NHØP (1973, with Niels-Hennning Orsted-Pedersen); IC-2005; Inner City.

Axis (1977, solo); 37.38.33; IAI.

Alone, Again (1979); 37.38.40, IAI.

MARIAN
McPARTLAND

March 20, 1920–

Marian McPartland is erudite in the jazz piano tradition. Her concerts will normally include Dixieland staples, such as "Royal Garden Blues," Duke Ellington's dissonant "Clothed Woman," some show tunes or ballads by her friend Alec Wilder, and compositions by Chick Corea and Herbie Hancock. She also composes, and one of her more lasting pieces, "Ambiance," was recorded by the Thad Jones-Mel Lewis Orchestra during the early 1970's. McPartland's piano style is eclectic. She absorbs the sources of her material, reinterprets songs of different jazz eras, explores every piece with sure harmonic footing and an infallible ear, and when she gets her left hand going, she can make the piano seem to be strutting across the stage. McPartland has become a conduit for the spreading and channeling of a wide range of jazz piano styles. This has perhaps been her own strongest contribution.

Marian emigrated in 1946 from England, where she was brought up to be proper and refined by a family who never recovered from the shock of their daughter's becoming a jazz musician. She arrived in Chicago with her new husband, cornetist Jimmy McPartland, whom she met playing on a USO tour for American soldiers stationed in Europe. Until 1950 she worked in Jimmy's band, which played in the Chicago Dixieland style of the 1930's influenced by Bix Beiderbecke. Eagerly soaking up more modern sounds, Marian left the group and led her own trio or performed as a soloist, working regularly at the Hickory House in New York from about 1952 to 1960. Apart from Jimmy's group and a brief tenure with the Benny Goodman Sextet in 1965, Marian has never worked for another bandleader. In 1969 she started her own record label, Halcyon, which continues to distribute a modest catalog of her own albums, a collaboration with violinist Joe Venuti, and LP's by Dave McKenna and Jimmy Rowles. McPartland leans toward swing, a rich diet of chord changes, and good taste; she has less of an affinity for passion, percussiveness, and outright blues.

McPartland has done a great deal to further the jazz piano tradition through channels other than performing live or on records. For years she taught jazz to schoolchildren at various clinics and workshops around the country. Since 1979 she has hosted *Marian McPartland's Piano Jazz Show,* a thirteen-part series broadcast annually on National Public Radio. These shows include her elucidating commentary on music and conversations and spontaneous duets with such guests as Oscar Peterson, George Shearing, Billy Taylor, and several other pianists.

I first heard Marian perform at El Matador in San Francisco in 1976. Seated in the front row next to me was George Shearing, her compatriot and contemporary. George commented on her marvelous ability to carry any tune solo, a facility born of many years on her own. (The following year, when Marian played the Monterey Jazz Festival, Bill Evans made precisely the same comment about her playing after hearing her solo before an audience of 7,000.) Marian and I spoke during an intermission at El Matador, seated at a small table in the downstairs dressing room. A few weeks earlier Teddy Wilson had been sitting across from me at the same table, and I suppose that is what prompted my first question.

Teddy Wilson has said, "There's nothing in the feeling of nineteenth- or even twentieth-century European music that has the jazz feeling at all." You've had years of classical training in London—do you agree with him?

Teddy's approach to the piano is very different from mine. He's a more linear player, and if you were going to compare him to classical composers, you'd say Bach or Mozart. The long, flowing lines. Now I love all the lush harmonies of Debussy and Ravel, and I suppose it's natural that I'd be influenced by European music since I'm from there. But I was even influenced by European *jazz*. One of the finest groups I ever heard was the Hot Five of Paris with [guitarist] Django Reinhardt. Of course, I had American jazz influences, too. Duke Ellington, Teddy himself, all the pianists I listened to while in England, like Joe Sullivan and Bob Zurke, two white pianists during the Bob Crosby era. Jess Stacy, too. Art Tatum. Now there's a man with a great harmonic conception. Actually, I listened to everybody. I'm like a sponge. I absorb everything I hear. Oscar Peterson, George [Shearing], Lennie Tristano. Especially Teddy, though. I never dreamed I'd come over here and make a record with him [*Elegant Piano,* on Halcyon] or that we'd be as close friends as we are.

How did you get started in the States?

When I first came here, I was working with Jimmy's band, which was more or less Dixieland. Though he stayed with the more traditional form of playing, he influenced me to leave the band. "You're playing more advanced things," he told me. "You're going to get out of this Dixieland style." In a way I feel bad about not going through an apprenticeship, as most musicians do, playing with different bands and working with different leaders. I've never worked for anybody except Jimmy and Benny Goodman, the latter for only six months in '65. I also began at the Embers, once a top club in New York, so I started out doing something I really wasn't ready for, not having gone through the intermediate stages. Well, maybe I went through them later, a little less conspicuously.

You mention Lennie Tristano as an influence. Have you done any formal piano study with him or any other teacher in this country?

Not really. I've listened to Tristano a lot and once went to him for a criticism of my playing. Boy! He really gave it to me. He said, rather cynically, something like: "If you want to be a romantic player who doesn't keep strict time and lets the time wander, I suppose that's all right. But if you want to play with good time, go home and start practicing with a metronome." I was a bit crushed, but I did it. As I think about it now, I should call him up and tell him that his criticism really paid off. I may not have perfect time, but it's certainly improved.

Who modernized you while you were playing with Jimmy's band?

I was going out to listen to everyone in Chicago. One of the first people was Roy Kral [later part of a piano/vocal duo with Jackie Cain], who was playing with Charlie Ventura's Band out on the South Side in a place called Jump Town. We'd finish up at three A.M.., but they'd still be playing for an hour, so we would catch the last set. We heard everyone who came into the Blue Note and the Silhouette. I heard George Shearing when he was just starting out with the quintet. There was also a wonderful pianist named Mary Southern. She was a big singing star in those days, but she's retired now. Lennie Tristano came to town, and then there was the Dave Garroway radio show, and he used to have Dizzy Gillespie on, Al Haig and so on.

What's the story behind your long tenure at the Hickory House in New York?

They hired me for a couple of months, but after a year passed, they hadn't said anything about stopping. It turned out to be six months a year for years and years. It was a big barn of a place, sort of like a union hall. The choice seats were around a circular bar, and we played on a platform inside the bar. Toshiko [Akiyoshi] had her first job in New York there. They also hired Pat Moran, a fine pianist, and the guitarist Mary Osborne. I guess they liked women musicians. My trio was Joe Morello on drums and Bill Crow on bass. I wrote a whole section of Arnold Shaw's book [*52nd Street*] about the Hickory House.

You worked with Joe Morello just before he joined the Dave Brubeck Quartet, didn't you?

I practically discovered Joe Morello. When he came to town, he used to sit in. I couldn't wait to hire him, but then he joined Stan Kenton for a few months while Stan Levey was in the hospital. After that he worked for me for four years [1952–56].

What did you find so compelling about Morello's playing?

His touch, his technique, and his wonderful sense of humor, which I think is missing in a lot of drummers today. He'd play these funny rhythms and melodies in the middle of a four-bar break, with great skill and without being corny. I'm afraid Brubeck got him thundering like all the other drummers—too loud, you know. I think he was playing better early on.

What was your stint with Benny Goodman like?

I wasn't the right person at all. Benny had me play with him at his house for about a week, sort of live auditioning. I always thought he was pleased because he never said anything, like "Don't do this, don't do that." Then we got on the gig, and he'd give me these funny looks. We were with [vibist] Red Norvo and [trumpeter] Bobby Hackett at a rehearsal, and Benny would say to me, "Do you know that piece?" "Well, we just played it," I said. "Hmmm." He'd give me this look. He was, well, needling. I must say, though, he's a fabulous musician. My basic mistake was probably playing those "accursed" harmonies, flatted fifths. Benny, I realized later, loves those sheet-music changes. We were playing Dallas when the President [John F. Kennedy] was shot [November 1963], and the tour kind of ended right there. Nobody was in the mood to hear music. We got back to New York, and I never went back to work for him.

Have you noticed any evolution in the pianist's role, in the way the piano is being used, since you began playing in this country?

The first thing that comes to mind is that after this big, loud rock thing we've been going through, Keith Jarrett can come out with acoustic solo piano, making a great hit. There's really been a swing back to soloing, as there was in the days of Jelly Roll Morton and Fats Waller. It has something to do, too, with the way the world is going. People say music is always on the upswing during a depression, and it does seem that way. Everyone's complaining, but in my part of the music business, it's never been better. I'm playing colleges, getting grant money, more work than I can handle. It's very gratifying. I'm thankful for Keith, especially, because he's made people realize you can play with just the piano and no paraphernalia, not that I don't enjoy the Fender Rhodes.

How do you feel about free time playing, and playing that's not song-oriented, like the music of Cecil Taylor or Keith?

I like to do that kind of thing, too, but it's somewhat like eating all ice cream or all strawberries, you know. Although if I play a college, like [the] Eastman School [in Rochester, New York], where all that the kids listen to is Cecil, Chick Corea, and Keith, then I'll do much more free music or tunes by Chick or Herbie Hancock. Otherwise, you can't do too many free things when you're playing for people. The El Matador audience, for example, heard me years ago, and I think they expect me to do tunes I did then. I do play some of the same music, but not the same way. Then, of course, I like tunes, so I do them for that reason.

You've played more solo than most pianists. Everyone else seems to feel it's too difficult. How did you overcome the obstacles?

Well, more people are playing solo now than even a few years ago. In my case I used to be chained to the rhythm section. Now I'm just as happy if the other guys don't show up. I just decided to do some soloing at the Cookery in New York. It wasn't easy putting myself in that situation, but afterwards I knew I could do it. Some of these things that made it easier were playing some of those one-finger bass lines, some implied rhythms, like Bill Evans will do, a little stride piano with some tenths in the left hand, and I even started doing some far-out lines, like you hear now from that wonderful pianist from Spain, Tete Montoliu. When I was soloing once, somebody paid me the ultimate compliment. He said, "Oh, my God, your bass line is so good it has hair on it!" I thought about that for a while and decided it must be a compliment.

When you take up a new tune, how do you begin working on it?

It depends what it is. Right now there's a ballad I want to learn by Johnny Mandel called "Close Enough for Love." First, I hear the tune as a whole in my head. I'll write out the changes for the bass player, try it on the job, and see what happens. Usually the chord changes and melodic line you can apply to the tune are what appeal to me. Now, when I started playing "Send in the Clowns," I saw the show first and got the sheet music. It's such a strange tune anyway. I started out with Stephen Sondheim's harmonies, but after a while I changed the key and all the harmonies—he'd probably hate me. But I play the tune a lot, and I have to keep changing all those things or it gets stale.

Are there finger exercises you've used or you'd recommend for improving keyboard facility?

I did my studying at the Guild Hall Music School in London, and I worked very hard at scales, the Hanon book of scales, arpeggios, doubled thirds. I'd practice eight hours a day, doing Bach fugues and Beethoven sonatas. I had a very hard taskmaster for a teacher, and I built up a level of playing that stays with me even if I don't practice—which I don't. Of course, if I were going to play a Beethoven sonata, I'd have to practice a bit to get it back under my fingers.

Have you done any special work to acquire a jazz technique?

Well, I'd probably be able to do more "technical" things if I sat down and worked at it. But I'd hate not being spontaneous. I've heard that some people actually work out the runs they're going to play, but I'd rather live dangerously.

Do you work out your voicings?

Oh, they come naturally. I don't even think about it. I hear different ones every night, so I hardly ever play them the same way.

Are there certain types of chords and chord voicings that you have a tendency to work with?

I'd hate to have to describe them technically. On a slow tune I like to grab hold of a big chord and include as many interesting notes as possible. I'll use parallel things in an up-tempo tune because it's something I can do with my left hand. I don't want to play stride piano since I can't reach tenths as well as somebody like Teddy. Actually I do a little stride left hand on "Royal Garden Blues."

On those big chords, do you work around any particular color tones?

The ninth, the augmented eleventh, and so forth, but it's very spontaneous because I change key a lot.

Do you mean you'll play the same tune in different keys at different times?

Oh, sure, I can play in all twelve keys equally well, except on some up-tempo things. I like to do that with a trio if I have a good bass player. Right now I've got a very adventurous bass player, Frank Tate. I'll call out a tune and ask him if he minds playing it in B. "Sure, let's try it," he says.

You do live dangerously.

I've been able to do that all my life. You see, nobody ever told me it was difficult to play in certain keys, like F sharp. That's the problem with some teachers. They'll tell you a key is hard, and then it becomes hard. I'd start students out on the black notes. Personally, I find C a hard key. It's very sterile to me. Somehow all the keys seem to have colors and textures. I love B and E and A and F sharp. I actually associate them with colors, but Jim Hall, the guitarist, does, too, so I don't feel that ridiculous about it.

Have you found any particular type of ear training helpful?

I got what I have by listening to records, which people say is the hard way, but the more you do it, the easier it gets. I can take a complicated Keith Jarrett thing right off the record, though I couldn't even have attempted it years ago. So trying to play what you hear is the best thing you can do. I believe it's better than writing things out and then playing them, though it depends somewhat on the level of the student. There's probably no single method that applies to everybody. I've worked with such talented kids at [the] Eastman School that I'll sit back and ask them to show me something. Still, there are those who are just frozen and can't play a thing unless they see it in front of them.

When you present jazz on the piano to young children, what's the most effective level to reach them on? Harmonic? Rhythmic? Melodic?

It's a rhythmic thing, definitely. I'll start with something they know. I've got my preteen repertoire, my kindergarten repertoire, and so on. One of the great tunes I'm thankful for is [Scott Joplin's] "The Entertainer" because you can do a million things with it, a thumbnail sketch of the history of jazz. If I play a tune and tell them to listen for the way it's different the second time, it gives them an inkling of what improvisation is. Children never know the meaning of "improvise," not even the older kids. Sometimes I describe it as "being creative with what you know" or "doing your own thing," though I always come back to "improvise," trying to get the word across to them as something only *you* can do with a tune.

I wanted to ask you about your National Public Radio shows. How did that fantastic series get started?

Alec Wilder, who had a series of music shows himself, recommended me to NPR. They wanted to do something on jazz that was varied instrumentally. But I thought about it and came back to them with the idea that I wanted to concentrate on just the piano. It's been an enormous success, I suppose because of the millions of pianists and piano buffs on so many levels, from amateur to professional. I know there are students who taped those shows, like the one with Bill Evans, where he describes how he builds a solo from the ground up. You know, we'd name chords and explain how we do things.

You had Joanne Brackeen on your show, didn't you? Were you compatible with her in a duo piano improvisation? And how about the other important female pianist of the eighties, Jessica Williams?

I watched Joanne grow musically. I even have those early records she made for Adelphi. She's an enormous talent. Her ideas are her own. She's not everyone's cup of tea, but that's the sign of a true individual. We did fit together. I think it was a case of my going a bit further out and her coming a bit further in. In a way it was easy to accompany her because in all her flights of fancy she still has some root tone of the chord you can grab onto. I don't know Jessica's playing as well, but the first time I heard it I thought to myself, boy, I've got to meet her. So far I haven't been able to catch up with her. She seems to move around a lot.

How would you describe yourself stylistically?

I'm a sort of maverick. I don't think the NPR shows could have worked if I weren't able to adapt to whatever my guests were doing. Does that mean I don't have a style of my own? I suppose I don't in the sense of an Erroll Garner or George Shearing. I've never really wanted that unique thing because you get bogged down and then you have to stay with it. People expect to hear the same approach from you, and that stunts musical growth. Of course, without that you'll never be a great name. I know some people have branched out into more than one area, like Herbie and Chick, who went into those big-money fields using synthesizers and jazz/rock. I never had the urge to do that. I think I just don't have ambition in that direction. I love melodies and harmonies too much.

Selected Discography

At the Hickory House (1952–53); SJL-2248; Savoy/Arista.

Ambiance (1970); HAL 103; Halcyon.

Solo Concert at Haverford (1974); HAL 111; Halcyon.

From This Moment On (1978); CJ-86; Concord Jazz.

George Shearing and Marian McPartland (1981); CJ-171; Concord Jazz.

BILLY
TAYLOR

July 24, 1921–

Billy Taylor is an able and diligent spokesman for jazz, and his sophisticated, bebop-based piano style parallels the urbanity of his speech and manner. Taylor grew up in Greenville, North Carolina, and received a degree in music from Virginia State College in 1942. Taylor moved to New York and began working in Ben Webster's quartet at the Three Deuces on Fifty-second Street, where the numerous clubs were like a second home to the founders of bebop. In 1949 Taylor formed a quartet that was soon taken over by Artie Shaw and renamed the Gramercy Five. By 1951 Taylor was one of the house pianists at Birdland and worked with Charlie Parker, Miles Davis, Dizzy Gillespie, Milt Jackson, Art Blakey, and other founders of modern styles on their instruments.

Taylor played a less glamorous role in jazz than his colleagues, but one equally important. He was not an innovator on his instrument, but rather a talented communicator about it. If a single characteristic distinguishes Taylor from his peers, it is his conviction that *jazz can be taught.* Taylor's talents have been most widely recognized since 1977, when he began hosting *Jazz Alive,* a weekly National Public Radio show syndicated to more than 200 stations. Over the next four years the show received some of the network's highest ratings. It was Taylor's job to provide musical commentary and backstage interviews with the performers. Too rarely have education and entertainment been so closely linked in jazz.

Taylor continued his own studies in music, receiving a Ph.D. in music education from the University of Massachusetts in 1975. In the interview he explains the essence of his thesis, "The History and Development of Jazz Piano." In addition to leading his own trio during the 1970's, Taylor was the music director of *The David Frost Show,* a member of ASCAP's board of directors (replacing songwriter Harold Arlen), and a member of the National Council of the Arts from 1973 to 1978. Taylor is also the author of several instructional books on playing jazz piano. His book *Jazz Piano: A Jazz History*

(Wm. C. Brown Company, 1982) is based on his Ph.D. thesis and an NPR series called *Taylor Made Piano.*

I spoke with Taylor shortly after a lecture/demonstration he presented as part of the Summer Jazz Lab at Bennington College in Vermont. Students surrounded the baby grand as Billy played in his well-polished brand of bebop, stopping along the way to comment upon his treatment of the music or to demonstrate alternate treatments. Jaki Byard, also on the Jazz Lab's faculty that summer, was part of the intimate audience. Listening to jazz out in the rolling green countryside is a refreshing contrast to sitting elbow to elbow in smoky downtown clubs. After the class Taylor led me to a deserted performance hall and sat down at another piano to illustrate some of the points he was making about the instrument's role in jazz.

Where did you get your first musical experience and training?

Primarily I came from a musical family. My father was a keyboard player and also played brass instruments. Everybody in the family was a player, at least as an avocation. I could hardly get to the piano because it was in constant operation. Of course, I got the usual music lessons when I was seven years old—and hated it. I was studying with a lady named Elmira Streets in Washington, D.C. She gave me the fundamentals, but I was a terrible student at that time and didn't realize until later how much I had learned from her. I was lazy. If there was a recital, I'd practice. Otherwise, lots of luck—I'd go play ball.

Did you play any improvised music at that time?

No, I just liked to play. I loved the sound of the instrument. But a little later, when I was eleven or twelve, one of my uncles, who is a fine jazz pianist, introduced me to Fats Waller and Art Tatum on records, and it blew my mind. Then I got serious. But I wanted to play *that,* not the other stuff. I was very fortunate to live in Washington, D.C., because the Howard Theater had a great band every week: Ellington, Basie, Jimmy Lunceford, Chick Webb. Then Fats Waller played a solo concert at the Lincoln. I'd never heard anything like that. It just wiped me out. The sign outside said "Thomas Waller, piano." Thomas Waller? Piano—okay, I figured I'd check it out. It never occurred to me that this was Fats. Then I heard that first note and yeah! I spent the whole day there, listening to him, and it was one of the great experiences of my life.

Later the same uncle who had introduced me to Fats decided I was ready for Art Tatum. I'm glad he did it the way he did because if he had introduced me to Art Tatum first, I probably would have stopped [trying to play]. The first record I have of Art's was a thing called "The Shout," one of the few Tatum compositions on record. It's in G flat, and it was superstride. These were the two earliest influences I had in jazz—three really, including my uncle.

While this was going on, there was pressure from my mother to stay with my Bach and study traditional piano. I wasn't too thrilled about it, but I continued, until I met a neighbor of mine, Henry Grant, who was director of the high school band and a great music teacher. Almost all of the great jazz musicians who came out of Washington prior to '55 worked with him. He's one of the few people Duke Ellington actually studied with, and they were good friends. He was a fine pianist and masterful arranger. He was the kind of teacher who'd hear me playing something by Ellington, say, "Prelude to a Kiss," and show me a piece by Debussy with the same kind of harmony. He would relate wherever I was to something in traditional piano literature. The classical practicing I did was because he made me want to learn these things— all the little Debussy études and Chopin preludes. He'd show me my own voice leadings in a piece and blow my mind.

Did he encourage your improvising, too?

Oh, yeah. He'd just show me I wasn't alone in what I was doing. Debussy uses pedal tones and impressionistic chords, and all of this stuff exists in another kind of music, too. At Virginia State I ran into an equally good teacher, named Undine Smith [now Undine Moore], and she was remarkable. Her students ranged from Camilla Williams, the opera singer, to Phil Medley, who wrote for the Beatles, to me. But she treated everyone as an individual. She gave me new harmonic devices that I could use, not only in composition but in improvisation.

How long did you keep up an active study of written music?

Through college and even after I got to New York. I studied with Richard McLanahan at the suggestion of Teddy Wilson.

I remember his name. Teddy told me about him, too.

He was a tremendous teacher. You know, all these great teachers have something in common. Without taking music out of the Western European framework, they were able to show all the similarities and differences, the techniques that you'd need in order to do anything. An arpeggio is an arpeggio, no matter what the context. Essentially you've got to get over the keyboard from here to there.

You've gone into music education in an important way. Do you see any conflict between the role of educator and the role of performer?

I'm trying to keep them from being in conflict, but it's easy for them to be in conflict because academia is structured so that you must do certain things within the structure of the formal institution. That's a hang-up because the arts, especially the performing arts, have their own traditions and value systems. They must be carefully nurtured in terms of knowing what's happened in the past, building on it, and encouraging what's coming for the future. We don't do any of these things really. We ignore too much of the past; we keep reinventing the wheel. We act as if European classical music were isolated from all other types of music.

Is that attitude still prevalent in the university music departments?

Absolutely. People who teach are generally prisoners of the academic arena. Their teaching is subject to the censorship of their own music departments. From top to bottom we leave a lot to be desired. I'm insulted as an American that music schools in this country don't deal with the history of real American composition. You'd think a few white composers were the only ones writing concert music. They totally ignore people like Howard Swanson, Frederick Tillis, and even Dave Baker. Will Marion Cooke, William Grant Still, Robert Nathaniel Dett—their music is never played. Coleridge Taylor Perkinson writes some very interesting music, but I don't hear it. I hear lesser composers. These people have something to say which is unique. It's not jazz, but it should be heard. It's as American as Ives, Copland, or Bernstein.

Your dissertation was written on the jazz piano tradition. What's the central point of your thesis?

Jazz is America's classical music. It has been the traditional melting pot that we're so proud of. It's where the ethnic musical cultures that make up America come together. No other music does this. That's not to put down any other music. Rock has its place. Soul. Country-and-western. But none of them is as broad [as jazz] or covers the historical time period that jazz covers.

But what about jazz piano in particular?

My theory is that in the piano you have the whole history of jazz reflected, a focal point—in melody, harmony, and rhythm.

Piano styles are microcosms of jazz styles.

Absolutely. For example, Earl Hines and Fats Waller epitomized what was going on in all of jazz in the twenties and thirties. Their melodies and rhythms were the concepts of their generation. The generation which followed them— Teddy Wilson, Nat Cole, and Art Tatum—built on what they had done, so the music took a different turn. The generation that followed them—Bud Powell, Al Haig, and other people—took another turn. It went in five- or ten-year periods and really evolved—it didn't just spring from one place to another or turn a corner. It was a gradual evolution.

Do you believe that pianists were the leaders of their generations?

In many cases. If you look at the tradition, Scott Joplin, who set the pace for the ragtime writers, was a pianist. He also arranged his rags for instrumental groups. Joplin orchestrated the marching-band sound on piano and even used the form as the basic form of his ragtime pieces. He heard not only jazz but things from the European classical tradition and was able to incorporate them without changing the feeling of his music, which was the shout and other black music forms of his time. But he captured it in piano music.

Jelly Roll Morton took the ragtime experience and added another dimension. He wrote out a lot of his stuff. If you check the piano rolls and transcriptions, like on "Kansas City Stomp," you'll see that a lot of his orchestrations were based on his piano solos. So his piano solo was a miniature orchestration. This was true of many piano leaders, like Duke Ellington, Fletcher Henderson, and, to some extent, Count Basie–when he was writing. They all had the ability to visualize the whole orchestral texture of what they were playing.

Visualize or audioize?

Well, it's visual in a sense. Even though they hear the sound, they visualize it on paper.

To move to a more current topic, do you see a continuity in the piano tradition from these older, tune-oriented players to today's so-called free players?

Take Cecil Taylor. He's playing very much in the jazz form and is very aware of Fats Waller. When Cecil was studying in Boston [at the New England Conservatory of Music] he used to come down to hear me a lot at a place on Fifty-fourth Street called the Downbeat. Obviously what he heard didn't influence him to do the same thing, but he picked up the same points of reference I had–Tatum and Waller–and treated them in his own way. He's a remarkable player–his energy. In fact, his energy gets in the way of people realizing how very inventive he is and what good jazz structures he's making abstractions of. He'll play an abstract thing, and it may seem like it's not related to anything else. But it's definitely an abstraction of the Waller tradition or out of a stride or a swing tradition. He's fascinating to listen to.

Do you have equally favorable opinions of other free players?

I think much free playing is anarchy and not the best that that person can do. I think those who choose to play both tune-oriented and other techniques are a lot healthier than those who say, "I'm going to play everything with no point of reference, abstract." Of course, it's an artist's right to do whatever expresses what he's trying to say. But it's more meaningful to me as a listener to be able to hear the same guy do different things. Every person is more than one person. He's many people wrapped up into one, like husband, father, brother, and so on. I'd like to get more of that from players who just play abstractly.

For a beginning player, what kinds of procedures or material would you recommend?

Whatever grabs him in his quest to learn the instrument, learn to get over the instrument. Scales, arpeggios, different types of touch, use of the pedals, all the things he'll need to be able to express himself, no matter how he wants to play.

Hanon, Cramer, Czerny—are any of these particularly good?

They're all good, and they all have a use. I use different things, depending on the student and the circumstances. I'm one for the pragmatic approach. I don't believe all students should study Hanon or all should study Czerny. If a student is bored with an exercise, I'll tell him to take it through the keys or maybe try scales in contrary motion. You have to challenge a student constantly.

What about chord substitutions, voicings, and so on?

The best way to be any kind of jazz player is to start with the beginning, just as you would in Western classical music. Look at what went before you and see how you can apply these traditions to what you want to do. McCoy Tyner came from Art Tatum and other players. Erroll Garner came from Earl Hines. If a student is having trouble with voicings, I put him on Ellington compositions, like "Prelude to a Kiss," learning it from the sheet music in the old style. A lot of students are very sophisticated when it comes to playing a single line with a chord change, but what they don't know is how that chord looks when you spread it out on a piece of paper. When you write out chords and see them, it gives you a new concept of voice leading which you can't get from playing changes. You see that the flatted fifth is flatted because it's going down to something else.

I've talked to a lot of players who claim that studying with a teacher hasn't been very important to them. Horace Silver, for example, told me he took one year of lessons and, from then on, learned by ear. Do you think this is a valid approach for some people?

Absolutely, but musicians lie about what they do. Why? I don't know. They say they've never studied. Bull! I know what they've done, who they've gone to for study, and how they've studied on their own. You've got to be intellectually aware of what you're doing, or you're just a run-of-the-mill player. Erroll Garner is a brilliantly intellectual guy doing what he does. He's figured it out—you can't lose him in that style. Maybe he doesn't read music, but I'm not hung by terminology in that sense. He is self-taught.

Within his style, he knows exactly what he's doing. The fact that he didn't study with a teacher at Juilliard is irrelevant.

Yes, because he taught himself from the very best teachers. He abstracted what he wanted to do from Bud Powell. He isolated and intellectualized what he wanted to do. He's a brilliant melodic writer, but it didn't just come from the heart. It's very logical. You can analyze his music harmonically, just like you can a Bach piece.

Dizzy Gillespie was one of the most intellectual guys to come out of bebop. He and Charlie Parker decided intellectually how to extend the harmony, how to extend the line from four or six bars to ten bars, how to organize the rhythmic direction. I want the drums to do this, the horns to do that. The trumpet and alto sounded like one instrument. All these things were intellectual. They made a decision. They didn't just happen. I'm a teacher because Dizzy—at one point, before he began taking his elder statesman role to heart—and Charlie Parker and Duke Ellington refused to do that. I knew that these men knew intellectually what they were doing, but I read interview after interview where they came off sounding like idiots. The writers reported accurately what they were saying, but what they said was bullshit. It gave people outside the field reason to say jazz cannot be analyzed, it cannot be taught, because these men were leaders in the field and they were saying that it couldn't be.

Do you feel that made jazz less respectable in the eyes of the public?

I couldn't give a damn about respect in that regard. It was just that all this made it impossible to communicate with people I wanted to communicate with. They believed the writers who said the really great jazz musicians do it off the top of their heads, and it's all heart. There are no rules. You can do whatever you want. Bull! There's a tradition and a lot of things that go with good playing. Any musician can tell you who's a good player and who isn't, so there have to be rules, there are certain parameters to judge by. I'm still a player, but this is what motivated me to become a teacher. I don't think the two are incompatible. Some of the great classical pianists were supposedly the best teachers. Chopin was a teacher; so was Bach.

What's your feeling about electric keyboards?

I think they're totally different from the piano. Electronic instruments come closer to the organ tone because they sustain notes. They are valid instruments. Keyboards, yes, but not pianos. Anyone who plays one is limited only by his own musicianship, imagination, and mechanical ability.

Do you think the abundance of electric keyboards has been harmful to the pianistic tradition?

Not to the tradition, but to some specific pianists because the technique for playing these instruments is so different from playing the acoustic piano that many pianists have substituted electrical sounds for creativity. Of course, this is very subjective. I'm talking about my personal taste. I would rather hear Herbie Hancock, Chick Corea, or Joe Zawinul play acoustic instruments because they are all individuals who have a beautiful touch and do special things with voicings. I miss that when they play on electric instruments, although these instruments give them an opportunity to do different things and reach a broader audience. I don't put them down because they choose to go in that direction. It's just not my taste. The main thing—and I think Keith Jarrett has mentioned this—is that you are physically in control of an acoustic piano. With an electric instrument, you get intellectual control. You know that when you press a button, certain things will happen. That's mechanical, even if the ultimate result can be emotional for the listener. I've used the Fender Rhodes and the Mini-Moog, and when I directed the Frost show, I tried out a lot of different instruments. They have a place in creative music, but as a pianist, that's just not where I'm coming from.

Selected Discography

A Touch of Taylor (ca. 1965); 7664; Prestige.

Live at Storyville; 8008; West 54th.

Sleeping Bee (1969); 7096; Pausa.

Where've You Been: The Billy Taylor Quartet (1980); CJ-145; Concord Jazz.

JOHN
"JAKI"
BYARD

June 15, 1922–

More than any other performing pianist, Jaki Byard alludes explicitly to the jazz piano tradition in his playing. Consider his *tour de force* album, *Solo Piano* (Milestone). With equal authenticity and conviction, he plays a stride left hand like Fats Waller, atonal clusters like Cecil Taylor, and nearly every pianistic idiom that evolved between them. Of course, Byard has paid for his reliance on jazz tradition by giving up the pursuit of a clear stylistic identity for himself. It has hurt him commercially; the public, unless it is indulging in an occasional bout of nostalgia, demands individuality and novelty.

Musicians generally have more respect for tradition than their listeners have. Bandleader Charles Mingus, in whose work the roots of jazz are always showing through, took full advantage of Byard's historical sense in his great bands of the sixties. Byard also enjoyed a few favored years in the mid-sixties, when Prestige recorded him as a leader with groups that included Freddie Hubbard, Eric Dolphy, Ron Carter, and George Benson. One of the great thrills provided by these groups and the Mingus bands is hearing a tradition-oriented pianist like Byard with an iconoclastic saxophonist like Eric Dolphy.

During the late sixties Jaki was also a soloist at the Top of the Gate in New York. Byard prides himself on his adaptability and never affects the pose of "uncompromising artiste." He tells of playing a mayors' conference in New Orleans, where, despite the presence of two marching bands, he was asked to open the event with "The Star-Spangled Banner," probably the least improvised-upon tune in the entire American songbook. "Something told me before the job to check out the song," Jaki recalled, "and sure enough they asked for it. . . . So maybe it's good to have songs like that in your repertoire. 'The Battle Hymn of the Republic,' 'When the Saints Come Marching In,' Burt Bacharach, Blood, Sweat & Tears—I've used them all over the world and improvised on them. I go from that to Bach, to outside, back to inside, and all over the place." Not surprisingly, Byard is an excellent teacher, not only of piano but of composing and arranging. He has served on the faculties of the

186

New England Conservatory of Music in Boston, City College of New York, the Julius Hartt School of Music in Hartford, Connecticut, and several other institutions.

Jaki is a simple, direct man with little pretense about what he does. He understands intimately how varied and evolutionary the jazz piano tradition is. Through our interview I had hoped to discover the training and background that enabled him to re-create so authentically virtually all of jazz piano history. But Byard explains this versatility in his own terms. For him it all comes down to "tingling in your spine."

What were your first experiences at the piano?

I started with a lady named Grace Johnson Brown when I was seven years old. I had two or three years of training with her in European classical music, scales, and so on. I remember doing the *Waltz in C Sharp Minor* by Chopin, and after that I just sort of fooled around with the piano. [Elsewhere, Byard has said he recalled studying pieces like Dvorak's *Humoresque* and Cécile Chaminade's *Scarf Dance*.] Then there was a local high school band. My mother had suggested that I get into jazz, so I went back to Grace Johnson Brown and studied an arrangement of "Stardust" by Hoagy Carmichael. Then I stopped studying and just played with the bands.

Did you play piano with them?

Actually, I played trumpet with a lot of these groups, and my main ambition was to play sax. My folks couldn't afford a saxophone, but we already had a piano because my grandmother had played for the silent movies. Starting in 1938, my father used to tell me, "Listen to this cat." It was Teddy Wilson with the Benny Goodman Trio on the *Camel Caravan* radio broadcast. Teddy Wilson, Fats Waller, Fatha Hines, Basie, Fletcher Henderson—all these [pianists'] bands started me thinking about playing swing music and improvising.

I understand that most of your early playing was at the Saxtrum Club in Worcester, Massachusetts. How did you get involved with that club?

It was a private club organized by a few of us musicians. We used to jam and hold rehearsals there. The jam sessions usually started after midnight. There was a nearby theater where the big names played, and they used to come in to jam with us: Joe Venuti, Basie, the members of Stan Kenton's early orchestra. I was sixteen, and I guess I originated the name, Saxtrum, for sax, trumpet, and drums. I was playing trumpet at the time with a local band led by Howard Jefferson. I switched to piano two years later because the pianist quit, and they knew I could play. The doctor told me to give up trumpet and trombone anyway because I used to get headaches. He thought it was from playing. By the time I was eighteen I could get more gigs on piano, too, what they call cocktail piano. We called it intermission piano. Those gigs were really the birth of solo piano.

Speaking of clubs, I just visited this place called Asti's on Twelfth Street in New York. I was invited to have dinner there once, and then the owner asked me to play a little, so I did. This old fellow comes up and says, "Hey, you remind me of someone who used to play here back in the twenties. He was a big guy." Well, I knew it was Fats Waller, so I said, "Fats," and he said, "Yeah, that's it." Then I played some more, and he says, "Hey, you remind me of someone else who used to play here, and Fats would introduce him with 'Here comes God,' or 'God is here.'" So I figured out that this must be the place where when Art Tatum came into the room, Fats Waller would say, "God is in the house." You know, that statement got to be pretty famous.

Did you lose interest in the classics as a result of playing jazz.

No, I kept that up until I was twenty or so, and then I went into the army, where I [once again] played trombone. See, my father used to play in a marching band, so my folks had all these instruments in the house. In the army I got interested in Stravinsky's music and in Chopin again. I studied Chopin's *Fantasie Impromptu* and analyzed it. I began to analyze everything by Chopin, Bach, Brahms, Beethoven, and all these cats to find out what was happening in these compositions. I did this until about fifteen years ago, when I got more interested in the academics of improvising or jazz or whatever you want to call it. By 1969 I dropped playing the music of Beethoven and those cats because I had completely assimilated their styles. Practically every piano player is doing that now—improvising on their styles somewhere along the way, especially when playing solo. It's a good opportunity to dig into those styles. I've learned a lot from that in terms of knowing what their music is all about, or what it stands for, and understanding the feelings a musician gets from playing music, regardless of what style it's in. It's that feeling in your body. You get it tingling in your spine—the emotion behind the music and in the music, too.

What led to your playing with Charles Mingus?

Don Ellis, the [late] trumpet player and composer, was the one who introduced me to Mingus. Don was a student of mine in Boston. He studied arranging and composing with me. He sort of insisted that I come down to the Showplace in New York and play for Mingus. I sat in with him, and that was it. At the time Horace Parlan was playing piano for him. But about two years later (1963) Mingus asked me to join him. His front line was Clifford Jordan [tenor sax], Johnny Coles [trumpet], and Eric Dolphy [alto sax and bass clarinet]. Eric was always thinking about playing on top of the chords, like superimposing a C seven on top of a B flat seven, which is like [using] an augmented eleventh and thirteenth. It was a gas, accompanying him. He loved those changes on top of the chords.

How did that affect the way you accompanied him?

I played what we call combination chords, the root and the notes on top of the chord. Instead of playing the whole chord, with four or five tones, I'd play two tones, possibly the ninth and the root, or the eleventh and the root. Listen to that record *Outward Bound* [on Blue Note]. It didn't change the way I accompanied too much.

What was playing with Mingus like?

Hilarious. Sometimes because of his social behavior. You just had to tolerate it because he was a pretty interesting cat, musically and socially.

You two seemed to share an interest in the roots of jazz. Did you ever discuss that with him? What did you discuss with Mingus?

Mingus's group was one of the few where you could play anything you knew how to play, *if* he was in the right mood. We didn't discuss really, just a few specifics. He'd teach us by singing the music, phrasing it the way he wanted us to play it. I'd write it down for my own documentation. After he sang, we'd just jam it out.

Some of your solos with that band, like on The Great Concert of Charles Mingus *[on Prestige] were virtual capsule histories of jazz piano. Did he like you to do that?*

I'll tell you how that came about. Mingus did a funny thing; all of a sudden he'd stop the rhythm [bass and drums]. I remember the first time it happened. I said to myself, now why did he do that? What's going on? After a few times, I figured, the hell with it, if I'm playing alone, I'll play whatever I want, so I'd stride, play excerpts from concertos, anything. The public used to dig it, so I don't think he minded.

Why did he stop the rhythm like that?

I think it was because his fingers got tired. By the time we got to the piano solo, Eric had played five or six choruses, somebody else played a few, Mingus had solos for four or five choruses. He just got tired of playing, but he never gave you warning. He just stopped. I once told him, "You're a ham, Mingus, and I'm going to ham right along with you." He used to break up when I did that. I stayed with Mingus until about 1969.

Didn't you play with another tradition-oriented musician, Rahsaan Roland Kirk?

I never gigged with him, but we made records together. He used to buy old piano rolls and play along with them. When he was living in Philadelphia, he'd call me up, "Hey, listen to this. . . ." It would be someone like Jelly Roll [Morton], Pete Johnson, or James P. Johnson. He'd make a guessing game out of it. That was our socializing. Rahsaan did a nice album with me called *The Jaki Byard Experience* [on Prestige]. Very few sax players had his stamina. He had a very nice style, too.

The way he played reeds reminds me of the way you play piano in that he summarizes the history of his instrument. Did you consciously try to acquire all these styles?

When I came up, Fats Waller was in vogue. Then there was Nat "King" Cole and Basie. I played like Fats first, but the guys in the bands I worked with wanted something more modern, so I doodled around like Basie and played like King Cole. Then Erroll Garner came on the scene, and I listened to him. Throughout the years, as a soloist, I did different styles because it's a good way to do the gigs, playing popular piano styles. I remember being on a Bud Powell kick at about twenty-five years old. That's when I decided to get into music more and listen to everything. Bebop was an age of revelation. It made everyone want to study more. For me, listening to Bud, after a while, I could start to anticipate every change of chord, everything he was going to do. I decided there's got to be more to music than this. So I listened to lots of other people. I remember getting into Lennie Tristano's thing for a while. They all became part of my act.

How did you study? Did you go back to school?

No, I studied at the library, checking out the records and music. Chopin, Beethoven, Ravel, Stravinsky, and, of course, listening to piano rolls. I had learned the technique of writing and arranging in high school. That's the only formal training I had. When I tried to go to college after the army, I couldn't get accepted. So I used to get some books and work with other musicians, like [saxophonist/pianist] Sam Rivers. Sam and I both moved to Boston after the war. We used to play for singers and dancers, any type of show. Later on, before Mingus, I was associated with [trumpeter] Herb Pomeroy's bands with [saxophonists] Charlie Mariano and Serge Chaloff. In fact, I used to play tenor sax with that group at the Stables, where we played Tuesday and Thursday nights. I played intermission piano, too. Chick Corea used to come in—he was a kid then—and Dan Morgenstern [director of the Institute of Jazz Studies, Rutgers University]. These cats thought I was a tenor player because they heard me with the big band.

Has it been a disadvantage to you to be associated with so many styles, as opposed to developing a single identity within your own playing?

No, I have to play the way I feel. Some people have told me I ought to stick with one thing, if that's what you're getting at. But now my way is coming into vogue. You've got to dig into the piano historically these days. Just last night I heard Dick Hyman and Roger Kellaway playing duo, and they played every style you could think of. Johnny Guarnieri and Roland Hanna are doing that. [*Village Voice* critic] Gary Giddins, I think it was, paid me a compliment. He said I was partly responsible for this trend, for getting people to think like that. Of course, to some guys Fats Waller's music is just a point of amusement. When I worked for Eric Dolphy and Booker Ervin, on their dates, they were interested in music only from bebop on. You never played Fats for them. But with Mingus or Rahsaan, they took delight in hearing the way the piano used to be played.

Have the free-playing pianists expanded the potential of the piano?

Actually I think that's a bad term. There's no such thing as freedom, because when people play the piano, they're automatically governed by certain patterns that they've absorbed during their lifetime, and they're obligated to do what they know best. Cecil Taylor might play for forty-five minutes, but he's got some patterns in his mind. You can quote this: All humans have patterns of thought, and they come out musically. Nobody can change that. There's no argument on it because it's the truth.

So there's as much structure to free music.

There might be a little more endurance involved in the Cecil Taylor or the Keith Jarrett styles, but that might not last too long. When they reach the age of sixty, if they don't slow down, they're supermen.

Do you think less traditional tunes will be used by pianists as jazz progresses?

Less traditional tunes, yes, but traditional harmonies will be used, whether it's classical, impressionistic, or whatever's going on now.

Where is your own playing located in this spectrum?

I never thought about it, but there are times when I might go into anything. I seem to have become involved in using whatever I know of the piano, whether it's baroque, Brahms, Waller, Tatum, Bud Powell, or Jarrett. Whatever I hear gets incorporated into my interpretation and performance.

What do you recommend to players for acquiring technique?

I went through Czerny, the Bach *Inventions,* Scarlatti, and the impressionist composers Debussy and Ravel. Most of us are still involved in impressionism harmonically, with cascades of arpeggios and chords with ninths, elevenths, and thirteenths. Whenever I see that kind of chord, I think of Ravel's things. Practicing scales and studying their form were also a help. Knowing all the keys and the sound of the different keys is important; keys like B flat, F, E flat, and A flat are all associated with the sound of the trumpet and saxophone. Keys like E, A, and B are violin keys.

You played electric piano and celeste on Freedom Together *and organ on* Jaki Byard with Strings! *[on Prestige]. What is your feeling, however, about the use of electric keyboards like synthesizers? Do you think it's a healthy trend in music?*

It seems to be evolving according to the particular plan of commercialism. They're always looking for something new to market. Now they're exploiting, or experimenting with, the electronic sound, but you still hear the acoustic piano sound, too. I was telling my son this morning why I never bought him a bass guitar. I thought it would be foolish because he wouldn't play it forever. I told him I'd rather buy him a drum set because that will always be an instrument; it will always have a function.

What motivated you to do so much teaching recently?

I've always taught. When I was sixteen, I remember giving Don Asher [coauthor of the Hampton Hawes autobiography *Raise Up off Me*] a lesson for fifty cents. What really got me going was Gunther Schuller's calling me in 1969 to teach at the New England Conservatory of Music. I teach piano in the Afro-American Music Department, and I also teach a course in orchestration.

How did you acquire a system for teaching when you were sixteen?

By listening to and watching the local musicians and cats like Fatha Hines, [pianist/bandleader] Claude Hopkins, and Fats Waller—in 1939 you could get to hear him for fifty cents.

What do you emphasize with your piano students?

Scales, learning the keys, and the use of triads. I also show them the cycle of keys through fourths and fifths. The study of fourths covers guys like McCoy Tyner, analyzing their style and how it evolved. I tell them to learn the seven modal scales and to develop the cross-handed technique for playing arpeggios. You can cross hands and get two different sounds; if you use two hands, it can sound like a harp. I also encourage them to write down everything they play, like their own solos—document them, copyright them, and spend as much time as possible creating. Bach and Beethoven did it, so I tell my students to do it. It gets people off the ground in terms of composing.

What's the greatest asset to a student? Technique? Composition?

No. Experience. Many of them know how to play, so I just say, "Here. Add this to your knowledge or repertoire. Then you can create for yourself." The rest is experience and hard knocks.

Selected Discography

Jaki Byard: Giant Steps (1961–62); P-24086; Prestige.

The Great Concert of Charles Mingus (1964); PR-34001; Prestige.

Live! Vol. 2: The Jaki Byard Quartet (1967, with Joe Farrell) 7477; Prestige.

The Jaki Byard Experience (1969, with Roland Kirk); 7615; Prestige.

Solo Piano (1969); PR-7686; Prestige.

Jaki Byard: To Them–To Us (1982, solo); SN-1025; Soul Notes.

RAN
BLAKE

April 20, 1935–

Ran Blake is a friendly, frenetic man. His piano playing is idiosyncratic, and his attitude toward music, uncompromising. In his twenties Blake chose to work as a waiter at the Jazz Gallery and as a hotel desk clerk rather than play piano in a band that was not to his liking. While that sort of romantic idealism is often attributed to jazz musicians, when the chips are down there are few who actually make the choices Blake has made.

Blake is also one of the few musicians to have pursued single-mindedly the concept of third stream music. Blake's mentor, Gunther Schuller, defines this as a synthesis of jazz with modern European classical music. Blake's broader view of the third stream is that jazz is merged with ethnic musics from around the world. Although many pianists—such as John Lewis, Cecil Taylor, and Keith Jarrett—incorporate the classical idiom in their playing, Blake is unique in erecting his style upon a synthesis of jazz with ethnic music, especially Greek. His playing has been called oddball, quirky, and surreal. It is also humorous, imaginative, and artful.

In the interview below, Blake calls the third stream a "synthesized duality," and the phrase applies equally to his career. He divides his time between teaching at Boston's New England Conservatory of Music, where he is the chairman of the Third Stream Department, and performing. Sitting in his basement studio/office at the school, Blake predicted that he would remain there until he is fired or dies. "Ten years ago," he recalled, "this office was a mailroom, and I was licking envelopes. In the second year I did a little teaching. Five years ago, the Third Stream Department was created, and I was appointed to direct it. It was Gunther Schuller [the conservatory's former director] who kept me going."

I met Ran in his office at the New England Conservatory shortly after a performing tour designed to promote *Breakthru*. The album includes original music and interpretations that suggest highly polished and eccentrically cut gems. His music is full of open space and is based rhythmically on stride. As Blake notes in discussing his background, he is heavily indebted to Thelonious

Monk. Sadly, public excitement over Blake's intriguing style ebbed quickly, and he returned to teaching and local performing.

How did you get started on piano?

I worked with a variety of teachers. According to my parents, I've been playing since I was three or four. One of my teachers, Ray Cassarino, from Hartford, Connecticut, became very important to me, and I worked with him for about three years in my teens. He had gotten his playing experience on the road with [bandleader/clarinetist] Woody Herman. He put me through block chords and intervals and then encouraged me to explore on my own, which was very important because I didn't get encouragement to do that from anyone else. But if you mean practicing Hanon for hours each day, I did some of that on my own, and some Czerny, too. It bored me, and I couldn't wait to stop. Personally I wouldn't distinguish between learning technique and learning to play the piano. I developed more facility basically by playing my own music. I didn't want my hands to get ahead of my ears. I don't play fast right-hand lines, which people do expect of pianists, because until recently I didn't hear them at all. I'm just beginning to. I want to get other sounds, approaches, fantasies, angers, and dreams, and not just blow a bebop line like most people.

Are there any musical memories from your childhood that remain especially vivid?

Another part of Hartford for me was Bishop Jefferson's church, where I used to sanctify and protest. I sang anthems and got all this wonderful pentecostal black gospel music there. I went to Suffield Academy, Classical High School, and Bard College, but the church and Ray Cassarino were the two schools of music for me until I was nineteen.

What other teachers have you had?

I've worked with John Lewis, Oscar Peterson, Bill Evans, Mal Waldron, who gave me a lot, Mary Lou Williams, and a lady of rhythm named Laverne Powell, who taught at Hundred Twenty-fourth and Park Avenue in New York. In the cases of Evans, Peterson, and Lewis it was like a series of five-week courses at the Lenox School of Jazz [located in Lenox, Massachusetts, and defunct since 1960], with some follow-up in New York. I studied with Mary Lou a little longer, and with Mal Waldron for a good year.

What specifically did you seek out from each of these teachers?

I think I went to Mary Lou in search of tradition, background, Harlem identity, and her brand of reminiscences about Kansas City. Whenever things got philosophically heavy or my hands got tired of practicing, she would bring out the scotch or fried chicken. That was all very wonderful and important, and although I went only five or six times, she never slighted me on hours. I saw Mal Waldron faithfully each week for two or three hours, and I chose him because I liked the way he would pick and develop an idea and because I wanted to get some rhythmic flexibility playing with people. Lewis, Evans, and Peterson were on the Lenox faculty, so maybe I chose them at first just because they were available, although I still keep one part of what they've taught with me after all these years. John Lewis taught me about development and composition as you play. Peterson was a magnificent teacher; he was much more open than I might have thought he would be.

Since you don't play a lot of fast right-hand lines, one would think that you would have taken the opportunity to work on that with him.

I think he would have wanted to get into that if our lessons hadn't been cut off. He invited me to study with him in Canada, but I couldn't go. I hear a lot more for my left hand, and I'm working on some exercises that will allow me to play more of what I hear, but although my right hand has already developed a hell of a lot, judging from *Breakthru,* it will never go fast enough. It's that ability to think fast and be flexible that makes the difference. [Charlie] Parker and Bud [Powell] had it, but I've developed other resources. A lot of people play fast solos that are awfully meaningless, and I don't know if I want to do that. If I had time with Oscar, I would like to work instead on learning how to relax in playing situations. I think Oscar would have been so much more meaningful if I had worked with him after studying with Gunther Schuller because I didn't know what I was doing in the fifties, and I really felt that I had to be straight jazz or strictly classical. I didn't know of any other world until Gunther helped me on vision, clarity, and how to edit out the crap and tie your ideas together as you play. Gunther got me into my own music, which is what I want to do with my students at the conservatory.

Could you expand a bit on your definition of the third stream as a "synthesized duality"?

We might say that it means a way of making your own self-portrait, but then that would imply that I feel that the music Mary Lou Williams plays, for example, couldn't serve that function, so it's better not to say that. I think "synthesized duality" is a pretty good phrase.

What method for teaching piano do you use in the conservatory's Third Stream Department?

I am not a piano teacher, although I do work with students who are pianists. People tell me that nobody gets the tones, echoes, and pedal effects that I do on the instrument, but I don't teach that. I don't want to be conscious of those things. My whole educational approach is through the ear. The whole first year is ear training. I'll give students twenty-five or thirty pieces to learn and sing away from the tape or record. We try to develop the memory. We don't start with anything difficult; instead I'll begin with Billie Holiday, maybe some of my music, or Greek music, and eventually I'll add an operatic piece, or maybe a solo by [drummer] Philly Joe Jones. There's a great diversity. Finally they'll go find the notes on the piano or whatever their instrument is.

Why do you keep your students away from their instruments during the early stages of your instruction?

They study their instruments simultaneously in other classes, but I do feel that the ears should come first. What I have is an ear gymnasium. All pianists, horn players, and drummers have to do some singing—obviously not in public; God forbid that I ever will!—but they have to be able to carry a tune so at least I know that the melody is in the ear. Students say, "But I want to create now!" My answer is: "I know you can play improvisational tricks, but I want you to go through the whole process of developing the ear. It must be big, and it must like a lot of musics. You can't just go and add an East Indian gong sound to your latest recording because it's 'in' to have something international."

What makes your class different from the typical music school ear-training course?

What really makes it different is the fact that we try to have each student realize a self-portrait and that we understand that every person has a duality. We have people pick two opposite—or, if you will, two related—musics and really pursue them. In other words, we don't stress ensemble playing, although we have three ensembles, but we have a personal approach of "let's get your own internal act together and find out who you are."

How do you help your piano students develop technical facility at the keyboard along the way?

I don't. I send them to somebody more qualified. I work on taste and the imagination. I use the keyboard, that's true. It's wonderful to see the piano getting so many people right now. But honestly, I don't teach technique.

To get back to your students, what directions do they take after finishing the ear-training phase of their studies with you?

We start getting into performance. Instead of just memorizing, say, Miles Davis's solo on "Walkin'" [from *Walkin'*, on Prestige] they'll play it, too. Then they'll improvise a chorus, then imitate a chorus they've memorized, and so on. Eventually we make up what we call a grocery list. We find out the musician's likes and dislikes and the limitations of his or her ear. For example, some people cannot hear fast sequences, but they can hear harmonic density. They'll take a different direction from someone who hears very fast Coltrane "sheets of sound." We also find out taste limitations and ethnic musical background. Do they have an ethnic musical heritage, or was it only television, [singer] Barbra Streisand, and bubble-gum music? We find a few musics they can go into more deeply and eliminate the other styles, so they don't throw everything into the kitchen sink. Ultimately they integrate two kinds of music.

Do you feel that there are specific artists, like Streisand, or styles, like bubble-gum rock, that in no circumstances can serve as models for young musicians to pattern themselves after?

I probably do personally—everybody does personally—maybe because rock is so pervasive. I suppose that I might have to be intolerant of the most crass music from Broadway or certain kinds of rock, even though we all profess to being free from prejudice, but that's just because of my fear that a music such as rock could really take over. In terms of style, there are really just two musics—bad and good—and by the way, I've just become a tremendous fan of Earth, Wind & Fire, which is more of a soul-rock group. But I might still try to keep down the enrollment of young rock people because rock is the majority music, and I want more minority. It can easily eat out all other styles, and I think that if one thing gets so big that it begins to dominate everything else, then it's almost fascistic in its own way, and I might want to watch that.

So you're not as concerned with the music itself as with its position in the world today.

I think that's ninety percent true. I give my students Monk more than Streisand or [guitarist] Peter Frampton because I do feel that many people will succumb to the blander influence. I try to develop the ears of the freshman students so that they can perceive all the subtleties of music. But then again, we could say that singer Doris Day has subtleties, so the story would never stop.

Do students take to this approach readily?

At the very beginning the tendency is for them to say, "Let me be boss!" But it's too soon at that stage. Maybe they think music begins with Elvis; maybe they like the Boston Pops or, to take somebody good and hip, Coltrane. But that's still a narrow boundary, and it can make you self-satisfied. We don't want a lot of robots sounding like everyone else. Ultimately they have to teach themselves and become their own mentors, though while they're still here, they should hear my opinion and other opinions a couple of times a year.

Do you ever get into jam sessions or "musical dialogues" with your students?

Sometimes I'll say a few sentences and then get them to respond. Then they'll start out, and I'll respond. But I don't know about this idea of playing together. It's like five people talking simultaneously. Maybe you can synchronize in a nice crackling Philly Joe Jones/Red Garland/Miles Davis quintet format, but not if you're unpredictable. There are exceptions, like [saxophonist] Ornette Coleman and [trumpeter] Don Cherry, who have had enough "conversations" so that they can read each other.

Is this why you play solo more readily than with a group?

Well, people do need other people, in music as well as in the rest of life, and I have done some recording on Arista with [reed player] Anthony Braxton; [saxophonist] Sonny Rollins's new guitarist, Jerome Harris; my favorite saxophonist, Ricky Ford; and some others. But I have to tell you this. Gunther Schuller is publishing some music of mine that was transcribed by a young composer named Donald Fox. The music is from my album *Wendy,* and I had no idea of how rhythmically outrageous I am until I saw the transcription. If somebody gave me a piece of music with all those time signatures, it would be painful to play. I realize now how difficult I must have been to work with when I was growing up in Connecticut. I can see what a problem I must have been to other musicians, and why nobody would ever hire me to play at a dance.

Has your approach to playing solo piano been affected by the popular "ECM school" epitomized by people like Keith Jarrett and Richard Beirach?

I haven't heard Richard Beirach yet, although I've heard very good things about him, but I can say that certain ECM label releases sounded like very refined Muzak. I don't get surprised by it. To me, it's not really contemporary. What would still be contemporary in my opinion is Cecil Taylor. I hear he was fantastic when he played at the White House, and he did it all within five minutes, so he has the ability to shock you without going on and on in a thirty-minute piece. You can argue that the ECM piano albums are contemporary because they're being made now, but they're not any more new than what was going on years and years ago.

They haven't influenced your style at all then?

Well, maybe there are some new things happening in me. I've been listening to a lot of tango music since my tour to Argentina, for example. But I leave all that for the critics to say. I have no time to listen to myself, no time for social life, and no time to breathe because I'm so busy teaching and because my career is suddenly picking up.

Has your interest in tango music and Earth, Wind & Fire been reflected in your music yet?

The tango, not at all. It's so new. Anything that comes from that will not be evident in my playing for two years because I work very slowly at getting things into my system, and anyway, I don't think it's going to play much of a role at all. Although Earth, Wind & Fire are a sort of new interest, Stevie Wonder and Aretha Franklin are not, because they both come out of the church, which was one of my first musical experiences.

Yet these church-oriented performers play in a repetitious rhythmic cycle that seems totally foreign to your use of rhythm.

Well, I guess I'll never play that way, even if I want to. But I don't know why I gravitate toward some of their albums rather than toward music people think I'd be more apt to like, although I'm mad about [avant-garde saxophonist] Oliver Lake, too.

You seem to have an affinity for stride piano playing as well, although your work doesn't sound like stride in the traditional sense.

I do love James P. [Johnson] and Fats [Waller], but I don't know if that style of music is sad enough for me to listen to for a whole evening. I don't consciously take twenty stride records home and devote a summer to listening to them, as I'm doing now with Billie Holiday's Verve releases. Maybe I use stride to compensate for the absence of right-hand flourishes, or simply because I want to hear some action in the left hand, too. I'm not sure that's the answer, really. Another possibility is that I go out of time so often that it's important to stay in time occasionally. It gives the music a kind of whiplash and brings it back to earth.

Which pianists have influenced you?

Thelonious Monk, Thelonious Monk, and Thelonious Monk. Actually a lot of important influences weren't pianists. [Saxophonist] Ben Webster and what he could do with a ballad were very important to my development. Right now I like Mary Lou, Michael Smith, and Andrew Hill. I love Ray Charles and I have liked Cecil Taylor. Mildred Falls, who accompanied [gospel singer] Mahalia Jackson, is one of my great favorites. I also like Dollar Brand and McCoy Tyner, especially in the way Tyner's left hand interplays with the percussion. Believe it or not, I dig a lot of Herbie Hancock's stuff, like "Maiden Voyage" and his less commercial funk. I love Eddie Palmieri, the salsa pianist, though I'd love to hear a thousand more dissonances in there, and I'm not fond of that steady rhythm.

How has Greek music affected you?

Part of the Greek thing was the process of waking up to political oppression by hearing about a saxophonist whose lips were sealed because he wanted to play music by [radical composer Mikis] Theodorakis, for example, or a pianist whose fingers were broken. But the Greek experience also woke me up to the possibility of incorporating other ethnic musics into improvisation.

Do you think of your playing as pianistic?

I don't think about my own playing. I think about my dreams more often. I'm told that I'm pianistic, though, rather than hornlike, like Bud Powell. I don't have that kind of velocity. The sense in which the piano is like an orchestra pleases me most of all.

Which make of piano do you prefer?

I've had some very good experiences with Baldwins. I like some Steinways. Some Yamahas are good; some are bad. It's like talking about black people and white people, men and women; it's the individual that matters. Can I get something going with a specific instrument? Do we get along? Do we get into each other's head? I can't tell anything from the brand name.

What are your feelings about electronic keyboards?

Electronics don't interest me. Prepared pianos do. I'd like to work with microtones. But I really think there are a lot of sounds on the grand piano that I haven't gotten to yet, like horn sounds, very percussive sounds, sounds like a woodwind section, overlapping sounds. You can get into them by hitting the instrument, caressing the upper register, or pursuing degrees of touch and accent. The piano is an instant orchestra. It is the most complete instrument there is.

Selected Discography

Ran Blake Plays Solo Piano (1966); 1011; ESP.*

The Blue Potato and Other Outrages (1969, solo); MSP-9021; Milestone.

The Newest Sound Around (1972, with Jeanne Lee); LP-2500; RCA.*

Breakthru (1975, solo); 37.38.42; Improvising Artists, Inc.

Rapport (1978, quartet); AN-3006; Novus/Arista.

Film Noir (1980, quartet); AN-3019; Novus/Arista.

RAMSEY
LEWIS

May 27, 1935–

A boyish Ramsey Lewis met me in the lobby of the elegant Stanford Court Hotel, hours before his band opened for Earth, Wind & Fire, the headliner for that night's rhythm-and-blues concert at the Oakland Coliseum. His dress and manner were cool and conservative, conflicting with the glitter and garish hyperpromotion that preceded these bands into town. It had been more than a decade since Lewis's piano/bass/drums trio recording of "In with the In-Crowd" launched the Chicago pianist from local clubs into a national concert circuit. It proved a lucrative change of venue for Ramsey, but was not without its frustrations. Though "In-Crowd" expanded his audience numerically, it restricted him artistically. In his view, he became identified with funkiness; the audience expected to hear it from him and assumed he was capable of nothing else. "If I have any bone to pick," he said as we sat down in the plush armchairs of the hotel's bar, "it's that most people thought the 'In-Crowd' was me. No classical training, no exposure to Charlie Parker or Bud Powell, no recording with Max Roach and Sonny Stitt, no substantial background."

What is perhaps most remarkable about this bluesy modern-day stomp called "In with the In-Crowd" is that it foreshadowed the immensely popular fusion genre of the 1970's. Lewis's face came aglow when I expressed that thought to him because he feels that history has vindicated him from all the criticism his hit record drew from other jazz musicians.

During the early seventies Lewis played himself into a corner by immersing himself in electronics and rhythm-and-blues. He let his genuine jazz credentials dwindle to the vanishing point. Back in the late fifties he had seemed to be a product of two major influences, John Lewis and Oscar Peterson. In 1978, as we spoke, he virtually admitted that his subtlety as an artist had been trapped behind a tangle of patch cords and his bank of Bolex speakers. Ramsey Lewis had "fallen out of love" with electronic keyboards, but his career was plugged into them; he was a prisoner of his own success. Now, Lewis, however, believed he had found a way to extricate himself without leaving his seven-piece funk band behind, as he explains.

When did you first start playing piano?

I was six years old. I had a sister two years older, and my parents decided that she was going to be the musician in the family, so for no other reason than jealousy I wanted lessons, too. After about four weeks I decided I had had enough, but my parents said now that I started, I had to keep it up. From ages six to eleven I studied with the neighborhood teacher, you know, the person on your block who knows more than anyone else. She was the church organist and charged fifty cents a lesson. She told my parents that I had talent but that she'd taught me everything she knew, so they took me downtown to the conservatory, over my protests, and I met a wonderful person whose name was Dorothy Mendelssohn. She had an approach to life that carried over into music. She thought of life as one series of events, some good, some bad, but if it comes out positive in the end, it was worth it. Like in music, technique is important, getting through the piece is important, but the most important thing is whether you said something. She used to say, "Don't just play the notes; listen with your inner ear." Well, I was twelve at the time, so it took a while [for that] to get through, but now I know that's what a lot of musicians mean by soul. I stayed with Dorothy Mendelssohn until I entered the Chicago Music College, but I continued to study privately with her until I was twenty-one.

What was your curriculum like at the college?

Heavy classics. It was the usual: Bach, Chopin, and so on. Dorothy was making me write out my own scales and play them in all the keys. I used traditional fingering in the scales, but she taught me to experiment with other fingering possibilities in the passages of a work. The main thing I got out of classical music was discipline, the ability to think through a piece. Now it's the ability to think through a solo. Where am I starting? Where am I supposed to go? I don't think I'd have a feeling for the keyboard or the ability to think of notes as a means to an end if it weren't for Mrs. Mendelssohn. Anyway, the Chicago Music College was a great place for teaching ear training, harmony, and basic composition. [The college is now part of Roosevelt University.]

Do you still play written music?

Not as much as I'd like to. I mostly do it for the sake of challenging myself. In improvising we play only as much as we've experienced, so when you're improvising, it's difficult to challenge yourself.

The written music broadens your musical experiences?

Right, you lay away combinations, voicings, and so on in your memory, and they come later on. You can always tell a pianist who's never studied, unless that pianist is so gifted in his ear that he can just listen to records and fill his memory with what's on them.

What composers have been broadening experiences for you?

The Brahms *B Flat Piano Concerto.* The *D Minor,* although I didn't finish it. I love all the Rachmaninoff piano works, preludes, concerti. But I go to different composers for different reasons. I still play through the Chopin études mainly for technical reasons, and I still pick up *The Well-Tempered Clavier* for independence of finger movement.

Did you ever consider a concert career in the classics?

Yes. Dorothy Mendelssohn told my folks that she thought I had what it took to be a concert pianist, but that she had to be honest—and thank God she was—that it would be nearly impossible for a black musician to make a living concertizing. Therefore, she advised me to keep my eyes and ears open for other ways of making a living as a pianist.

My dad had already introduced me to Art Tatum, Oscar Peterson, and Erroll Garner when I was about twelve. At first I didn't know what Art Tatum was doing. If Bach was four voices, Tatum was twenty voices, but I did learn to appreciate him a bit. What impressed me most is that they were playing without reading. Of course, I had already been introduced to cadenzas in classical music, which at first were improvised. I guess after the composers heard what the musicians were doing to their parts, they said, "Never mind, we'll write it out."

When did you first start improvising?

The organist for one of my dad's church choirs had a dance band and invited me to play one night. He just had me come to the job; we didn't have time to rehearse. The first tune was a blues in B flat, and he kicked it off. I thought he meant boogie-woogie, so I went into this Meade Lux Lewis thing, and he said, "Hey, wait. Just lay out. Don't play." I don't know why he didn't fire me on the spot; probably because he's a born teacher. In fact, he's now a school principal in Chicago. Anyway, he showed me the changes and told me to listen to other improvisers.

The first year I was playing Erroll Garner licks and as many Oscar Peterson licks as I could recall. Maybe one or two Tatum licks. Eventually I started getting into the habit of demanding that my mind, or soul, tell me things. Real improvising! Pretty soon people began telling me that they could tell it was me playing and that it didn't sound like anyone else.

Was this the mid-fifties trio with Eldee Young and Red Holt?

Exactly. That's when we started recording, about forty albums ago. [The "In-Crowd" was on the eighteenth album.]

When did you begin to play electric keyboards?

Eldee Young mentioned them to me because he'd heard Ray Charles play the Wurlitzer electric piano and suggested I use it in the trio. This was in the early sixties, but I never got around to it then because I was in love—and still am—with the acoustic piano. Then Charles Stepney turned me on to using the electric in the late sixties on an arrangement of "Mother Nature's Son." [Before his death of a heart attack, Charles Stepney had played piano and vibes with Eddie Harris, written and arranged for Earth, Wind & Fire, Minnie Ripperton, and for Ramsey Lewis's *Sun Goddess* album.] He brought in a Farfisa and Wurlitzer. I don't think the Fender had come out then. At first it was great, like a new toy, so I started experimenting with keyboards and synthesizers. Then I sort of fell out of love with electric instruments altogether because I was spending more time planning new computer combinations, learning new keyboards, learning which keyboard worked best with which *wah-wah* pedal and which Echoplex wouldn't work, and so on. I was spending much less time developing my ability to improvise. During one show a keyboard went out, and I spent the whole show wondering what made it go out or what I could do to hook it up. Suddenly I asked myself, "What am I doing here anyway? I'm supposed to be playing the piano."

You were functioning as a sound engineer.

Right. That was about a year ago. Then, in January, we were recording *Solongo* for Columbia, and I had decided I wanted to be known as an acoustic pianist. They weren't too happy about that. On that session we were doing an up-tempo tune called "Slick," and theoretically I was supposed to be able to play it faster on electric. But I was brought up on an acoustic, so in fact, I can play faster *with control* on acoustic. After four or five takes the ideas still weren't flowing. We took a break, and I played the tune on acoustic, and everyone said, "That's it. Let's roll the tapes." So what I've done now is to hire another keyboard player who has all the electric stuff around him. I just play acoustic. He's a twenty-year-old named Bobby Bryant, and I'm always buying him new toys to fool around with. [Bryant has since left the group.]

That's a very simple solution to the problem of getting absorbed in electronics. I wonder why no one else has done that.

Right, because the electric instruments have their place in today's music. The sound is there now, and to do without it would be like removing salt from the dinner table. I do have one more hurdle to overcome, though. I have a seven-piece band, but only the drummer and I play natural instruments. So I'm experimenting now with the Helpenstill and Countryman, which are acoustic pickups. But I really haven't found a pickup that allows enough of the acoustic timbre to come through. There's still a false metallic ring.

Have you tried the Yamaha electric grand? Herbie Hancock and Paul Bley have told me it has a convincing acoustic sound.

Yamaha brought it here, rented a studio, and invited all the professional players to try it out. I was very impressed, and it's the closest thing to an acoustic I've played. But it *is* electric. If you take ten pianists and tell each of them to play the same notes, and if the instrument is acoustic, you'll be able to hear the difference between them. We all have a touch. The size of the finger, the weight of the arm, the mentality, the emotional output—they're all different. But the electric doesn't respond to that.

I thought the Yamaha had some touch control.

I didn't notice that it did. But the action was not quite so loose as most electrics, so the keys offered some resistance, therefore, some control. The harder you strike a note, the louder it will play—to a degree.

How do you feel about the electric as other pianists use it?

Well, Herbie Hancock, Chick Corea, George Shearing, Oscar Peterson—they have good piano tone. It has body; it sings; it lasts; it has character. All this is lost, even on the new Yamaha. I'm more concerned with my tone and technique. I spent a lot of years with Dorothy Mendelssohn developing a singing tone, as she called it, one that lasts until the next tone, that has a quality. I'm not satisfied to give that up to a computer. You simply lose your individuality of tone. I'd hate to go through life hearing piano players who all have the same tone. In my recordings the electric instruments will function as coloring, as icing on the cake.

Do you feel strange playing in the Coliseum to Earth, Wind & Fire fans instead of in a jazz club?

Well, I had moved into the concert halls after the "In-Crowd," so I'm used to that setting. The audience is a challenge on this tour because I can't be very delicate, and I miss that terribly. The end of the hall is two blocks away, and the sound has to be jacked up so much I keep telling them, "I don't want a song to be loud from start to finish." I hope you'll hear tonight that we've met the challenge. We're not just an opening group killing time until the stars are ready. I would have left the tour if it had come to that.

I've always thought that "In-Crowd" was one of the first examples of what is now called jazz/rock or crossover music. Do you agree?

I'm glad you said that. I have to tell you the musicians at that time really put me down. "You've got this rock element, rhythm-and-blues, gospel, what are you doing, man? No good, it'll never work." These were purist listeners who just didn't understand what I was doing. But I'd been playing like that since the mid-fifties in churches. That's black church music–getting down! I had all those influences on me, along with the classical, and the influence of Oscar Peterson and Charlie Parker. Now, ten years after "In-Crowd," the technique of putting emotional music on top, with a rocking beat underneath, has become a way of life. They call it jazz/rock, and there are those, like Chick Corea, who have extended it harmonically. Basically, though, that's what the "In-Crowd" was all about.

Selected Discography

Gentlemen of Jazz (1958); 627; Cadet.*

Hang On, Ramsey: The Ramsey Lewis Trio (1958); 761, Cadet.*

The Best of Ramsey Lewis (1973–81); FC-36364; Columbia.

Chance Encounter (1982, acoustic piano); FC-38294; CBS.

RANDOLPH
"RANDY"
WESTON

April 6, 1926–

Randy Weston is an imposing, almost regal figure. Large-limbed and graceful, he stands six feet seven inches tall. Wearing a dashiki and a colorful skullcap, he greeted me in his motel room overlooking San Francisco's Fisherman's Wharf. During much of our interview he methodically rubbed body oils into his hands, feet, and neck. Weston seems to glow with pride when he speaks of Africa, where he lived from 1967 to 1973 and operated a cultural exchange center for musicians called the African Rhythms Club.

More than any other jazz pianist, Weston incorporates African elements into his playing in an obvious way. He shifts meters frequently–between 4/4, 3/4, and less common metric patterns. He also uses the bass register of the piano as a kind of tonal drum. During a trio set the night before (with James Leary, bass, and Ken Marshall, drums) Weston demonstrated an uncanny ability to establish driving, hypnotic rhythms by using only one or two chords–sometimes only one or two notes–per measure. He has perfected what Bill Evans called the rhythmic displacement of ideas. There were times he made the whole room sway to his personal beat.

Weston's exposure to African culture and its derivative music began in childhood. His father, born in Panama, was of Jamaican descent and operated a restaurant in Brooklyn, serving West Indian cuisine. Realizing that Randy would not learn African history at school, his father educated him in his heritage at home. The restaurant was frequented by jazz musicians, who exposed Randy to the music of New York during the rise of modern jazz. He remembers listening to Bud Powell, Duke Jordan, Art Tatum, Willie "the Lion" Smith, and Erroll Garner. His most important influence, evident from the degree of space, or silence, he leaves in his music, was Thelonious Monk.

Weston began his career at the unusually advanced age of twenty-three, and his first job was accompanying the blues singer Bull Moose Jackson. He then worked with saxophonist Eddie "Cleanhead" Vinson, trumpeter Kenny Dorham, and drummer Art Blakey. In the late fifties Weston met historian

Marshall Stearns and toured with him on a lecture circuit, giving demonstrations of jazz piano styles. Weston became well known as a composer, especially of jazz waltzes like "Little Niles" and "Hi-Fly," which have become classics in the jazz repertoire. In 1960 Weston composed "Uhuru Africa" for a big band and vocalist, with text provided by poet Langston Hughes. In 1967, following a State Department-sponsored tour of fourteen African countries, Weston moved to Tangier, Morocco, where he established the African Rhythms Club. In 1973 he moved to Paris. Since then he has done most of his playing in Europe and Africa.

Weston is very disturbed by the picture of Africa presented in America. "All we hear about are the problems of Africa," he said, "like wars, famines, and racial problems. That's what makes the news. But there are tremendous musical and cultural experiences there." His own African experience, he explained, made him aware of spirituality, nature, and the historical role of the musician in African culture. "He was a communicator, whose task it was to spread knowledge of the traditions of the people. He was a healer, too; scientists in the West are just beginning to look into music as therapy. There is music for weddings, funerals, and virtually every aspect of life. In Africa today the musician is still an integral part of all community life."

Weston sees jazz piano as part of the black man's Africanization of European instruments. "I would like to have been there when our people first came into contact with these instruments," he said. "Can you imagine the excitement, the freshness of the first encounter? To me, what Louis Armstrong did was fantastically modern, really avant-garde." My line of questioning began with the origins of jazz.

What is your vision of the connection between African music and American jazz?
Let's go back as far as we can, farther back than [cornetist] Buddy Bolden, and imagine the first African who was brought here as a slave. His instruments were taken away from him because they were a means of communication, a way of keeping the traditions alive, a way of keeping the people together. The music we developed here on new instruments, which we call jazz, or gospel, or blues, calypso, bossa nova—they all have the same basic traditions.

What makes our music different? The rhythm is tremendously complicated, especially in most indigenous African music. Improvisation is very important. The individual sound of each player, of every handclap, is very important. The music is based on flatted thirds, blue notes, as we call them. When you hear the religious songs or the songs of sadness in Africa, you can hear the beginning of the blues. Creating something new out of the blues is the real genius of our music [jazz].

It's also very important in this tradition to see the artist work, not only to hear him. Each musician does a completely different thing when he plays. So you're losing something in both jazz and African music if you only listen to a recording. There's also an extremely evident spiritual quality in Africa which you can also hear in Louis Armstrong, Charlie Parker, or Monk. Getting back to these original sources nourishes our newer ideas.

Has your closeness to African drumming and rhythms made you more critical of American jazz drummers?

Not at all. It taught me what tremendous creativity there must be in this music to produce jazz drumming. I hear jazz drums as a collection of African drums, and I think drummers are working more and more on producing direct African sounds and rhythms.

What is the response of Africans to jazz or to jazz piano?

First I have to say that I think it's a miracle that African and European influences came together to produce jazz. It's an act of God. That's the only way I can understand it. How the Africans respond to jazz in its present form has a lot to do with who is playing it. Any group heavily into the blues form would be fantastic. If the musicians were avant-garde, half the audience would probably walk out. What's the most important element of our music? To play the blues—that's the way I was taught. Incidentally, that's the way our music is always taught, not from books, but aurally, by hanging out with other musicians. Playing the blues was always the test while I was young.

My band played for audiences from Morocco and Tunisia as far east as Beirut. We played for audiences who had never heard a concert, not to mention a jazz concert. But I always had an African drummer with me. I would say to the audience, "This is your music after it crossed the Atlantic, after it came into contact with European civilization. Your music has changed in our hands, but the basic traditions are still the same. This is what happened to your music."

I wrote something called "African Cookbook"; it's in 6/4 time. The music goes in waves, not in a strictly divided beat. It's jazz, but the similarities [with African music] are very deep. On occasion the audience would raise their hands in the air and take the song away from us with their handclapping. They never lost a beat. They'd keep the song going and wouldn't let us stop playing.

Can you recall your first experiences with the piano in this country?

I remember very well. When I was a teenager in the forties, we had the most fantastic music all around us. My father had a great record collection: Louis Armstrong, Jimmy Lunceford, gospel groups, and so on. But he would never have described it as jazz. It was so much a part of our lives; it was just music, our music. It didn't have a name. Like a lot of musicians my age, I was a first-generation New Yorker. My father came from Panama by way of Jamaica. My mother was a Virginian.

I didn't want to study music at first. As you can see, I'm physically big, and I was six feet tall when I was twelve years old. So I wanted to be an athlete. But my father was very wise. He knew that the streets were rough and that the best way to keep a boy off them was to give him a musical instrument to study. Of course, I was in complete revolt. My first piano teacher started me on Bach, which seemed to have no relation to my life at all. The battle was waged for three years with my father physically forcing me to practice. Finally the teacher told him to save his money. "This cat will never play," he said.

After a while I got to know some musicians who showed me some melodies that caught me. I got another teacher who realized that I wanted to swing everything, so he gave me some popular music along with the classical. In the army I started to learn theory from other musicians, and afterward I went to a GI school in Brooklyn, where I played with some fine people.

I should also mention that the influence of the black church was very powerful. Naturally I didn't want to go there either, but my mother took me every week. I heard gospel music regularly and suddenly began to understand the piano better—and how much it meant to our people. Churches were the only place black people could congregate because it was assumed the pastor had things under control. Certainly everyone could be watched. And that's where the piano was kept—a European custom—and Christian/European music was played there. But we responded to it, as Africans.

Were there particular pianists you were aware of at the time, pianists who influenced you?

"Influence" is an interesting word. I'd say there are pianists whose souls have entered me, like Monk. From other pianists, maybe one melody, or one bar, enters me—and it remains with me. To be more direct, there was a time that I started to play like certain people I was hearing. I was successful with Count Basie. I really could imitate his style, which was probably one of the easiest to play. Yet I was fascinated by his sense of rhythm and space. He could say so much with so few notes.

Next came Nat "King" Cole. I'd never heard a piano played with so much beauty and taste. That's also one of the qualities I like in John Lewis. Each note is sheer beauty. Art Tatum shattered me and frightened me, so I never consciously thought I was playing anything like Art. But when I play, I *hear* Art. Like I hear four or five notes from one of his runs. He taught me to be more daring. I guess Monk came after the Tatum thing.

Another musician I've been close to since my teens is [bassist] Ahmad Abdul Malik [who played bass with Monk and the oud, an Egyptian stringed instrument]. His father was Sudanese, so he had a definite Eastern influence. In fact, on an album with [saxophonist] Johnny Griffin in the late fifties they recorded jazz with Eastern and African music, probably one of the earliest records to do that.

Coleman Hawkins has been very important to me. In fact, I got to know Monk through him. For a time I tried to play piano like Hawkins played saxophone. Anyway, Monk played for Coleman, which is how I first heard him. I remember thinking, this is it! This is the direction we have to go in. It's like going back to the source in order to progress. Of course, a lot of artists are taking other directions, new directions, but I think there's only so far you can go that way. We can go further by continuing the source of the tradition. That means going back to the East, to Africa, Asia, and India.

Yet electronic instruments seem to be leading us in a technological, Western direction rather than back to the sources.

Yes, I think so, but I also think it's temporary. Although we're using electronic, complex, and mechanical devices, away from nature's instruments, we're also searching for a more natural existence in other ways. There's a great increase in the interest in natural foods, exercise, natural medicine, and so on.

When I left America and was without its contact for six years, I came back without a recording from 1965 to 1972. People told me I just had to make a record, so I complied with several compositions about Morocco for the album *Blue Moses*. Then I was told, "This is the electronic age, and you've got to use an electronic piano, too." Well, I don't like the electric piano because my sound is my voice, and my voice is what makes me unique. You don't hear my sound on the electric. But I listened to these people. I compromised and played it their way. Well, this record was a blessing for me—it got tremendous air play, and I'm very grateful for it. But I don't ever want to make another record like it. When I hear myself on electric piano, I cry a little because I don't hear my sound.

In our music that sound is very important. A personal sound is the most difficult thing to achieve; it's an extension of yourself. Years ago Coleman Hawkins would walk into a club, and all he had to do was play one note—he wouldn't have to play a lot of notes because he had that sound. I've heard Monk stop an audience dead by hitting one chord. That's part of the African tradition. We've got to maintain this tradition even though we've come in contact with other cultures; it's our nourishment.

When you play the [acoustic] piano, which type of instrument do you prefer?

Each individual instrument has a soul, a certain spirit or quality. You do have a name on that piano: Steinway, Baldwin, Bösendorfer, Bechstein. These are my favorites. But in Venice I played on a full concert grand, a Steinway, in a beautiful theater with twenty-five hundred people in the audience. It was like a battle. I really had to work to play that piano, and I couldn't explain it. When I listened to the tapes later, I realized I could not get in tune with that piano. Then, a month later, I played in France on exactly the same type of piano, and I couldn't do anything wrong with that instrument. It was pure pleasure to me.

Could it have been you? One night you were "on," but in Venice, you were "off."

That happens, too, but not in this case. It was the instrument. Pianos are made by men, so their spirits enter into it. Each individual instrument becomes different regardless of the brand name.

There's another thing I've thought about piano companies: I'd like to see them make their instruments more available to jazz artists in return for endorsements. My impression is that the companies are more classically oriented.

Some jazz artists do get terrific cooperation. Oscar Peterson is now supplied with Bösendorfers.

The Bösendorfer is more than a piano; it's an orchestra with those nine extra notes in the bass.

Yet Oscar told me he doesn't use them, that they'd have to be written for.

Yeah, but I use them, maybe because of my African direction. There's a whole octave of drums down there. I've been able to use that piano quite frequently in Europe.

What types of pianos did you find in Africa?

They tend to fly them in from Europe. The weather just isn't very good for pianos there. It's too humid, and most of them have to be "tropicalized." I don't think the Africans make pianos at all.

Do you think there's anyone who is showing the way to the future of jazz piano music?

McCoy Tyner, without doubt. He's showing the way to the future, yet he's maintaining the tradition, the rhythmic quality, the spiritual vitality, the humor, the sadness. If he only knew what a fan I am!

It's gratifying to see how well received his music is, too.

That's right. You've really said something there, because what he's doing is so important. When Monk and the other giants stopped playing, the other cats had no idea where to go. They were without a leader. Some of them have become more involved with European classical music, and others are searching for something new in electronics. The idea is to get back on the track, and McCoy is on the right track.

Selected Discography

Zulu (1960's); M-47045; Milestone.

African Nite (1975); 1013; Inner City.

Randy Weston; 7017; Pausa.

BILL
EVANS

August 16, 1929–September 15, 1980

Bill Evans was a warm, good-hearted, and extremely intelligent man. He stood for honesty, integrity, and beauty in music, and he never backed away from those high standards. Evans was the most influential pianist of the 1960's. The tone, touch, texture, and harmonic richness of his playing affected the majority of pianists who followed him.

Bill Evans grew up in Plainfield, New Jersey. As a boy he studied piano, violin, and flute. During high school he played in local bands, occasionally working with Don Elliott, guitarist Mundell Lowe, and bassist Red Mitchell. He won a music scholarship to Southeastern Louisiana University, where he continued to study a classical repertoire, as well as playing jazz in bands. While in the army (1950–54), assigned to play flute in the band at Fort Sheridan, Evans worked in Chicago with Tony Scott and studied with the composer and theoretician George Russell. Russell's idea of applying the Lydian mode to jazz improvising had a strong impact on Evans. In 1959 he collaborated with Miles Davis in structuring and playing the music on *Kind of Blue,* a timeless classic of modal improvising. Evans was also the piano soloist on other historic recordings: Russell's "All About Rosie," John Lewis's "Odds Against Tomorrow," and Oliver Nelson's *Blues and the Abstract Truth.*

Beginning in 1960, Evans led his own trio. With bassist Scott LaFaro and drummer Paul Motian, Evans set new standards for interplay among the trio's instruments. It was clear almost immediately that Evans had a new way of treating harmony and melody on the keyboard and a personal touch as well. Evans was shattered by LaFaro's death in an auto accident in 1961, and he isolated himself for the next year, hardly playing the piano at all. Gradually, he returned to performing over the next few years. In 1965 Evans recorded a unique overdubbed album, *Conversations with Myself* (Verve), which involved taping a second piano part over one previously recorded. The album won a Grammy Award and helped to boost Evans back to a position of some prominence. (Contrary to certain press releases promulgated by a record company on Bill's behalf, but without his approval, Evans was not the inventor of overdubbing. As noted in Part One, that innovation in the jazz piano field must be credited to Lennie Tristano, who had overdubbed three tracks of an album in 1955.)

In 1966 Evans began working with bassist Eddie Gomez, who—like La-Faro—became a sensitive, melodic partner with whom Evans communicated on an intuitive level. Two years later, drummer Marty Morell joined Evans and Gomez to form the second important Bill Evans Trio, which remained together for nine years. After Gomez and Morell left the band in search of their own personal niches in jazz, Evans led several different bands and worked as a soloist. By the mid-seventies, he was too much of a master to be greatly affected by the particular talents or even the absence of sidemen.

Though acclaimed as a pianist, Evans was probably underrated as a composer. His "Waltz for Debby" and "Peace Piece" are acknowledged as classics, but Evans wrote other fine compositions, such as "Blue in Green," "Show-Type Tune," and "T.T.T." Like his improvising, his composing was typified by clear, melodic lines and rich, colorful harmonic sound on the acoustic grand.

Prior to my conversation with him at the Monterey Jazz Festival in 1976, Evans had become a father for the first time. He rejoiced in the birth of his son (Evan Evans) as an apt symbol for a regeneration that was apparent in his music. "I think the most important element is the spiritual content of whatever you're doing," he told me. "My personal life has become so happy in the last couple of years, getting a whole family thing going, buying a home, becoming a father—all of this contributes to my motivation, which is a mysterious element in anybody's life. You can't turn it on or off very easily, and I feel like my motivation is returning. I'm just feeling more alive now, alive in a broader way than just being a musician. . . . When you have children, it seems you're more tied to the future and to everything that's going on in the world.

The earliest evidence I had heard of Bill's enlivened playing was on the 1973 album *Intuition* (on Fantasy), a collection of piano/bass duets with Eddie Gomez. Compared to his earlier work, the melodic lines are longer, the ideas more definite, and the rhythms more forceful. There is new weight added to the bucolic lyricism of his past. He uses primary colors instead of pastels. Bill was articulate on the subject of his own development. His style was built on his personal interpretations of both classical and jazz influences. His acutely sensitive and lyrical technique or touch is unsurpassed on the keyboard. Bill worked ceaselessly to develop his music, and his achievements were hard-won. Tragically Evans's sense of well-being did not last long. His health deteriorated rapidly during the late 1970's. A prolonged period of drug use during the fifties and sixties was partly to blame for his compromised health. He continued to perform until only weeks before his death, of a bleeding ulcer, in a New York hospital.

Most of the interview ahead comes from the conversation with Bill in his motel room at Monterey; the first six questions and answers, however, are excerpted from a conversation we had at the Fantasy Records studios in Berkeley in 1974.

In terms of style, what musical influences are you aware of? The role of bebop in your melodic lines is evident, but there's a lot more. Where does it come from?

It's more a personality characteristic of putting things together in my own way, which is analytic. Rather than just accept the nuances or syntax of a style completely, I'll abstract principles from it and then put it together myself. It may come out resembling the [original] style, but it will be structured differently, and that may be what gives it its identity. I've often thought that one reason I developed an identity, which I wasn't aware of until recently – people were telling me I had an identity, but I wasn't aware of one! I was just trying to play – is that I didn't have the kind of facile talent that a lot of people have, the ability just to listen and transfer something to my instrument. I had to go through a terribly hard analytical and building process. In the end I came out ahead in a sense because I knew what I was doing in a more thorough way.

Do you mean because of analyzing the elements in your own music?

In other people's music, too. If I liked something and wanted to be influenced by it, I couldn't just take it whole hog like some people can, like getting it more or less by osmosis. I had to consciously abstract principles and put them into my own structure.

Whose music did you analyze?

Everybody's. Everybody's I could play. Everybody I loved, and I loved everybody. From Dizzy [Gillespie] to Stan Getz to Bird [Charlie Parker], the whole works.

When you say structure, do you mean the voicings of [selection and order of notes in playing] chords?

That's part of it, but I'm thinking in terms of the language of music, which is more in the melodic [quality], the way one idea follows another. Why does it have meaning? Why does it say something? Because it relates to the idea that precedes it or the one that follows it. It's that kind of structural thinking. It's a way to handle musical tones. If you're a painter, you should be a draftsman, too, and an architect. You should have a compositional sense and a structural sense. When you think about people like Michelangelo, they're great architects, sculptors, painters—everything that encompasses that kind of art. You have to have an architectural sense and a real respect for the building blocks in music. It doesn't mean much to memorize the changes to a tune, unless you really understand why everything is there. It's no less a consideration in a folk tune than in Bach or Bartók.

Did you play classical music or learn very much from it?

Yes, but it's difficult to pin down exactly what. My heritage is classical, too. I've played a lot of Bach and up through the contemporary composers.

Is the music you play in performance worked on or worked out with the trio?

We never have rehearsals. If something sounds worked out, that's the result of playing it over and over. I try to keep things loose. I don't come in with arrangements or anything of that sort. We just agree on the basic structure.

From hearing you live and listening to your new albums, I get a strong impression that your playing has developed markedly. Do you feel that way about it?

There has been development, but the development I'm looking for is right through the middle. I don't try to go to the edges of what I'm doing and spread out that way. I try to go through the middle, the essential quality, and extend that. Consequently a lot of listeners might not hear any development for a long period of time, but there is inner development going on.

It might have something to do with ideas or the rhythmic displacement of ideas, but that's speaking technically about something I'm not thinking about technically. What I'm trying to do is *say* something in the context of my music. What I'm learning how to do is say it with listenable, understandable musical language that gets deeper into meaning. The best example I can think of is what Philly Joe [Jones] can do with an eight- or four-measure solo. Using the same rudiments that other drummers use, he can do something that makes you say, "Wow! Yeah, what a beautiful way to put those things together, so simply and to say so much."

I'm trying to say strong things, strong ideas. I'm speaking as if it's a technical consideration, but when I'm playing, I'm thinking of being in the flow of the music, allowing it to develop over a period of time.

To be more specific about my own observation, you seem to be digging in harder. I feel that there's more "definiteness."

Really? I hope that's true. I think it may be true. I play almost everything I play now with conviction and without much equivocation in my feeling about the music. I went through a lot of confidence problems when I was coming up. It seems like you go off in one direction or another, and each time you return to yourself you have a little more confidence. Maybe when you have enough experience and get old enough, you have enough courage to really believe in where you're at and realize that it's the only place for you.

Things like avant-garde or the acoustic versus electric controversy couldn't interest me less now. And I'm not saying one is better than the other. I'm only interested in making good music within the context of my own experience and abilities and out of the tradition I come from. The best thing I can do is communicate with myself on honest terms. That will make me happy, and I think it'll make some other people happy.

How did the The Tony Bennett/Bill Evans Album *come about?*

It was one of those things that was in the air for years. I always figured that if Tony would do any of my tunes, I'd be overjoyed. In fact, he did record "Waltz for Debby" once. Debby's my niece. I wrote that for her when she was three, and she's getting married this year. Tony and I have always had a mutual respect and a distant acquaintance with each other. It so happens that my manager [Helen Keane] and his [Jack Rollins] are good friends.

It was my idea that we make it only piano [and voice], though it kind of scared me. It seemed to be the best way to get that intimate communication going. It was pretty much off the top of our heads. We picked the tunes and then went in to do them.

The voice/piano combination is very traditional, but given all the heavily produced vocal albums that are played, it was very fresh and pure.

That's exactly what I wanted, but it's very chancy, because a lot of the public wants that big sound—the studio orchestra, highly produced or over-produced. So I thought we'd go all the way in the other direction, and I think it's timely because a lot of young people are looking for that personal quality. It's been lost in much of the rock and pop music. That big electric sound. It worries me. It seems desperate. The elements are coarse. There's no element of greatness. It makes me worry about the state of the world. What qualifies for greatness now is whatever sells the most records.

Do you think this happening in jazz to any extent? Herbie Hancock, just for an example, has been criticized for what you might call popping out.

I don't know that much about what he's doing, though I understand that he's simplified and funkified and sold a lot of albums. But I was thinking more in terms of rock and pop. Actually I don't feel qualified to make many comments on the current scene because I don't follow it that closely. I may have superficial opinions about a lot of these things.

Well, did you feel the duet album with Bennett succeeded?

I thought it came off nicely. I haven't done much accompanying or solo playing in the last twenty years, so it worried me a bit. But we got a relaxed, pure feeling going. It couldn't have been much better. The piano itself is great. I love Tony's singing.

How did you feel about the lyrics to some of those old songs?

I never listen to lyrics. I'm seldom conscious of them at all. The vocalist might as well be a horn as far as I'm concerned.

Intuition *seems to go in that personal direction, too. Without mincing words, I thought it was successful and very accessible. People I know who never listen to jazz seem to love it.*

I'm glad to hear that. I find myself putting it on at home, too, and I don't listen to many of my own records.

How did you get that unusual sound out of the Rhodes? Was it a filter?

There was something on the piano that Don Cody showed me how to use, but I don't know what it was. [Cody, a Fantasy Records engineer, later identified the device as a Maestro phaser, which cancels frequencies in a more varied pattern than a normal filter, giving the sound a "swirling effect."]

Following this move toward a personal and a pure sound to its logical conclusion, wouldn't you be due for a solo piano album—like Alone *[on Verve]—one that's not overdubbed, like* Conversations with Myself?

I just haven't played enough solo, but I think it's kind of necessary. If I get my studio set up in the new house, I may be able to work on that. I'd have to prepare for a solo album by playing solo at home. I was talking to Marian McPartland about that after she played solo the other night. It sounded marvelous. She's working a solo gig in New York, so I said, "Now I know why you sound so good solo." It's the best practice in the world for a pianist. I wish I could play a solo gig for about a year; but I am interested in the trio, and to keep it together I have to keep it working. My conception of solo playing is a rhapsodic conception that has interludes of straight-ahead jazz.

Have you felt an evolution in your technique? I was discussing with Oscar Peterson an essay by LeRoi Jones. I said that technique is inseparable from content and that a player like Monk is not limited technically any more than Peterson is. Oscar disagreed, saying technique is purely physical.

I can tell you that, for me, technique is the ability to translate your ideas into sound through your instrument. [Thelonious] Monk does it perfectly, though he is "limited" in the sense that if you put a Mozart sonata in front of him or asked him to play an Oscar Peterson chorus, he couldn't do it. I'd agree, though, that technique is separable from the context of ideas in this sense. In playing a keyboard instrument, you should develop a comprehensive technique. This enables you to go in new directions without worrying about your hands.

What you have to remember is that your conception can be limited by a technical approach. Someone who approached the piano technically the way Oscar Peterson does could never have the conception that Monk has. If you play evenly, attacking notes in a certain way, you wouldn't conceive of making the sound that Monk would make. If you could develop a technique like Peterson's—which is practically unmatched, I guess—and then *forget it!* Tell yourself to try anything you can conceive of. . . . I think a great technique would be to develop an entirely new articulation and make it happen on the piano.

Like Cecil Taylor?

That's an example. Or being able to breathe into the piano, make vocal nuances come through the piano. That's a great technical challenge. The classical tradition never utilized a real vocal utterance. Sometimes there were vocal utterances, but they were translated through a very great architectural tradition in classical music. To really breathe through the piano. . . . Well, Erroll Garner did it some, but in a limited way. I mean to go [sings a figure].

Like on a reed instrument?

Right. This is a comprehensive technique which goes beyond scales and so on. It's *expressive* technique.

Would you call it touch?

No, I wouldn't. Touch seems to connote being very sensitive or tender. I don't mean that this has to be tender. What I'm talking about is a feeling for the keyboard that will allow you to transfer any emotional utterance into it. That's really what technique is all about. I think that's what LeRoi Jones was talking about. He was right, but Peterson was right from a different stand-point. What Jones might not realize is that this type of direct technique isn't enough today. A musician has to cover more ground than that. That's one of the criticisms of pop and rock music. Kids get into being creative before they've experienced enough on their instrument. You need both. You need a comprehensive, traditional technique.

Mechanical?

You could call it that. Whenever I was practicing technique—which wasn't that often—but if I spent a couple of days playing scales and so on, I found that my playing became a shade more mechanical. What has to happen is that you develop a comprehensive technique and then say, "Forget that. I'm just going to be expressive through the piano."

In terms of touch, I was thinking of it in a broader sense, the sense in which the piano is a percussion instrument. Does it only mean being tender? I think of McCoy Tyner as having a distinctive touch, though he's certainly not a soft player. Or is this what you'd call his expressive technique?

Absolutely, although touch probably does have this other connotation, too. The more you express yourself through your instrument, the more identifiable your touch becomes, because you're able to put more of yourself, your personal quality, into the instrument. The piano is very mechanical, and you're separated from it physically. You can control it only by touching it, striking it, and pushing a key down. Playing a wind or a stringed instrument is so much more expressive and so much more vocal because of its contact with the player.

So pianists go through long periods when they're putting themselves into their instrument only to a limited degree. There comes a time after pushing very hard against the problem when they suddenly break through. Oscar is right. That's a very physical problem. You have to spend a lot of years at the keyboard before what's inside can get through your hands and into the piano. For years and years that was a constant frustration for me. I wanted to get that expressive thing in, but somehow it didn't happen. I had to spend a lot of years playing, especially Bach, which seemed to help. It gave me control and more contact with tone and things.

When I was about twenty-six—about a year before I went with Miles—that was the first time I had attained a certain degree of expressiveness in my playing. Believe me, I had played a lot of jazz before then. I started when I was thirteen. I was putting some of the feelings I had into the piano. Of course, having the feelings is another thing, another matter.

When I last spoke with you, you had just signed with Fantasy via your relationship with Orrin Keepnews, who had produced your first Riverside recordings. But between the Riverside and Fantasy affiliations there seemed to be a lot of label hopping. What happened? Did you feel you were getting some bad deals?

Yeah, kind of. I was talking to Chuck Mangione about that today. We agreed that it was disappointing to be with record companies as jazz artists. You tour, but you don't get backing. They won't help out. There are no displays, no coordinated advertising.

The stint I had with Columbia: I thought I'd finally arrived at a company that had the money and the interest. Clive Davis and I just didn't hit it off. I never even talked to the man, and he was already directing my career, changing me, making me "creative," "communicative," whatever.

And before that was Verve.

Verve: I was with them for quite a while. Creed [Taylor] was very shrewd and did a lot of good things. He got some commercial success out of jazz artists, which no one else had been able to do: Stan Getz, Wes Montgomery, Jimmy Smith.

He's still doing it, it seems.

He's still doing it, and it's to his credit. I was with him for seven years. Then came Columbia and Fantasy.

I was under the impression you felt Fantasy was being cooperative and supportive.

They are, but it's the old story. If you have a record that makes it by itself, they'll be overjoyed and interested. I feel good about the *Intuition* album, but I think more could have been done with it. I don't know what's been spent, but I don't think very much has been spent on advertising. Aside from that, distribution is always a big problem. You can go to big cities and people say they can't find your records. Well, that's an old, old story in jazz. Record companies are a business. I can't fight that.

I've spoken to a lot of musicians who believe jazz is quite identifiably black American music in the sense that the innovators and creative forces in the music have been black people. Interestingly, you're often cited as an exception to the rule. How do you feel about this issue, and do you feel you're an innovative force just as Teddy Wilson was in the swing era or Bud Powell in the bop era?

I think whether I've been innovative is for somebody else to judge, not me. But I think it's sad that these questions come up. There's a sense of the hurt child in the people who want to make this only a black music. They haven't had much, so they want to make jazz one hundred percent black. Historically, I suppose, the black impetus was primarily responsible for the growth of jazz, but if a white jazz artist comes through, it's just another human being who has grown up loving jazz and playing jazz and can contribute to jazz. It's sad because all that attitude does is to turn that prejudicial thing right around. It makes me a bit angry. I want more responsibility among black people and black musicians to be accurate and to be spiritually intelligent about humanity. Let the historians sort out whether it's sixty-seven point two percent black influenced or ninety-seven percent. To say only black people can play jazz is just as dangerous as saying only white people are intelligent or anything else like that.

I hope I didn't present this sentiment in an oversimplified way. The usual point of view is that in fact, all, or almost all, the innovators have been black.

An innovator. That's even more ridiculous. Now there could be an argument in the case of soul music because the black culture has been separated from the white culture to such an extent that there could be a spiritual content in the black culture lending itself to "soulfulness," which the white culture may have less of. But to say only black musicians can be innovative is so utterly ridiculous I can hardly consider the question.

To be a human being is to have creative potential, and where this is realized is a matter of what a person commits himself to and is dedicated to. White, yellow, black, green, or whatever, a person who loves and dedicates himself to jazz music can be creative, depending on his talent and commitment. I'm just sorry that this is an issue because at bottom you're going to find a racial attitude involved, and a racial attitude is a prejudice, pure and simple, as bad as the plantation owners. I don't care whether you're black, green, or red—man, if you're prejudiced, you're wrong.

Do you have any aversion—as many musicians do now—to having your music classified as jazz?

Hell, no. I think jazz is the purest tradition in music this country has had. It has never bent to strictly commercial considerations, and so it has made music for its own sake. That's why I'm proud to be part of it.

Selected Discography

Peace Piece and Other Pieces (1959–61); M-47024; Milestone.

Miles Davis: Kind of Blue (1959); PC-8163; Columbia.

The Village Vanguard Sessions (1961); M-47002; Milestone.

Conversations with Myself (1963); V6-8526; Verve.*

Intuition (1974); F-9475; Fantasy.

Alone (Again) (1977); F-9542; Fantasy.

STEVE
KUHN

March 24, 1938–

Steve Kuhn's tone production and keyboard dynamics set him apart from other pianists. Those assets were developed under the guidance of the Boston piano tutor Madame Margaret Chaloff, the teacher of Ran Blake, Toshiko Akiyoshi, and other prominent pianists. (Margaret Chaloff was the mother of Serge Chaloff, the talented baritione saxophonist in the Woody Herman band of the early fifties.) Madame Chaloff schooled Kuhn in "the Russian technique," which has enabled him to make the piano's lower register hum like a string bass, and its upper register ring like chimes.

Kuhn was the first (and only white) pianist to work with the John Coltrane Quartet. I had always wondered about the source of this musical affinity, but it turned out to be Steve's temerity that got him the job. Kuhn had simply called John in 1960 to ask for an audition because he knew the saxophonist had left Miles Davis's band to go out on his own. As a result, Kuhn worked with Coltrane for two months at the Jazz Gallery, until McCoy Tyner took over. In the interview below, Steve offers some provocative insights on Coltrane's use of chord progressions.

In 1961 Kuhn worked with Bill Evans's bassist, Scott LaFaro, who had organized a rhythm section for a new Stan Getz band. Although LaFaro died a few months later, Kuhn remained with Getz's group until 1964. Next, Steve joined trumpeter Art Farmer's band, playing in the company of drummer Pete La Roca and bassist Steve Swallow. After that came a brief stint with vibist and arranger Gary McFarland. In 1967, when jazz was in its commercial doldrums, Kuhn moved to Stockholm, Sweden, where the competition for jobs was less fierce. Among Kuhn's other stories of his life in Europe, he tells of discovering an abandoned nine-foot Bösendorfer piano, at least seventy years old, stored in a castle, a find that can be likened to a wine connoisseur's stumbling across a forgotten case of Lafite-Rothschild. Kuhn bought the piano, which had four extra bass notes, for $5,000 only to find it did not hold a tuning very well, which is comparable to learning that some of the Lafite-Rothschild corks had developed leaks. Kuhn returned home (without his piano) in 1971 and began rebuilding his career. He feared his absence would mean "the kiss of death" but found that his ECM albums placed him more in demand than ever.

Trance and *Ecstasy* are an interesting pair for comparative listening because they present contrasting aspects of Kuhn's playing. The first is a hard-driving quartet with Steve Swallow on bass, Jack DeJohnette, drums, and Sue Evans, percussion; the second, recorded within days of *Trance,* is a pensive and impressionistic piano solo, perhaps because of the way it originated. "We had just finished mixing *Trance,*" Steve explained, "when [producer] Manfred Eicher told me he'd like me to do a solo album. I hadn't prepared at all, so I stayed up all night trying to figure out what I was going to do. I went into the studio the next evening, played for ninety minutes straight, and that was it." At the time we talked, Steve was writing new music for his upcoming collaboration with singer Sheila Jordan (later released as *Playground*), which became Kuhn's best-selling work.

Steve Kuhn and I had our sole conversation on the third floor of a family-operated Chinese restaurant called Sam Wo's. It is famous for authentic cuisine that bears no resemblance to the Americanized Chinese food served nearly everywhere else in Chinatown. Most of the clientele is Oriental. As we watched the outdoor fruit and vegetable vendors below, we must have been a curiosity ourselves, with my tape recorder and mike propped up on the table centerpiece and with Steve wearing oversize rose-colored butterfly-shaped sunglasses.

What was your musical background prior to your studies with Margaret Chaloff?
I started piano lessons when I was five, although I had already shown a great interest in jazz. In fact, my father was buying me records when I was a baby because he could see how well I related to it. I'd get up at six A.M. and start putting his records on. I used to have a photographic memory, which is pretty well gone by now, but even before I could talk, my father would hold up a record and I'd tell him what it was in baby talk. Actually I was written up in 1943 in a book called *Low Man on the Totem Pole* by H. Allen Smith [a book of oddities, like Ripley's *Believe It or Not,* now out of print] because of my ability to recall these records. Well, I learned how to play the instrument from lessons, but I had to undo my technique seven years later. I always had a great feeling for jazz music, so as a reward for a good lesson, my teacher would give me a boogie-woogie piece to play. Even at that time I was bored by the European repertoire because I had to play a song the same way each time. The reason I was drawn to jazz was the improvisation and the rhythmic differences between the two musics. To this day I feel the same way.

When did you start your studies with Margaret Chaloff?

When we moved from Brooklyn to Boston in 1950.

What music were you listening to then?

My father used to buy the seventy-eight [rpm] records of Benny Goodman. He'd also bring home records of the boogie-woogie pianists Meade Lux Lewis, Albert Ammons, and Pete Johnson. Duke Ellington records, too. I listened a lot to Art Tatum, Bud Powell, Erroll Garner, and Teddy Wilson, and I was influenced by all of them at one time. Bill Evans was probably my most recent influence. I heard him for the first time when I was in high school, and it seemed that we were going in the same direction, except that he had it together and I didn't. I remember thinking, well, there it is. What am I going to do now? Ironically, I had the opportunity later of playing with Scott [LaFaro], who had been with Bill.

Did LaFaro's bass playing affect your piano style in any way?

Scott had an incredible knowledge of standard songs, and I do, too. We would pick out very obscure songs that no one had heard of, and what we could do harmonically was a kick for me. We could hear each other taking the songs out, stretching them at certain points. It wasn't playing without harmony, but it was using the harmony in a way that freed us. I had never played with a bassist who could do that.

It's surprising to hear that you know a lot of standards, since you never seem to include them in your repertoire.

When I was a kid, I went through the fake books page by page and learned the tunes. It helped me subsequently because I've done—and still do—commercial jobs, where you go through one hundred songs in a night, from the 1920's to the seventies. I do these jobs for financial reasons, and I don't really mind doing them because a lot of the players are very good within that context. Most young pianists know the tunes from ten years ago, but there's an incredible number of standards that are good to know because they can show you what's been done. John Coltrane had an incredible knowledge of standards, too. When I was working with him, I realized, for example, that the release to "Have You Met Miss Jones?" had the same harmonic sequence he was using in *Giant Steps*. The tonal centers were related by an augmented triad—E Major to C Major to A flat Major in the key of C, for example. He would precede each one of these tonal centers with its dominant and interpolate this sequence, if he had eight bars to fool around with. He did it in "I Can't Get Started," "But Not for Me," and other standards we used to play.

What exactly is the Russian technique?

Basically, it's an approach that enables you to do anything dynamically, from the softest pianissimo to the most incredible sforzando and anything in between. It enables you to play as fast as you need to with projection and without getting tired. I call it the Russian school because they were the ones who came up with the approach. All the great European pianists have used it.

What is the essence of this technique?

You breathe as if you were playing a horn, from the diaphragm. You think of your fingertips as a reed and the keys as a mouthpiece. The sound comes out of you; it travels to the soundboard and out of the piano. It's a complete flow that should not be broken. If you're playing with a heavy arm or dragging weight down in your hands, the sound will stop somewhere in the elbow and you'll feel tension in the forearm. If you feel tension, you'll know you're not playing correctly. If you want an incredible sforzando, the sound should come from the bottom of the feet, and you should push off the floor so that the sound travels up through the feet, the knees, the hips, the torso, through your shoulder and elbow, and out through the fingertips. It requires a very light arm. Actually there should be no weight in the arm because that will slow down the flow. Most pianists will bring their wrists down, and you can just see them physically stopping the sound from flowing into the piano.

It sounds like a fairly traditional method of tone production.

Most pianists aren't even aware of it, though. Unfortunately they don't go beyond "How fast can I play?" They don't think about how to allow the sound to get out. The acoustic piano is capable of producing incredibly beautiful sound.

That must make playing the electric piano, as you did on Trance, *very frustrating, or very different, for you in terms of producing a satisfactory sound.*

Right. I don't even think about it when I play the electric. I play it a lot on commercial jobs, though, because the acoustic pianos are often so bad. It's like a toy, a color, but I've been playing it long enough to have an identifiable style. You can't voice chords on an electric as you would on acoustic. It gets muddy.

You've written some songs yourself for your upcoming album with Sheila Jordan. Is this the first time you've composed tunes with lyrics?

No, I'd written a bunch of songs with lyrics when I was living in Sweden, and a couple of Scandinavian singers have recorded them. Basically I wrote them thinking melodically, so that they could be sung, although they're not easy to sing. The lyrics are perhaps a little bit "out," but I don't know. That's for other people to say. But there's so much you can learn from the standard repertoire. It really opens your ears up to other things. It enables you to play without harmony so that it means something, although I don't believe there is complete freedom in playing.

What do you mean by playing "without harmony"?

Using a pedal tone, which Coltrane got into after a period of very dense harmonic playing. He would use one or two harmonic references throughout a song, as he did on "So What" [from Miles Davis's *Kind of Blue,* on Columbia]. It was basically D for sixteen bars, E flat for eight bars, and then back to D. Ultimately, he worked with only one harmonic reference point, and then in "Ascension" [from *Best of John Coltrane: His Greatest Years,* on Impulse] there was nothing harmonically.

Why don't you believe in totally free playing?

Because I think there has to be a reference point. If you brought an elephant out of the jungle, sat him in front of a piano, and let him swing his trunk to hit the keys, that would be *free!*

If all players have reference points, what distinguishes the innovator?

When the frame of reference is completely in the subconscious and you can play *you.* Of course, there's nothing new under the sun, but there comes a point in every player's development when he is no longer imitative. The player's influences can still be identified, but they are no longer that important. Bill Evans is an example for what he did to further the harmonic concept and the voicing of chords in the left hand and the way he was so careful about harmonizing songs.

What is "harmonizing" a song?

Well, he reharmonized them actually. It's being able to understand what the composer had in mind and creating something personal out of it. Even the songwriters themselves often use very naïve chords for their songs. Now I don't mean simply changing chords just for the sake of doing that. That's really corny, though a lot of people do it. It has to mean something. Bill could use the basic harmony and make it much more sophisticated. Bill is a great song player and an innovator. One should play the total sum of one's experiences, but this can be done by an innovator in a personal way.

Selected Discography

Trance (1974); 1052; ECM.

Ecstasy (1974); 1058; ECM.

Motility (1977); 1094; ECM.

Non-Fiction (1978); 1124; ECM.

Steve Kuhn/Sheila Jordan Band: Playground (1980); 1159; ECM.

McCOY
TYNER

December 11, 1938–

When I visited the Tyners in rural Connecticut, they had recently moved from Newark, New Jersey. Woodlands bordered their spacious Colonial-style home and backyard. Aisha Tyner, McCoy's wife since their teens, was concerned about how their three boys, who were still in school, would adjust to the new setting. There were few black families in the district, and, as Aisha noted, "there's no sense of neighborhood. After school all the kids go home to their own little worlds." McCoy seemed content with their new house and his new studio, where he keeps his Steinway grand and modest record collection.

McCoy is an unpretentious and basically private person. He is most relaxed puffing on a pipe in quiet conversation, much of which typically revolves around his family. Backstage, before a performance, he is tense and preoccupied. At the keyboard his broad-shouldered, powerful frame hunches over, and he attacks the keyboard with the strength and determination of a pit bull. Tyner has a prominent religious streak in him, at least for the spirit of Islamic belief, if not for its institutionalized practice. Although he answers certain questions about his musical background in down-to-earth terms, he looks at other issues as spiritual or emotional.

McCoy discusses his career in detail in the following interview, but it is worth keeping its broad outlines in mind. After a brief tenure with the Benny Golson/Art Farmer Jazztet in the late fifties, Tyner played a historic role during the 1960's as part of the John Coltrane Quartet, which also included drummer Elvin Jones and bassist Jimmy Garrison. Tyner's use of modes (or scale-patterns) developed quickly under Coltrane's influence. But during the 1970's Tyner himself had a lasting impact on jazz piano when he began to use a more complex modal-harmonic system in conjunction with a fierce, distinctly percussive keyboard attack. Tyner has led his own quintet since 1973 and recorded one of the great solo piano achievements of the seventies on the album *Echoes of a Friend,* which comes from a period of his music that is examined in the interview ahead.

Part of the McCoy Tyner interview was taped immediately following the recording of the LP *Trident* in 1975 at the Fantasy Records studios in Berkeley, California. The conversation about his philosophical and religious outlook occurred later over dinner at a restaurant near McCoy's hotel. The segments of the interview that concern Tyner's composing and the role of the piano in larger ensembles come from the visit to his Connecticut home.

What have you found helpful in developing technique?

Technique depends upon what you need to express at the time. If you're able to express yourself, that's all that's important. The need has to be there first, and then the acquisition of technique comes. You see, I consider music a form of self-expression. A lot of people can play an instrument, but whether they're using it to express themselves is a totally different thing. Personally I'm just not the technical, analytic type. I'm not like a lot of players who sit down and plan things out. Herbie Hancock might be an example. Of course, you have to do a certain amount of planning if you use synthesizers. I like to keep things on a spontaneous level because that's the type of performance that's most effective.

But didn't you work on technique at some point, say, at the Granoff School?

At Granoff, I just studied theory and harmony, which amounted to basic eighteenth-century composition. But when I was young, I practiced scales a lot and a few compositions, though not many exercises. Most of my technique comes from scales and actual playing experience. I did use Hanon, Czerny, and Macfarren, which are all fine. When you're acquiring the tools of your craft, you have to put in a lot of time. I'd spend hours practicing after school until I was politely asked to stop. I would advise young musicians to practice as much as possible and consistently, if not for long periods of time. Twenty minutes a day is better than four hours one day and ten minutes the next. I used to practice at the neighbor's because we didn't have a piano until a year after I started.

Were there any particular musicians you were listening to at the time?

Well, I didn't have a record collection. I couldn't afford it. I had a string quartet on a seventy-eight [rpm] record, and somebody gave me a Miles Davis record. I had some seventy-eights of Charlie Parker, and as soon as I found out who Bud Powell was, I bought some of his records. But these were things I picked up when I got older. I started off just playing pieces.

What motivated you toward improvising?

I had a little group I formed when I was about fifteen. There were seven pieces, whenever I could get them to practice. We used to have sessions in my house or in my mother's shop—she was a beautician. I started realizing that I had to give these guys notes to play, and most of it came from trying to play tunes I heard on records or the radio.

How did you meet John Coltrane and become part of his quartet?

I met him in the summer of 1955, when I was seventeen. It was at [trumpeter] Cal Massey's gig with Jimmy Garrison and [drummer Albert] Tootie Heath. Cal and John were close friends. Coltrane struck me as very quiet and serious. At that time he was at the inception of his style. He hadn't blossomed yet, but there was something about his sound and approach to improvising that was captivating. We kept in touch when John came back to town, especially during this period when Miles had let him go [during 1957]. I was working as a shipping clerk in the daytime and as a musician at night. John and I played together, and he had improved quite a bit. I think he was working on some of the ideas that went into *Giant Steps*. Coltrane went back with Miles again, but we had sort of a verbal understanding that if he ever got his own group, I would play piano.

By the time John had his group going Art Farmer and Benny Golson had come through town [with the Jazztet], so I joined them. I think that I heard, while I was with the Jazztet in San Francisco, that John had a group. Steve Kuhn was playing piano. I don't think John wanted to ask me to leave the Jazztet because he was friendly with Benny Golson, but I believe Naima [John's wife] encouraged him. John left it up to me—he asked me what I wanted to do. It was a hard choice, even though I knew what I *wanted* to do. There were probably some bad feelings at first with the Jazztet, but I think they understood better later on. John's group was where I belonged.

Aside from the obvious musical influence, could you assess the importance of your years with the Coltrane quartet?

When I began with John, I accepted the responsibility of being an accompanist. I figured if I did the best I could in that role, I'd have to learn something. I wasn't interested in telling John what I wanted. I wanted to find out what he had to say. So I submitted to leadership, although the submission didn't take the form of his telling me what to do. I think the saying is true that you have to be a good follower before you can be a good leader. In any business you've got to have enough experience to stand up in front and say, "Okay, I'm ready to take charge." In a sense I was in the first stages of preparing for leadership.

How do you feel about your first recordings for Impulse as an individual artist during those years?

I tried to record some things that made me sound different from the group, not realizing that the way I played with John was really the way I played. We just happened to be able to play together. Our personalities complemented each other. We were that compatible.

What prompted you to leave the group in 1965?

Well, I felt if I was going to go any further musically, I would have to leave the group, and when John hired a second drummer [Rashied Ali], it became a physical necessity. I couldn't hear myself. John was understanding. In fact, I think he admired my courage.

What happened next?

There wasn't enough interest in me as an individual artist at Impulse, so I left them and began doing sessions for Blue Note, though only a few as leader. But I didn't work consistently enough to really be working on anything. I wondered whether it was meant for me to continue playing music. I was actually considering working during the day—I had reached that point. It's funny, though; along with the pressure, it was also one of the happiest times of my life. I didn't travel much. I became very close to my family. It renewed my faith in the Creator. Despite the adversity, this was a fulfilling period because it was a test of my ability to survive, personally and as an artist. I had a chance to compromise, and I didn't do it.

You mean you were going to quit, or play pop, or what?

I was thinking about hacking, you know, driving a cab. The guy I went to see about the job couldn't believe it. He used to drive me to the airport when I was working with John's band. He just didn't believe I needed a job, and he never called me back. Also, I had offers to go on tours with Benny Goodman. A lot of guys I knew were going electric or into rock to become more commercial—I just couldn't.

Who was it who said, "It takes pressure to create diamonds"? Sometimes you can only learn through adversity. If a man's faith isn't tested, I don't think he'll learn anything. You can see it in people who have achieved some margin of success in life—meaning peace of mind and happiness, at least some of it. They have struggled to get it and sacrificed to learn. Faith in the Creator is what brought me through, and my wife. She's really a jewel. It takes a special kind of woman to live with a musician, especially a musician, or any artist really, who's not making it. We went through some pretty tough economic times. I had a log-cabin bank full of pennies—I still keep it.

It seems that about 1971, just before you left Blue Note for the Milestone label, your music acquired a new character and identity. What was the breakthrough?

It's very difficult to pinpoint a particular period when you take that big step. All you know is, you're there. Once you've dedicated yourself to something and you work at it, it takes shape and grows.

A specific difference is your use of the piano as a percussion instrument. Theoretically the piano is a percussion instrument, but there are few jazz pianists who explore that dimension. Do you think you play percussively?

Yes, I suppose I do. When you reach a certain point, you look for something else in the instrument to express your emotions. The piano became more of a rhythmic instrument to me, more like a drum, I guess. You see, after all these years, the piano and I have really become friends. I can truthfully say I have a friend there. It's like an arm or a leg, part of me. I can use it for almost total expression.

Would you say that your style of playing the piano has had an influence on others?

I'd like to believe that what I'm doing makes a difference. It takes that type of belief in your music to give you the firm belief that it's meaningful in terms of what's happening today. To me, influence is an indication that what you're doing is valid for the times. It's meaningful if people hear the music and get some beautiful feelings from it, or inner emotional release, or just learn something. Music can educate people, too, not in the ordinary sense of education. You take people on an excursion. The artist should be able to convey his adventures musically to the people. You can entertain, and you can also broaden people's perspectives through music. If your ideas mean something to you, you should be able to communicate them. Some of the simplest things are the most beautiful, and simplicity is coupled with complexity. That's the way life is, simple and complex at the same time.

How do you view your own music historically speaking? Is it derived from bebop, from modal music, or do you think of it as black American music?

My music is an extension of bebop, but all these other things are interconnected. You really have to be aware of the interrelationships and of the roots of the music in order for it to have its identity. Historically, though, there are different ways to look at this. The music had its roots in the black community. Music played a very important part in self-expression within the black community. The form of the music is very expressive of how black people felt, especially with bebop because it was such a major change in that particular idiom. I'd say the selection of music now is very commercial, while back then it seems people really liked good music. But the music has grown, and it's become an individual experience, which is another level from just historical categories. You might hear Indian music in it, or Stravinsky—I happen to like Stravinsky's orchestration. The thing is that the roots of the music must be felt for it to be truly what it is. If you look at the top of a tree, it can be blowing in many different directions, but once it's broken off from its roots, it's dead.

What's the connection for you between religion and music, or religion and your music?

Jazz started as religious music. Music, generally, started out as a form of praise to the Creator. That was the original purpose of it. In fact, the church was about the only place the [early] black Americans would make music, which was an indication of the seriousness of the music and how it was taken by our people. Religion is not in the church or mosque or synagogue, at least in my opinion; it's in the person. Religions should make you conscious of what you are in relationship to the Creator.

Why do you say "Creator" instead of God?

I believe that the idea of man was conceived out of love. I like the word "Creator" for that reason, because instead of something sitting in judgment, it denotes a deity that loves His creation. I've been with this since I was a teenager, and I feel I really understand the function of religion in life. It's just a word unless you've lived through enough to know what it means. In a sense it has to be tested, like a marriage or faith, so you know whether it's served its purpose so far as your life is concerned.

Do you consider your music religious music in some sense?

I hope it's on that level, though it can be other things at the same time.

What about composing? Are you doing much of it now?

I'm approaching some new concepts in my writing, but I think the best is yet to come as far as composition is concerned. I'm hearing more motion, more mode changes in my solos, so I want to compose in that framework. What I really want to do is write things that complement my mood when I'm soloing.

Can you describe the role composition has played in the history of your musical endeavors?

My interest in it goes pretty far back—to when I was a teenager with a seven-piece band. We were just a group of guys going to school together. I liked that band sound, and I tried to pull everything together into a tighter sound, which was the most I could do at the time. We went so far as to tape a few things.

It got more serious when I was with John [Coltrane]. He tried to get me to do some writing and orchestrating for larger groups around the quartet setting. But I was so engrossed with what we were doing in the small band I didn't pursue it heavily. The only thing from the early sixties was "Greensleeves" from the *Africa Brass* album, where we used my orchestration involving French horns and a trumpet. I guess I did feel a lot of voices in my music, and my own [pianistic] style reflects it. I remember John saying that he heard it in my approach to comping [accompaniment]. Incidentally, the tune "Africa" was written from my voicings by Eric Dolphy. He asked me to show him what I was doing so he could get the same sound I was getting from the piano.

Even though the seeds of orchestration and composing were planted many years ago, I feel they've just begun to take root. It's like another horizon for me. It's been a challenging one, too, and I think it's always a good idea to have a new venture.

Song for the New World actually preceded *Fly with the Wind* *as an album of significant writing for you. Did you feel a lot of progress had been made between the two of them?*

I look at it this way: Piano is my instrument, but in writing I'm beginning to use the orchestra as another instrument. You have to learn a lot by trial and error.

So you're taking up a new instrument?

Exactly. And it's an especially exciting one to me because I always look forward to hearing how things sound after I write them. At this point I really can't tell until the music is played. So in answer to your question [about my progress] I don't feel *Fly with the Wind* is the ultimate in terms of depth. I was a little bit cautious when I wrote it. It was successful for what it was, but it's not the epitome of what I could do with strings. I'm looking ahead. I'd rather look ahead to see what my potential is than look back to see whether I've fulfilled it already. It's important to look at your music and feel you can do better.

While Fly with the Wind *was being recorded, I remember your telling me you had consulted a book on orchestrating for strings.*

Yes, and it was valuable in that I had a reference for the instrument's capability—its capability in normal circumstances, taking into consideration who was playing it. If you don't write for strings all the time, it's very helpful to have that kind of information available. I was using Walter Piston's book [*Harmony*], but Forsythe has one which also seems to be very good [*Orchestration*].

Hadn't you studied orchestration at Granoff?

No, I never did. Looking back on my life in music, I can see that things happen in stages, by development. I like that. I'd rather see how I've grown in the past ten years than feel I've reached some sort of pinnacle. In other words, I hope I haven't climbed the highest mountain. *Fly with the Wind* let me know that what I hear can be translated into forms other than piano and brass, that I can use the orchestra, that I can be less conservative when I write. Incidentally, I wasn't afraid of what the record was going to sound like, but I think I was surprised. I didn't realize how powerful strings could be when they're used properly. Many people assume that strings have to be used very commercially, as a sweetening track, but that's not so.

Did you compose "Fly with the Wind" at a table or at the piano?

I always use the piano when I write because it helps me to hear the weight of certain tones in developing chords. You can tell more easily which colors in the chord stand out and then use the elements you find most important. Personally I like to use the piano not for the security of it, but because I can relate so easily to the sound of the instrument.

After hearing it on the piano, were you surprised at all by how the orchestration sounded played by other instruments?

Yes, but pleasantly. The weight seemed so balanced. There's a real science of balance. Notes that are strong on one instrument in a register have to be checked by notes on a different instrument. You have to be aware of the weights of tones. One of the surprises was that the simpler things sounded stronger than the more sophisticated chords. It's a very mystifying aspect of writing. Right now I'm thinking of a particular chord on the title tune, "Fly with the Wind"; it comes in just before the main theme during the introduction.

You once mentioned that Stravinsky impressed you very strongly. Do you think his work has influenced your sense of orchestration?

Stravinsky and Debussy are two of my favorite composers. Stravinsky was definitely inspirational. I should also include Duke [Ellington] in there because he was so heavy into the harmonic concept of the orchestra. Producing a sound with an orchestra is a unique talent. Just like I listen to Art Tatum to get inspiration at the piano, it's nice to be able to be inspired by composers. It's not that I want to copy them, but it's a stimulating thing. I think it's good to listen, but I don't think it should be too deliberate. Then you'll be inclined to copy. The inspiration is good, but it should be left at that level so that your own creative emotions can flow. You don't want another creative individual to overshadow you. That's not the purpose of listening. To me, its purpose is to be inspired, not stifled.

"Fly with the Wind" had a captivating theme to me. It gave me the same feeling as Gershwin's "American in Paris" in terms of the lightness of the strings. Is this a valid impression from your point of view?

Well, I know what you mean, because I was in a happy mood at the time.

At times in my career I have felt heavy and gone into heavy things harmonically. But there are times when I feel light, and I think I should express that side of me musically, as well as the very serious side.

What can you tell me about the album for voices that you're about to record?

I'm using four trumpets, five saxes, trombones, and an acoustic guitar [played by Earl Klugh], and then the voices. Bill Fischer, who did *Fly with the Wind*, will conduct and work with the voices. He's a very flexible musician, which is important to me because I want to work with different contexts. Actually that's why I'm writing. I don't write music because I want to be popular. I write because I want to experiment with different settings.

Do you think there is also a presumption that voices—like strings—are a sweetener?

Yes, I suppose so, but I don't think my material will reflect that.

How can you expand the seriousness with which voices are used as an additional color?

Well, the way I'm using them they will be like instruments. I don't anticipate any words being used.

Why voices?

It seemed like the next step for me. Orrin [Keepnews, his producer on Milestone] and I work very well together. He often suggests things for me, which we then discuss. For example, the last trio album which used different rhythm sections [*Supertrios*] was his idea. It was a way of making that album different from *Trident*. After we expanded the number of players involved, we thought about the next thing we could do with a larger size group. He suggested voices, and I had been considering it myself, so that's how it came up.

Did you listen to any vocal music for inspiration or to stimulate your ideas?

I did pick up a couple of religious pieces written quite a long time ago. One was a record of church chants sung in Greek by a choir of priests. It was just to get the sound of the voices in my ear, although what I'm writing has nothing to do with that music. Yet I am going to do some a capella things, some with piano accompaniment, some voices with the larger group. Actually it will be a mixture of formats.

We'll probably use about twelve singers, but there will be some overdubbing of voices, too, for a bigger sound. We're overdubbing for technical reasons; it's not economical. The voice is so delicate that in a studio you have to be careful. A chorus has to be working together a very long time before it can succeed in a studio. As an alternative to bringing thirty singers into the studio—they wouldn't be able to hear each other in a situation like that—we felt that we'd get better tone quality and definition by overdubbing.

How do you feel about performing your orchestral compositions live, as you did with "Fly with the Wind"*?*

I played it once with a professional orchestra which was right in the middle of an internal dispute, and I think they had had some bad experiences collaborating with jazz groups, too. We really walked into the middle of something there, and I wasn't very happy with the result. But the Oakland Youth Symphony performance and the performance at Newport this summer were both very exciting. I'd want to do a live performance with voices, too, but right now I have to concentrate on recording the music.

Can you foresee functioning strictly as a composer, writing an album of music on which you wouldn't perform?

Well, I'd rather be involved with what's going on. I don't think I could orchestrate for a living because I enjoy performing too much. It's an important part of my makeup as an individual. Performing is a wonderful release of emotions. Performing is like emptying the cup in order to fill it again. That's the joy of it.

Considering Chick [Corea], Herbie [Hancock], Keith Jarrett, and a few others, it seems that composition is becoming a more important part of a player's repertoire. Do you see that as a trend, too?

Yes, composition is taking a larger role, which is a good sign for the music. It means that we're hearing other forms. When changes take place in the music, it often happens compositionally. Guys start to write differently, and pretty soon you'll hear a concept change. Of course, it depends on the artist. John created a change through his playing. His writing complemented his style. In a way I think that's true in my own case. I write my own music best, as a complement to my style as a player.

Some players seem to have a very good understanding of form. Even though Chick and Herbie are involved in the electronic thing very heavily, I have to admit that they are very fine writers. In Herbie's case, I'm thinking of his more interesting compositions, not the commercial ventures. I guess I'm still growing as a writer. I've yet to put down all the things I hear. I need to spend more time at the piano writing.

Do you have a writing schedule?

No, it's whenever I can fit it in. The same is true of practicing. I haven't had a practice routine since I was a teenager.

When you speak about "form" in music, are you distinguishing it from the content of the piece?

The advantage of writing your own music is that you can create a form that you enjoy playing on. You know, I sometimes feel that I have to learn my own music–that is, the ideas that are in it. A song is like a good book. It takes a while to get familiar with it. Of course, you can always play it, but after you've played it for a while, it becomes more revealing. It becomes like a good friend. You can get more deeply into the material. Then the form begins to flex a little bit more. Look at the wall over there. At first it looks like one solid mass, but you can get down to looking at the particles on a microscopic level, the atomic structure, and so on. A piece of music can look like one entity, too, but then you learn it better and you can break it down into an abundance of things that are happening.

Remember "My Favorite Things," which I played with John? I didn't like the song at first. But after we played it for a while, the song began to flex and become part of the group. It's a very good thing at times to take a standard and shape it to your own needs as a player. Of course, the whole process is easier with your own music, your own compositions, because you are writing them to complement your style. And I don't mean the writing of them is easy, but only that it's more integrated with your playing.

Is there anything else you'd like to add on the subject of your writing?

Well, I haven't exhausted all the things I hear. Frankly I hope I never do.

It was surprising to hear you using a harpsichord on Trident *[on Milestone]. How did that happen?*

I was trying to find a keyboard instrument that would be different from the piano and yet have a good sound. The first time I saw one was in Europe with John. I plunked away at it, and the sound stuck in my mind. The action is different. You have to lay on the key. If you jump off it, the tone will disappear. The harpsichord I used on *Trident* had two keyboards on it, and there were certain gadgets you could push to get both keyboards playing in unison, as well as a staccato button. I didn't use any of these devices on the recording.

What kind of piano do you prefer?

Generally the Steinways. I have one myself. I especially like the European Steinways. The studio at Fantasy Records [in Berkeley] has a Yamaha, though, which is very fine. *Echoes of a Friend* [a solo album on Milestone] was recorded on a Steinway in Japan. When I go to Japan, I get Steinways. They gave me one Yamaha, and they apologized.

While we're on the subject of keyboards, what's your feeling about electric pianos?

To me, electronic instruments have more of an artificial sound. Emotionally I couldn't function on them. It's too easy, physically, to play, and it weakens you. You can push a button and get a gigantic sound. I think it interferes with some of the human vibrations.

What kind of music do you listen to now?

I like Stravinsky, especially the way he orchestrates— *The Rite of Spring* and *Petrouchka* particularly. I also listen to music from different parts of the world, from Japan, Turkey, North Africa, Central Africa. At a certain stage you have to listen to good music, no matter where it comes from. But I enjoy jazz more than other forms.

Do you listen to jazz?

Very little nowadays, because there's so much electronic stuff. I'll go back and listen to Art Tatum's collection, that Pablo series [*Tatum Solo Masterpieces*], or I'll listen to Leadbelly, Sarah Vaughan, and Billy Eckstine. I like a lot of different things.

Are you practicing anything new on the piano?

Well, I've reached the point where I want to do some practicing. In the group with John, we were always able to give each other inspiration, but it's hard to find a setting like that. Now I have to do it all myself. Practicing won't solve that problem, but I do want to do more playing on the piano. I know everything doesn't lie in the practicing, which is just limbering the muscles and so on. Music doesn't lie in that. It helps, though. John even practiced between sets in the back room. He worked hard, like a person who didn't have any talent. As great as he was, he practiced constantly. So who am I not to?

Have you considered teaching? Would you do that one day?

A friend of mine asked me to lecture to his class at the University of Santa Barbara. I couldn't. About what? I don't look at music like that. Music is a form of self-expression to me. Music is a part of nature— it's sound. I don't stop to analyze. I play from sound, from what I hear in my head and from what I feel.

Why do you think jazz has such a hard time getting played, distributed, and supported in America?

Because there's a lot of junk— manufactured music that's not personal— that has been thrust upon people. Art is placed on a much higher level in other countries, where symphony orchestras and jazz are supported by the government. It's disappointing. But I don't think the American public has poor taste. They've just been misled.

Selected Discography

John Coltrane: A Love Supreme (1964); A-77; Impulse.

Expansions (1970); BST-84388; Blue Note.

Echoes of a Friend (1972, solo); M-9055; Milestone.

Enlightenment (1973); M-55001; Milestone.

Supertrios (1977); M-55003; Milestone.

TOSHIKO
AKIYOSHI

December 12, 1929–

Toshiko Akiyoshi adds a new dimension to the role of the pianist as bandleader, extending the tradition established by Fletcher Henderson, Duke Ellington, Count Basie, and Earl "Fatha" Hines. Toshiko organized and nurtured the sixteen-piece Toshiko Akiyoshi/Lew Tabackin big band as an outlet for her composing. Her husband, Lew Tabackin, is the group's featured soloist on flute and tenor sax, which he plays in the rhythmic, logical, and hard-edged style of Coleman Hawkins and Sonny Rollins.

Akiyoshi is a charming and personable performer. Her petite frame and lighthearted manner belie her seriousness as a composer and her deep-seated ambition. Her model is no less than Duke Ellington. Toshiko has a command of hard-driving bebop, which is the basis of her piano style. She also writes Ellingtonian works of mood, color, and texture and some strikingly original jazz that incorporates traditional Japanese instruments and themes.

I spoke with Toshiko on a sunny afternoon at the Monterey Fairgrounds in 1977, prior to her band's Sunday night concert. The year before, her band had provided the festival with a rousing grand finale. I feel certain that her closing position on the 1977 program was an indication that the festival directors, producer Jimmy Lyons and musical director John Lewis, knew the band would leave the audience excited and wanting more.

The first step of Akiyoshi's journey from her native Japan to the Monterey bandstand was taken when Oscar Peterson heard her perform in a small Tokyo nightclub in 1953. Peterson was in Japan with Norman Granz's *Jazz at the Philharmonic* show. "Oscar told me to come to the hotel to meet Norman," she recalled. "When I got there, Oscar said some things to Norman, who told me, 'If Oscar says so, I take his word for it. Let's set up a session.' Oscar even gave me his rhythm section for that record. It was [guitarist] Herb Ellis, [bassist] Ray Brown, and [drummer] J. C. Heard." The album, originally recorded for the Clef label, has been reissued in Japan but is out of print in America.

Upon her arrival in the United States Akiyoshi enrolled as a student at the

Berklee College of Music in Boston (1956–59). There she met her first husband, alto saxophonist Charlie Mariano. During the 1960's she performed with her own trio and in a quartet with Mariano, and she recorded for Granz's Verve label. In 1969 Toshiko married Lew Tabackin, and in 1972 they moved to Los Angeles. There they put together their first big band, with local studio musicians. The band had unity, spirit, and musicianship but little work; most of the players, however, remained loyal to Akiyoshi out of enthusiasm and respect for her prolific and personal style of writing.

The group's earliest albums (*Kogun, The Long Yellow Road,* and *Tales of a Courtesan*) were very popular in Japan before RCA began distributing them in America. *Insights* (1976) contains Akiyoshi's most impressive composition, "Minimata," a tone poem about the fishing village tragically decimated by mercury poisoning. Despite the band's winning top honors in *Down Beat* polls from 1978 to 1981, their albums did not sell in big enough numbers to satisfy RCA. Akiyoshi and Tabackin decided to form their own label, Ascent, which has been distributed by JAM records since 1981. During the late 1970's Toshiko also recorded as a trio pianist (*Dedications,* on Inner City; *Toshiko Akiyoshi,* on Concord Jazz), proving that she is not limited, as are many composers, to playing the sparse, punctuating chords known as arranger's piano. She is a fluent rhythmic and articulate improviser and plays in the tradition of her primary influence on piano, Bud Powell.

Toshiko's career is of special interest because, more than any other Japanese musician—and jazz has an intense following and many superb artists in Japan—she has become part of, and a contributor to, jazz in America. In addition to offering keen insights into the work of several master bandleaders, Toshiko discusses the differences between playing jazz piano and using the piano in the context of the big band.

When did you start playing piano?

Although I'm Japanese, I lived in Manchuria and started playing piano there when I was seven. I studied with an insignificant piano teacher, who was very good for me, but no one you would know about. When you start piano there, you start like anyone else: Bach, Hanon, Czerny. I'm sure those exercises were helpful to me, and it's also helpful to start when you're young. There are certain instruments, like violin and piano, that will not become second nature if you start late. It involves so much coordination, not only left and right hands but arms and every finger. There are a lot of notes to be played. In sight-reading, too. if you start young, you are usually a better sight reader.

What was your first jazz experience?

It was accidental. I got into the music business—in other words, playing for money. The war had ended, and my family lost everything in Manchuria, so we had to come back to Japan. I was fifteen at the time [1945]. Money had to be made, and I loved playing the piano, so I found a job in an occupation dance hall. That's where the best jobs, and money were. It was a small group: accordion, drums, violin, alto saxophone, and piano. The music was terrible.

After your classical training, how did you learn to improvise?

By listening, as a matter of fact, to a seventy-eight [rpm] of Teddy Wilson's "Sweet Lorraine." The first time I was exposed to it I was very impressed. I copied a lot of records and then analyzed them. I used to practice my improvisations, too. I would write them out, and then practice them. I went on to other groups and eventually into big bands, going from one on to the other. Later I formed a quartet with [alto saxophonist] Sadao Watanabe, who's well known now. He was eighteen at the time. The other two are good players, but not known in this country.

Was Teddy Wilson the only pianist you listened to?

In 1947, yes, but I was exposed to a lot of other pianists later. Most people neglect to think about this, but just because you are a pianist, doesn't mean you are influenced only by pianists. In my case, drummers influenced me a lot. Max Roach, Arthur Taylor, and Roy Haynes. But Sonny Rollins and Miles Davis influenced me a lot, too.

What was it about drummers' work that helped you?

You know that development doesn't happen suddenly—it comes very slowly. You pick up little things that come out in different forms, so it is not a black-and-white thing. You can't say this influenced that. Generally speaking, the drummers influenced me in terms of jazz rhythm. Like Duke Ellington said, "It Don't Mean a Thing If It Ain't Got That Swing." That's my musical philosophy. Today, though, young players don't want to define jazz. They want to play crossover music or think of what they're doing as just plain music. To me, the jazz is one of the elements that attracts me: the dynamic, rhythmic pulse. The drummers showed me the accents of this rhythmic style. But Powell influenced me predominantly on piano, by the way. I was impressed by Bud Powell at a time when I was growing very fast musically, and I think this is fortunate.

What gave you the opportunity to come to the States?

The album that Norman Granz recorded on Oscar Peterson's recommendation. The record came to the attention of the Berklee College of Music back in 1953, and I got a full scholarship to the school. I had a very good piano teacher while I was there, although she wasn't part of the regular faculty. Her name was Madame [Margaret] Chaloff. She taught me how to practice.

What does that mean? How did you practice?

It means I practiced very, very slowly. The idea is to program your brain to move the fingers. Before, my method was to move the fingers and let the brain remember the movements by repetitive playing. She taught me to reverse that process. Am I making this clear? She had me learn music so that I could tell her the order of the notes backwards. What I learned from her about practicing slowly saved me a lot of time because I didn't have to practice as much to learn something.

I used to practice Hanon exercises a lot to make my fingers strong. I have very small fingers, and being female, I had to develop more power. I also played scales—not ordinary scales, but a certain phrasing of a scale—and in different keys. Each person has to find his own fingering for his own hands. I practiced voicings and harmony, too. I think what's important is to do everything in all the keys, not just in C. Do it in D flat. Any exercise will help if the person is musical. If a person is not musical, exercising sometimes becomes the playing. That is, when he plays, it sounds like exercise. That's terrible.

Did you have a chance to work professionally while you were a student?

Yes, at Storyville, George Wein's club. I started working three months after I came to Boston. I was also working with Charlie Mariano soon after we got married in 1959.

How did your playing change as a result of coming to America?

My ideas changed, so I'm sure my playing did, too, although I was still strongly influenced by Bud Powell. Soon after I got here, I realized I'd have to develop my own style and self-expression. I grew to like Bill Evans a lot. Bill was influenced by Powell, as he admitted once, but not so much in how he played as in the spiritual sense, especially on ballads. So many people influenced my ideas just by working with them—Oscar Pettiford, Roy Haynes, Max Roach, Sonny Rollins, Miles Davis, Charles Mingus, and a few others I was lucky enough to play with.

Except for Mingus, I never realized you played with any of those people.

Not officially, no. But I was working four nights a week at Storyville from 1956 to 1959. These other bands came in to play, and in those days Boston was a seven-night-a-week town. They even had a matinee. Miles and the others used to let me sit in. I worked at the Coke and Bib, which was a weekend club on Long Island, and I worked with Roy Haynes there. I came to America at a very good time, when all those great players were free enough to work occasional jobs. Later on in New York I met Lew [Tabackin], when I was subbing for the pianist in Clark Terry's band.

What was your experience with Charles Mingus like? It seems he provided a much looser context for his musicians than Ellington did.

Well, Mingus wasn't so capable of writing down his music anyway. For the larger orchestral works he hired an arranger. In the small groups, when I was with him [for about ten months during 1965], he taught us by ear. In that band we had Lonnie Hillyer on trumpet, Charles McPherson on sax, Julian Priester on trombone, Pepper Adams, sax, Booker Ervin, sax, and even another bassist sometimes, Henry Grimes. Mingus was unique in that he wrote a lot of music that bordered on being corny. At least if anyone else did it, it would sound corny. Because he did it, it came out great.

What you were saying about looseness—Ellington was loose, too. I've heard he arrived at the studio with very little written down, just the form. What he wrote was like a mosaic, if you know what I mean. It was vulnerable. If you pushed on one point, it was felt throughout. This is in contrast with someone like Basie, whose music—although he didn't write it himself—was pretty solid and healthy. Ellington had weak spots, which, if you hit them wrong, the whole piece came down. That's why Duke's music is so hard to play, especially for a high school or college band. There are only certain pieces they can play because the others are so vulnerable.

Did you pick up any tricks from Mingus as far as leading a band is concerned?

I hope I have. I don't think I can say specifically what it is. I felt something happened in my heart, and I like to think I use all my experiences. Influence is a spiritual thing. I hope my music is a reflection of my thoughts and experiences. Mingus was extraordinary, though, and he had very warm feelings toward me, which made it easier to be influenced by him personally.

What attracted you from the small combo to the big band?

When I played in the small group, I was just interested in the instrument. Later I became interested in writing, and the reason for that was that I couldn't express myself with just two hands and the piano. I didn't have big hands or that kind of virtuosity. There was not enough color to me. If you compare piano music to a black-and-white brush painting, the big band is a picture with color, and that's what I wanted. It's very difficult for me just to play piano. I need the band as color. Like a painter needs a yellow or a blue, I need a horn.

It seems that a lot of big band leaders have been pianists—Duke Ellington, Fletcher Henderson, Count Basie, Stan Kenton.

One reason that the piano player leads the band, I think, is that piano players usually write, although Basie doesn't write, so he's different. The role of piano playing in a big band is very limited, too, unless you write music specifically to feature the piano. Basically, the piano can almost be eliminated from the band. So it's logical that the pianist, who doesn't have to be at the instrument most of the time, should stand up and conduct.

Do you include many piano parts in your own arrangements?

Since I'm the only writer for my band, I always know what I have to do. When I have to conduct, I eliminate the piano. I play only when the piano has to be played as a background for a soloist. Some solo players prefer that background, and others don't want it. You have to know all that and write accordingly. That's the object of big band piano playing, and it's very difficult. The most difficult job of the rhythm section, piano and drums, is how to give solo players what they need, and how not to give what they don't need. Many piano players overplay. But it's very hard, and you can spend your whole life working on it. The only thing to say is that the function of a piano in a big band is to play the minimum possible. Still, there are certain places where it's needed. For example, horn players use their mouths, so they have to breathe sometime. There will be a hole at the end of a phrase, and you have to pick those up. That little playing to fill in has to match up with the quality and tone of the music. That's what Count Basie and Duke Ellington do so well.

Have you ever used an electric keyboard?

No, I don't consider that a piano. It's another keyboard instrument, but not a piano. It has a different sound and function. I'm narrow-minded, I guess. I like acoustical instruments. I'm a traditionalist in the sense that I don't want to lose what jazz has had in the past.

What type of acoustic piano do you prefer?

When you're a pianist, you have to learn to play whatever you're given. We're not fortunate because we can't carry our own instrument with us, so you really have to meet a lot of instruments in your life. Some take an immediate liking to you, and others refuse to like you ever. The brand doesn't always matter because each piano is different. Baldwin, to me, is like a cat. It doesn't care what you're thinking. It's very independent. It will ring anytime it wants, no matter what you want it to do. I like Steinways, generally. The Steinway is more like a dog: it's very responsive. I have a Model B Steinway at home, which I like, but we're not that intimate with each other. I once bumped into a piano at Top of the Gate in New York, a five-foot eleven-inch grand. It was so good to me that as soon as I touched it, it made me feel like a queen.

Has becoming primarily a composer affected your playing?

I've gained a bit and probably lost something, too. I guess that's always true when you change; you just have to hope that what you lost isn't necessary. I've probably lost my athletic quality at the piano—you know, playing hard and fast. Jazz piano playing is a little like a sport. You have to be athletic. I can't do this as easily because I need to put so much time into my writing that I don't practice as much as I'd like. In terms of my content, my piano playing is richer and thicker because of composing. My notes are probably much more selective than they were.

I've noticed that a lot of pianists, who think of themselves as pianists and not really bandleaders, are starting to organize large ensembles. McCoy Tyner and Chick Corea are the ones I have in mind. They seem to be playing a kind of orchestral jazz rather than big band music. Do you know what I mean or see a difference?

I don't think of these groups as big bands either. It's more like a small combo, only with more people. Whatever they do is an extension of their own playing. Nowadays everybody has the schooling and training to be a writer, if he wants to be. McCoy has a very strong voice which you can hear in any group he writes for.

Chick is an extraordinary musician. I heard some piano solos of his recently on tape that are not quite jazz, but a little more like Bartók. They're beautiful. I think the best big band recently has been the Thad Jones-Mel Lewis group, which isn't around anymore. They were terrific. To me, a band is a book, a book of material.

And its soloists?

Yes, but even with great soloists, you need the material. It's easier to make the soloists sound good with good material than for good soloists to make the whole band sound good.

Selected Discography

Toshiko-Mariano Quartet (ca. 1962, with Charlie Mariano); JAZ-8000; Jazz Man.

Insights (1976, with big band); AFL-1-2678; RCA.

Dedications (1977); IC-6046; Inner City.

Finesse (1978); CJ-69; Concord Jazz.

A Tribute to Billy Strayhorn (1981, trio); JAM-5003; JAM Records.

ARMANDO "CHICK" COREA

June 12, 1941–

Chick Corea has probably done more to expand the role of alternative keyboards in jazz than any other pianist. A sensitive player with a singing tone and crisp technique, Corea has successfully adapted himself to the electric piano and synthesizers (especially the Mini-Moog), using them in a way that preserves his jazz feeling and personal voice. Corea epitomizes the "keyboardist," a term that began to replace "pianist" on record jackets and in jazz criticism during the mid-1970's. There were even critics and press agents who, for emphasis, coined the mouthful *"multi*keyboardist." While several other individuals appearing in this book warrant the title of keyboardist–specifically Ramsey Lewis, Herbie Hancock, and Josef Zawinul– these jazz pianists gravitate to rhythm-and-blues or rock with a synthesizer at their fingertips. Corea fits the description of (pardon the expression) *"jazz* multikeyboardist" better than anyone else.

Like his music, Corea is energetic, extroverted, and fun-loving. When I met him, he had recently moved to California with Gayle Moran, also a keyboardist and the singer with his enlarged thirteen-piece Return to Forever band. The two had been close friends in New York for many years. Philosophically, Corea is a disciple of Scientology, which he calls "the second greatest discovery of my life." At that time his two teenage children, a boy and a girl, were attending the Delphian Foundation School in Oregon, which implements the educational theories of L. Ron Hubbard, Scientology's founder.

Part of the interview following, concerning Corea's background and musical credo, was taped one evening over tuna fish sandwiches in the offices of his management company, Chick Corea Productions, which then operated out of a two-story house in North Hollywood. Our second conversation, about his composing and studio technique, occurred after a three-hour concert at the Greek Theater in Los Angeles. At that concert, between band segments, Chick and Herbie Hancock played a set of duo piano that included bebop, free playing, and even playing on the strings inside the piano. Since the concert was the last on a long tour, Corea had planned a postconcert party for the musicians, traveling crew, and friends. The backstage area was in chaos with the preparations, but Corea appeared on schedule in a private room, lit a cigarette, and shut out the distractions for the duration of our talk.

Chick is a master of focusing attention. That may explain why the versatility of expression in his work has not been achieved at the expense of its quality. Corea's accomplishments have been varied. He improvised free-form music as a solo pianist and collectively in the avant-garde band Circle. He set a high standard for future jazz/pop with singer Flora Purim and bassist Stanley Clarke in the original Return to Forever group. RTF played jazz/rock after guitarists Bill Connors and Al Dimeola had joined it. After that Corea wrote strong thematic music, involving string and horn sections, for his thirteen piece band. And all that between 1971 and 1976! In each of these genres Corea shows originality and a sense of purpose. As reflected in his conversation, which documents his career methodically, he is a man of extraordinary control, concentration, and clarity.

What made you want to become a musician?

My father, who is a trumpet player and bandleader in the Boston area. I couldn't imagine a more perfect relationship than I had with my father. He helped and supported whatever I got interested in, and he showed the same kind of care and support in my musical training. He didn't force techniques or ideas on me that I wasn't ready for. He played enough piano to show me a few things, but it was more like talking me through the piano and showing me how to read and write music, which was all very important groundwork. He'd often write out arrangements of popular tunes that he played with his own band, but he'd write them for my level, so I learned notation in a very meaningful way. I learned the language of music.

Basically my mother and father provided me with a very safe environment. They let me grow and hang out and have my own thoughts and be myself—whatever I wanted to be. But there was still some discipline, just enough for it to be a help instead of a suppression.

So did that make you a serious student of music when you were young?

I wasn't serious in the sense of being ponderous. I didn't have serious goals or a deep commitment in the first few years. I didn't even practice the piano very much. But at about six or seven years old I knew that I dug music and that I was a musician, although I didn't feel I had to be one. I felt very playful about music, not solemn. My father took me to Salvatore Suolo around that time—he was a classical piano teacher in Boston—and then I started to put more time into music. When I was ten, I remember knowing that I would smile and "glib" my way through school, that I wouldn't take the whole thing too seriously because music—which was something I did at home—was my real life. With Suolo, I studied classical piano music, like Bach, Beethoven, and Chopin. He introduced me to very traditional piano technique.

During high school I put together bands for dances and rehearsing. I had a trio back then [about 1957-58] and copied Horace Silver's entire repertoire from his albums with [trumpeter] Blue Mitchell. It turned out to be a very good way for me to learn how to duplicate a piece of music from hearing it. My father got me into the society-music circle, so I started making some money, too. I had a rented tuxedo and went out to play weddings, *bar mitzvahs,* and coming-out parties. But just like school, I was never really into it. I liked making thirty dollars a night, but never for a minute did I think of myself as doing that kind of thing indefinitely. I sort of liked the idea of providing a service, too, like finding out what was needed and delivering the music. The only thing I had consciously in mind was playing the best music I could for whatever the purpose was.

Back in the middle fifties I used to play jazz by putting groups together to play in small clubs. There were different figures I admired and aspired to along the way, like Miles Davis. It wasn't till I moved to New York in the early sixties that I made any money playing jazz. I went to New York because that's where the musicians were at the time—although I did go to Las Vegas for one summer after I graduated from high school in order to play for a show band. When I got home, I was accepted at Columbia, where I lasted one month. For the next eight months or so I practiced ten hours a day on a [classical] repertoire that would get me accepted at Juilliard [School of Music]. I had an audition, was accepted as a piano major, and didn't last more than two months there. Suddenly I started saying to myself, "All right, cut out the protocol. Get into what you really want to do." So I took an apartment on Seventy-first Street and became a New Yorker, working with as many bands as possible.

What was your apprenticeship like in New York?

There were a whole lot of different learning experiences. I worked for two years with Stan Getz, who had Roy Haynes on drums and Steve Swallow on bass. That band had very high musical integrity. Then came Miles. It happened like this. Herbie Hancock was away on his honeymoon, somewhere in South America, I think, and he couldn't get back for his gig with Miles, which was in Baltimore. It was also around the time Herbie was thinking about going out on his own, so maybe it was part of that process. Anyway, [drummer] Tony Williams, who I knew from Boston, called me out in San Francisco, where I was with Sarah Vaughan. I hit the ceiling! I just freaked out on the phone. Playing with Miles was one of my oldest goals. I went wild on the phone, trying to call someone to replace me for Sarah. Finally, I got Bob James, who had been Sarah's accompanist previously, to play at least that gig for me.

I called Miles on the phone just to see if it was real. I asked him, "When are we going to rehearse?" He said in that hoarse whisper, "Just play what you hear." Uh-oh, I thought. So in Baltimore I made an attempt to find out what the band's repertoire was, but it didn't make any difference. [The band also included Wayne Shorter, sax; Tony Williams, drums; and Ron Carter, bass.] That quintet didn't play things the way they did on the albums anyway. I'm talking about *Nefertiti, Miles Smiles,* and so on. I got up onstage with that one instruction: Play what you hear. The band started and took off like a rocket ship on the first piece. It was "Agitation." I'll never forget it. I just hung on. It was like the shock of suddenly traveling at five hundred miles per hour. I knew they were playing tunes, but they had the tunes so facile and abstracted that even a musician's ear couldn't tell what chord changes were going by. After that first set I went up to the bar to buy myself a drink. Miles came up behind me and whispered in my ear, "Chick, you're a muthafucker." That did it! What more could I ask for? I stayed with that band for three years.

What was it like working for Miles?

Miles was a man who had a vision of what the music should be like. Every time he put the horn to his lips, creation happened. His state of being had the certainty of creativity, which means he creates easily and naturally, directly from himself. His music is full of life. It's great art. I became a blotter, trying to absorb every ounce of it. I also dug trying to find out what was needed from me. At first I tried to play like Herbie had with the band, but I realized pretty soon that Miles wanted his musicians to be unique individuals, like he is. With Miles, there was never any sitting down and discussing the music: "Hey, I'd like you to play a little more of this or that." No instructions, no analytical conversation. There were grunts, glances, smiles, and no smiles. Miles communicated, but not on a logical or analytical level. As it turned out, the more I played for myself, the more Miles liked it.

When [drummer] Jack DeJohnette joined six months after I did, we began to treat the structures and Miles's compositions very freely. I couldn't tell all the time whether he [Miles] liked it or not, but there was some real vibrant music created by that quintet that never showed up on records. On records Miles came in with something new for us to play, usually a set of chord changes, or just a vamp to play on—real sketchy.

What about the group Circle, which was so important to the avant-garde movement in the early seventies? Why did you leave Miles's group?

For me, the heart of Circle was my relationship with [bassist] Dave Holland. We became very close friends while we were in Miles's band, and we both had lofts in the same building in New York. We discussed music a lot and shared life together. We were also attuned to what was happening between us when we played. It was like constant conversation going on. We also wrote music with that communication in mind. We played that way with Jack and Wayne in the band sometimes and encircled Miles's statements with a background and support that he could jump into. Sometimes he got involved in our conversations, and that was really interesting. At one point Dave and I went over to Miles's house and told him we wanted to get into more of this other thing.

What was the goal of Circle for you? [Circle included Corea, Holland, drummer Barry Altschul, and reeds player Anthony Braxton.]

The quality of communication between us. The goal was to investigate it and expand it. It was based on the game of pure improvisation, meaning that we would improve on the structure of what we played as well as the content. Free improvisation means we had no prior agreements about what we would do melodically, harmonically, or rhythmically—no limits, no hold barred. That game can be fun, but it can be weird. When you don't have rules or agreements, you start to wonder what you're doing. The only controlling factor was that we had to be communicating with each other.

Did that go for Anthony Braxton, too?

Not as much as with Dave and Barry. Anthony had another type of thinking about what we were doing. I felt I should have a real grounding in the basics of music, no matter what I played. That is, I should know rhythm, harmony, melody, and be familiar with the great tradition in music to some extent. Anthony bypassed grounding in a way. What constituted grounding for him was his relationship to his horn. [Braxton played mostly alto saxophone and bass clarinet in Circle.]

Recently I put on a tape of the Coltrane quartet in my car and caught the middle of this tune where there was this far-out dialogue between Trane and Elvin Jones. I was thinking, what the hell are they doing? A minute or two later it became clear: They were playing the blues. They had really abstracted the form, but then they landed where it was really coming from. There's something powerful in hearing that grounding come through. It's not possible to understand that very abstract stuff without understanding a basic blues. That's the kind of discrepancy that occurred with Anthony. What allowed some of our music to become beautiful was a friendship and the desire to create something together.

Was Return to Forever a return to some basics?

After Circle, I realized there was a missing ingredient in what I was doing musically, and it was an extra-musical thing. It's about people. If there's anything real in the world, it's people. What did my piano playing have to do with people?

You must mean the audience. You were certainly relating well to other musicians.

True, true. I knew how good it made me feel to communicate well with other musicians and how bad I felt when it didn't happen. It started to get very important to me. I had a similar realization at home. My father has thirteen brothers and sisters, so we have a large clan in Boston. It was difficult for me to communicate what I was doing in music to my family. That didn't feel right either.

An intimate part of this growing awareness was my contact with L. Ron Hubbard's writing. I got introduced to it during my last months in Miles's band in about 1970. A bass player, Jamie Faunt, who is still a friend, showed me some books, and I immediately got interested in what he [Hubbard] was saying about communication. I began to apply it to myself and to my music. He made a lot about life seem simple and down-to-earth. I dug that.

There's an interesting parallel there to Herbie Hancock's career. He was also playing a rather esoteric kind of music, he became involved in a philosophical idea [Buddhism], and he suddenly began playing more accessible music. Is that more than a coincidence?

We had a chance to talk about that on this tour, and we recognized the similarities, too. Whenever your mind is opened up to something new, you can expect some changes to occur. You have to get into what people are all about, and the first step in that process, in what people are about, is communicating. One of my personal goals in life is to bring into my everyday experience the kind of awareness and uplifting feelings I get when I'm playing music. I'm very clear. There's nothing in the way. It's just me and the music and the people I'm playing with. There's a subject in Scientology called Dianetics, which is the study of the operation of the mind. The mind is the thing which causes the opposite of clarity—muddiness, or whatever you want to call it. The uncontrolled mechanisms of the mind get in the way of a person's intentions. If you learn to make your mind a useful thing to you, instead of a hindrance, you can attain clarity in what you do. Especially when you create or play music or use your imagination, the best way to operate is without mental mechanisms. You simply see what's necessary and do it. Bringing that kind of clarity into my other activities in life is something I accomplish only to a degree.

In what you said about playing music, it sounded as if you were talking about spontaneity or instinct?

Sort of.

But it's an educated instinct that involves lots of schooling.

Oh, yeah, I'm not talking about magic.

How about an example? I'm interested in how you re-created Bartók's "Bagatelle No. 4" on The Mad Hatter.

I had been listening to some Bartók records on an old Hungarian label. They were posthumous performances of very early orchestrations which the composer had put aside. I was also listening again to the string quartets and the Concerto for Orchestra. In a biography I was reading, I discovered Bartók's interest in folk music, and I realized "Bagatelle No. 4" wasn't something he'd composed, but an arrangement based on Hungarian folk music. The whole thing impressed me as a blues—that was the basic communication. Something mournful, from another culture. I started messing with it at the piano and imagined the piece with a choral background and some wailing going on on top of it. That was the basic concept.

The piano made the basic track for the record. I play the song through three times. For the second and third choruses, I added the Oberheim 8-Voice [synthesizer] with a choral sound, and on the third chorus Gayle [Moran] sings the same notes as the Oberheim. After all that, I improvised some Mini-Moog [synthesizer] over the last two choruses. Originally I had another overdub that I decided to leave off the final record. Did you ever hear Sonny Murray play drums? I had my drum set in the studio, put some pads under it, and played in that fast, sporadic way for the second and third choruses, too. Well, if you were in New York and went to the clubs in the mid-sixties, you'd have said, "Oh, yeah!" But to anyone else, it would have sounded like someone dropping oil cans in the background. So that was one overdub that didn't make it. For me, the record really enhanced the communication of the original folk song.

When you work with a group, to what degree do you feel comfortable with orchestration or any preplanned music, as opposed to improvisation?

It varies, depending on the effect you want to create. As an artist, there's some result you're working for. You use whatever resources you have to accomplish that aim—knowledge, musicians, budget. . . .

So it's a practical question, not a theoretical preference?

For me it is, especially since my tastes range from complete formlessness, demonstrated by the second piece Herbie and I played tonight, which had a little melody at the beginning but was completely open after that. My tastes range from that to note-for-note composition, when that's the effect I want to create. Fortunately I have musicians in my band who can do both.

Historically it seems there's been a shift toward more orchestration in jazz. Do you agree?

Are you asking for a general observation?

What I'm getting at is asking to what extent jazz allows for note-for-note composition. Some of Ellington's fully composed and orchestrated work, like "Concerto for Cootie," is jazz by anyone's definition. But Gershwin's Preludes *for piano don't qualify as jazz, to my ear, even though they imitate a lot of the changes jazz musicians use.*

You have one aspect of this backward, to my way of thinking. The style doesn't dictate the use [of orchestration or improvisation]. The user is the one who creates the style. I don't ask myself, "Does this work as jazz?" I'll create the music I need without thinking about style. Now the historical observation: The reason there's more orchestration being used now in jazz-inclined areas is that there are more structure-inclined artists—musicians who are both jazz-based and more desirous of controlling the effects they produce with their music. Herbie and I are both examples of that. Also, there are more musicians able to compose. Structuring music is a manifestation of trying to program music and gain a clearer idea of what you want to communicate.

As Herbie explained it to me once, he works with the studio, not just in the studio. It sounds as if you're doing that, too, judging from what you said about "Bagatelle No. 4." When you overdub, what happens to spontaneity and the interplay you get with other musicians?

But I'm aiming at a different concept when I overdub. The art of overdubbing is being able to re-create a mood or feeling. You can actually interact with tracks you've already laid down. I agree, it's a time warp, but it can be done. You see spontaneity is not the same as differentness. You don't have to play something different every time for it to be spontaneous. The only prerequisite for spontaneity is having all of one's attention on the moment. It's fully experiencing the world around you.

Like love? You can love someone with spontaneity even if you've known the person a long time.

Yeah, I'd say that analogy holds.

Let's get to synthesizers. What's your attachment to the whimsical, whistling kind of sound you get from the Mini-Moog?

That's the solo voice I grabbed onto. If I could play trumpet or sax, that's just about how I'd sound. I like the synthesizers because I like having the ability to bend a note, modulate a tone, and do things with timbres that the piano doesn't offer. As a jazz pianist I'm basically in the rhythm section, so unless conditions are A-one optimum, I never really get to sing that solo line, which is what I get to do with the Mini-Moog. In relation to people like Malcolm Cecil and Tomita, I'm a dilettante at the synthesizer. But I do have an interest in electronic music, so I'm hoping I can remedy that.

How do you bend pitches on the Mini-Moog?

It has two wheels instead of the usual levers. When you roll it forward, the pitch goes up; backward, and it goes down. There's a notch in the center where the pitch is stable. My hands have grown real comfortable with those wheels, so I can express myself very easily with them. The left hand has a whole new function in the single-voice synthesizer. Except for the case of multifingered runs where you have to use both hands, the left hand is used for things like pitch bending, expression, modulation, and timbre or octave changing.

Have you ever thought about doing a solo multikeyboard album, overdubbing all the keyboards you play?

Well, I do that at home with my four-track [recorder] when I practice. It would be fun, but it's not of great importance to me right now. I'd rather interact with other musicians or play solo on a great piano.

Do you practice the acoustic piano at home?

I do, but it isn't very regular. Sometimes I'll develop routines, whatever I want to get into at the moment. Usually I'll take out my classical repertoire. Alban Berg's *Piano Sonata* is one of my favorite piano works. I'll play anything by Bach, some of Chopin's études, Mozart sonatas, or [Olivier] Messiaen's piano music.

By the way, you're not always confined to the rhythm section as a pianist. Didn't you just complete a solo album [Delphi 1]*?*

That was recorded at the Delphian Foundation [in Oregon] where my kids are in school, and it was done on one of the best instruments I ever played, which was a big reason for my recording there. About a year ago I met a man—Mark Allen—and a piano. He built a concert grand with his two hands which is par excellence a fantastic instrument. His one prototype is at the school, and he has a workshop in the basement of the chapel where he's training assistants to help him. The care and quality of the materials are what makes this one different. The improvements are instantly noticeable. The structure of the case is different, and so is the tension on the strings. The piano, from the lowest note on the keyboard to the highest, is very clear and sonorous, as opposed to the muddy base and mechanical, clinky top of most pianos—even the good brands. The low register, if played caressingly, sounds like an organ. The upper register sounds like the bells of St. Mary's.

Another thing I discovered from playing the Mark Allen is that all other pianos have a natural distortion built into them when you play clusters of notes loudly. Take eight or ten notes in the middle register and really hit them. The sound breaks up, cracks; it distorts. The pressure doesn't get contained and resonated evenly. The Mark Allen doesn't distort no matter what you do to it. It plays softer and louder than any other piano I've seen.

In your earlier solo albums, I understand your improvisations were based on mental images. Is that how you recorded this time?

No. That was sort of a game, like musical portraits of scenes I imagined. These were just improvised on the spot, and I gave them titles later on.

The Return to Forever albums with the large ensemble, like Mad Hatter, *seem to be suites. What's your concept of a suite, and how are the pieces related?*

A suite to me is almost like a collage of themes with transitions between the themes. It's like you're traveling down a road. There's one walk you're taking, but there are different scenes along the way. It's episodic music, as opposed to playing one theme, varying the theme, and then returning to it.

You're incredibly eclectic, involved in so many different types of musical activities. Do you ever get confused or worry that you're spreading yourself too thin?

Music is pure joy and fun for me. Let me explain something. I can sit down and play the piano from the perspective of the piano. Or I can sit there and play the song, not just the piano. Then my attention isn't on the song, but on the music. You can expand that into a group. That is, I can play the group, not just my instrument. My attention and intention is going through all these musicians—and theirs through me, I hope. We're not just playing a song, but a whole performance, a two-hour performance—that is, a single, large communication. We focus on the effect of all that. The playing field is getting larger, and I can be freer with the music. That's what's going on with me now.

Selected Discography

Circulus (1970); LA882-J2; Blue Note.
Circling In (1968–70); LA472-H2; Blue Note.

Piano Improvisations, Vol. 1 (1971); 1014ST; ECM Records.

Where Have I Known You Before? (1974, electronic keyboards); PD-6509; Polydor.

My Spanish Heart (1976, large ensemble); PD2-9003; Polydor.

The Mad Hatter (1978, electronic keyboards); PD1-6130; Polydor.

Delphi 1 (1979, solo piano); PD1-6208; Polydor.

Trio Music (1981, improvisations/music of T. Monk); ECM2-1232; ECM.

HERBIE
HANCOCK

April 12, 1940–

Herbie Hancock, like his close friend and occasional collaborator Chick Corea, merits the title "multikeyboardist." As he explains below, Herbie was initiated into the rites of electronic synthesizers during a dramatic recording session in the early 1970's. Hancock, once an engineering student at Grinnell College in Iowa, has grown increasingly interested in electronics. On July 5, 1982, his picture turned up on the first page of *Infoworld,* a newsweekly of the computer trade, in a story reporting his use of the Apple computer to create new synthetic sounds as well as to expedite his office work. Using electronic keyboards primarily in his funky fusion music, Hancock returned to (acoustic) jazz in about 1977, happily with his touch and technique on the piano undiminished. He continues to work with his two most sympathetic accompanists from the sixties, drummer Tony Williams and bassist Ron Carter. Hancock also records as a sideman for horn players and in piano duos with both Corea and a longtime admirer of his talent, Oscar Peterson.

Hancock's career may be divided into three phases. During the sixties he played a very improvisational type of modern jazz typified by superimposing rich keyboard harmony over modal, or scale-based, patterns. He worked for trumpeter Donald Byrd (1962–64) and Miles Davis (1964–68), and he led several studio bands of his own throughout the decade and his own sextet from 1968 to 1971. Hancock excelled as an accompanist in the Davis band, which also included Tony Williams on drums, Ron Carter, bass, and Wayne Shorter, saxophone. For his own recording groups, Herbie wrote lyrical, sophisticated compositions that became classics in the repertoire of the period, for example, "Maiden Voyage," "Speak Like a Child," "Riot," and "Dolphin Dance." Later, with his sextet, Herbie began to explore electronic keyboards and odd time signatures in a freely improvised music.

The second phase began in 1973, when Hancock first applied electronic keyboards to jazz-influenced rhythm-and-blues. After his first album in that style, *Headhunters* (on Columbia), went "gold," Herbie abandoned the piano for several years, occasionally playing the Yamaha electric grand as a substitute. As noted in Part One, his contribution as a keyboardist in these years was to explore the role of the synthesizer, electric string ensemble, and the electronic Clavinet in the fusion style.

In about 1977 Hancock inaugurated a third phase in his career with a series of acoustic piano concerts in duo with Chick Corea, and in a well-publicized touring band, dubbed V.S.O.P., with trumpeter Freddie Hubbard and Herbie's colleagues in the Davis band of the mid-sixties. Since that time Hancock has remained active in both the acoustic and the electronic worlds.

The following interview has been constructed from several meetings during the latter two phases of Herbie's career. One of our conversations took place at the Automatt recording studio in San Francisco, another in an apartment that Herbie rents during his frequent work trips from his home in Los Angeles, still another in my car en route to the Xerox Corporation headquarters, where he was scheduled to demonstrate a new gadget that would instantly transcribe solos onto a video screen, store them, and later print them out on paper. On that occasion Herbie began by playing his earliest popular piece, "Watermelon Man" (1962), but the computer, or its program, malfunctioned, leaving the small audience disappointed. Herbie himself had disappointed much of his public when he limited his interests to electronic rhythm-and-blues. But he won them back easily with his return to jazz. The jazz piano tradition will surely be enriched by his return to it.

When did you first start playing piano?

I started at seven years old, and when I was eleven, I performed at a young people's concert with the Chicago Symphony. I played the first movement of a Mozart concerto. In fact, I studied classical piano all the way through college, until I was twenty.

Was all that training ultimately helpful, technically or otherwise?

Definitely. It was a great help, although there are areas of jazz technique that aren't included in classical training.

Did you have any particularly influential teachers, in either classical or jazz keyboard work?

I never had a jazz teacher, as such, but my very first piano teacher was a Mrs. Whalen, who gave me lessons on the second floor of the Ebeneezer Baptist Church in Chicago. She taught me how to read, but I had no sound, no feeling for music. Then, when I was ten, I went to a Mrs. Jordan, who's since passed away. She was my favorite teacher. She realized that everything I played sounded the same. She showed me how to play nuances on the keyboard and talked in more philosophical terms, trying to get me to understand what music was all about. That's when I started getting a touch.

I've heard that you went through a period of transcribing Oscar Peterson and George Shearing solos.

That's how I learned harmony and ear training. Actually the vocal group the Hi-Lo's were the greatest aid to me in harmony. I loved the harmonies they were using, especially Clare Fischer's arrangements, which I used to take off the record. By the time I studied theory in college I breezed through it. I also listened to mood-music orchestras a lot, like Robert Farnon's orchestra from England. He'd take a tune like "Laura" and—although he might have some corny things in there—by the time he got to the third chorus he'd go all kinds of places with the harmony. I learned a lot of progressions from listening to his music. Farnon's got quite a jazz following over here. In fact Quincy Jones's score for the film *The Pawnbroker* will give you some idea what Farnon is like. [Trumpeters] Dizzy Gillespie and Donald Byrd dig him, too. They'd probably do anything to get one of his scores.

How did your relationship with Donald Byrd begin?

When I came out of college in 1960, I went back to Chicago, where I had a gig in the post office. I also had a gig with Coleman Hawkins as part of a local rhythm section. That was in October. Later Donald Byrd came through town with his group during a big blizzard. I got a call from the manager of a local club because Donald's piano player had somehow gotten stranded. I played with them three days, and they asked me to move to New York and become a permanent member of the group. I was with Donald from December 1960 to May 1963, when I joined Miles.

And how did the job with Miles Davis come about?

There were these rumors, people were telling me that Miles was looking for me, that he was going to call me. I didn't believe it at first, but enough people started telling me to start me thinking that it might be true. At the time not only was I working with Donald, but we were also roommates. He told me, "Look, if Miles calls you and asks if you're working with anybody, tell him no, and take the gig. More power to you. I don't want to stand in the way of your moving forward." I thought that was a beautiful thing to say. Anyway, that's exactly what happened, or almost.

Miles called, asked me if I was working with anyone, and I said no. Then he asked me to come to his house on Thursday at two-thirty. I said okay. Then he hung up. I didn't even have his address. About a half hour later Tony Williams called me, and he had Miles's address. We both went there for the audition, and George Coleman was there, and Ron Carter. Miles's basement was his music room, but he didn't really play with us. He told us to go downstairs and play. Every once in a while he'd come down, stand in the doorway, and then go up again. We were there three or four hours. This went on for three days.

The second day Philly Joe Jones and Gil Evans showed up. Miles played about three notes, put down his horn, and walked upstairs. The third day Miles told us that we were meeting the next day at Columbia studios on Thirtieth Street to make a record. I said, "Miles, does that mean I'm in the band?" He says, "You makin' the record date, ain't you?"

Did your playing change dramatically working with Miles, Tony, and the other people in that band?

Yes, those were my very formative years. I was at the point of transition between being a good piano player and being one who had a personal style. During the time I was with Miles, I started to hear music on the radio and caught phrases or something in another pianist's solo that sounded like me. I realized that suddenly I had a sound that could be recognized.

Before Miles, while you were with Donald Byrd, were there pianists who influenced you, people you listened to in order to learn what their styles were all about?

Oh, definitely. I was listening to McCoy Tyner, Wynton Kelly, Bill Evans. But that's a little misleading. I also felt that I was influenced by horn players as much as by pianists. Miles Davis, for one. I was listening to Trane [John Coltrane], Lee Morgan, and really everyone playing in those years.

What specifically did you learn from the other members of Miles's band—Tony, Wayne Shorter, and Ron Carter?

From Tony Williams, I learned so much about cross rhythms, about Indian rhythms. I got turned on to avant-garde jazz, say, from Coltrane on, through Tony, who was listening to that stuff carefully. That was his thing. He helped me get beyond hearing it as funny notes and really appreciating it like a piece of sculpture. He also turned me on to a lot of contemporary classical music. Tony and I used to hang out together. He was probably my closest friend then, and he was only seventeen. I was twenty-three, practically an old man.

Now Ron Carter was the first bassist I really listened to. He could find the notes that allowed you to be free in your improvising, but they were grounded enough so you didn't get lost.

I always liked the way he connected his notes. He was so smooth and flowing, even up-tempo.

Absolutely. His tone, too, was great, but of course, without all those things together his playing wouldn't have the impact it does. For me, the

thing that made the most difference was his selection of notes. His compositions were special, too. They had a kind of European flavor in the way the
chords were laid out, say, in a piece like "Little Waltz."

The master writer to me, in that group, was Wayne. He still is a master.
Wayne was one of the few people who brought music to Miles that didn't get
changed.

Now Miles himself: He rarely told any of us how to play. Also, when
anyone brought in music, he'd take it down to its skeleton, just bare bones.
When we played it, all of the flesh and tendons were improvised. That meant
we could create a whole new being out of that song every night. Miles always
said, "Never resolve anything." I remember when Ron Carter brought in the
song "Eighty-one" for the *E.S.P.* album, Miles took the first two bars of
melody notes and squished them all together, and he took out other areas to
leave a big space that only the rhythm section would play. To me, it sounded
like getting to the essence of the composition. He'd take the inherent structure
and leave us room to breathe and create something fresh every night. There
were the basic elements of the song, but not used exactly as they were in the
composition. That's why it was always fun to play with Miles.

Why did you leave that band?

Because I wanted to develop some of the things I had learned there and to
play some of my own compositions that wouldn't have sounded right with
that group. That band couldn't do everything. Miles knew I was planning to
leave at some point, although I hadn't given him an exact date. The band had
just hired a new bass player, Dave Holland. It was 1968. I got married on
August 31, after the first job with Dave on bass. We went on our honeymoon
in Brazil, and I was supposed to be back two weeks later to play a gig. The first
night in Brazil I got food poisoning. So the doctors wouldn't let me leave on
time because I was still on medication.

When I got back, Chick had taken my place, and Jack Whittemore,
Miles's agent, told me that Miles realized Chick could handle the job. Miles
decided it would be better for him if I left the band then because he knew
Tony was going to leave sometime later on, and he didn't want me and Tony
leaving at the same time. Then he'd have to break in too many people; it
would be starting out with a whole new band. I said, "Cool," mainly because
of my ego. Of course, I didn't feel that way really. I had no intention of
coming home from my honeymoon with no gig. In essence, I didn't leave
Miles. I was asked to leave. The timing wasn't the greatest for me, but I also
realized I'd probably need a push to leave no matter when it happened. It was

hard to break away because we had our own sound, plenty of work, and it was very comfortable.

Were the songs that you wrote during the mid-sixties written for Miles's band or for your recording sessions on Blue Note?

The things I recorded on my records were written for my group. "Maiden Voyage" was written for a television commercial, although I sort of had Miles in mind. We were advertising Yardley men's cologne. "The Sorcerer" was an exception; it was recorded by Miles, but I never played it on record.

Were you surprised that "Maiden Voyage" was taken so seriously, considering that it started out strictly as a commercial?

Not really, because I always liked the piece, and I was serious about it, even though it was for a commercial. When I decided to record it, I took a lot of time selecting the right title. The title was the last thing that came to me.

What's the story behind your first popular piece, "Watermelon Man"?

That was written to help sell my first album. It was the first time I ever wrote a piece with a commercial goal in mind. Of course, Mongo Santamaria is the one who made it popular, but as the composer I paid my bills with that piece for about five or six years. I don't mean that the song was a sellout, by the way. Compositionally, from a structural point of view, "Watermelon Man" and "Maiden Voyage" are probably my two strongest pieces. I'm talking strictly about craft—the balance, the relationships that are working throughout the piece. They're almost mathematical. Also, on "Watermelon Man," I tried to get part of my life in there as a black person, which is one of the reasons it has an R-and-B feeling.

Did the title come first? The speech rhythm of those words are such a perfect match for the melody!

Yeah, they are, "Heeey, Watermelon Man . . ." It's probably the only piece of music I've written where the title came first. Another thing about "Maiden Voyage": I was originally trying to create a different rhythmic framework. We usually have accents on [beats] two and four. I wanted accents that were strong, and different, but not like R-and-B. So what came out was the opening [to "Maiden Voyage"], sort of a new rhythmic vamp.

If we could switch to the subject of improvising, how do you approach a new piece of music. How do you analyze it, absorb it, or make it part of your repertoire?

There are a lot of different approaches I might use. I could look at the shape of the melody—whether it's based on wide intervals, or descending notes, chromatic notes, clusters, or maybe some central theme or concept. The idea is to get some central idea to use, to work off of. It could be a harmonic theme instead. I like what I do better when I'm exploring a theme, rather than just playing licks across the chord. It doesn't have to be a theme in the song; it could be a theme you develop from the song as a starting point.

That's one of the things I like about Wayne's playing. He develops a theme that leads to another theme and so on. It's just great the way he can do that. It's not just clever; it makes it easier for someone to hear what you're doing. There's a thread that goes through the improvisation. It gives it more substance.

What drew you into funky music?

A realization of values that was triggered by my religious practice of Nichiren Shoshu Buddhism and chanting *nam-myoho-renge-kyo.* When you chant, you chant for things that you want—desires, whether they're spiritual or physical. You set goals for yourself or try to overcome certain obstacles. One day, after the sextet had broken up, I was chanting for a solution to the problem of what I was going to do next. Write movie scores? Get a new band? My mind wandered to an old desire I had to be on one of Sly Stone's records. It was actually a secret desire of mine for years—I wanted to know how he got that funky sound. Then a completely new thought entered my mind: Why not get Sly Stone on one of my records? My immediate response was: Oh, no, I can't do that. So I asked myself why not. The answer came to me: pure jazz snobbism. Here was a kind of music I really dug, but I felt it wasn't "good enough" to be included in my own repertoire. I was really disappointed in myself for that narrow-mindedness. Since that was the kind of music I really dug, and since I had to do something new anyway, I decided to give it a try. But I wasn't accustomed to playing that way, so I figured I'd better get some people who were really into it. That's why I got Paul Jackson on bass and Harvey Mason on drums. I took Bennie Maupin because the woodwind instruments he plays have a great variety of contrasting colors.

How would you define or describe funky music?

The best way would be by example, people I feel are playing funky, though not necessarily keyboard players. Sly Stone and James Brown are the two best examples of funk. Certain things Stevie Wonder does, and the Temptations, are good examples, too.

The first time I ever heard the word "funky" applied to music, it was in reference to Horace Silver.

Well, that's some of the first funky piano playing, though it's applied toward a jazz sound in the rhythm section. That kind of playing overlaps what I'm talking about, but they're not the same thing. Horace is within the jazz

framework, and I'm closer to the R-and-B framework. There's a stylistic difference, even though there's a common ground.

What's the common ground that unites jazz funk with R-and-B funk?

Certain phrases unite them. Horace Silver is more than just a melodic line.
There's also his accompaniment and phrasing. The language of funky R-and-B
is different from the language of jazz funk. The jazz musicians don't know
that, though. They think it's easy to play funky. They think anyone can play
funky. Now, certain configurations may be the same, like some of [organist]
Jimmy Smith's licks. He'll alternate between a single note line and using two
notes simultaneously. He'll play the interval of the fifth and octave, going
down to the lower octave with his thumb; then the fourth and sixth simultaneously, then down to the lower octave; then the minor third and fifth,
and so on.

So that's a funky figure which could fit into either jazz or R-and-B?

Right. I think the rhythm actually makes the difference. There's a definite
leaning toward staccato playing in the rhythms of R-and-B funk. That's what
I've gone into, more or less.

*Last year, you told critic Ray Townley that you were "just learning to play
funky." How does that translate itself onto the keyboard? What, exactly, were you
learning to do?*

First of all, the music has to go into your head—you have to be able to hear
it, so I had to orient myself to being able to *think* funky. Next, there's a
greater use of dynamics and accents, as opposed to, say, McCoy Tyner's playing
or even Chick's. Of course, those styles use accents, but when I'm playing a
line, I use very strong accents. It's related to bebop, but I'm using a different
language of accents in what I'm playing now, especially in accompaniment.
There are a lot of spaces, and I use the *wah-wah,* which doesn't change the
pitch, though there's a psychological effect that makes it sound like the pitch is
bending.

*Oscar Peterson said recently that you were the best equipped of the younger pianists
to play solo, if you wanted to go in that direction.*

Wow! Maybe that means I carry twenty-seven pieces of equipment or
something like that. Seriously, though, I doubt it's true, but it sure feels good.

How do you feel about doing a solo album?

I'm more comfortable playing with other instruments. Accompanying is a
specialty of mine. It's part of my style. I enjoy playing colors—like creating
environments—behind other players, and I don't like being out front all the
time.

But you were in some of your sixties albums, especially Maiden Voyage *and* Speak Like a Child.

Right. But my whole purpose in doing *Speak a Child* was to satisfy a lot of people who were telling me I ought to do a solo album. I didn't want to do one, so I made an album that *features* the piano along with other instruments.

Why did you do a solo concert with electric keyboards at the '74 Newport Jazz Festival?

Well, Keith Jarrett was the first one on the program, and he really blew me away. Then McCoy [Tyner] came up. Now nobody can follow Keith Jarrett, right? Only McCoy followed him, and it was burnin'. He was so strong, I was saturated, and I thought the audience was probably saturated, too. I felt everyone needed a contrast, and since I'd been playing electric instruments currently, I wanted to represent myself as I am. Since I had just acquired the ARP 2600 synthesizer and the Digital Sequencer, I was hoping the audience and I could have some fun, because I wasn't ready to bowl them over with a polished performance.

Do you feel inclined to do another solo gig?

Not yet. I'd consider playing a keyboard solo concert, including acoustic piano, but it would take some preparation. See, there's even a technique for moving from one instrument to the other. I've got it down as long as there's a rhythm section with me, but solo, I'd have to compensate for all that. My experience is too limited so far.

Then you consider yourself an ensemble player?

I definitely feel that way. As far as Oscar's statement about my being equipped to play solo is concerned, if he means the potential is there, perhaps he's right. I really don't know. The thing I don't have at this point is the technique for solo *thinking.* Sometime I'd like to try it.

What drew you into synthesizers and the electronic approach of your new style?

It all began when we [the sextet] were doing *Crossings* and *Sextant.* Patrick Gleeson was playing synthesizers for us, but we weren't doing much with overdubs. Then during one session our equipment manager turned on a random resonator which picked up and filtered all the noises in the studio. We really liked parts of the tape and made a loop by stretching it across the desks, file cabinets–everywhere! We spliced together what we wanted and used it as a rhythm track for "Rain Dance" on the *Sextant* album [on Columbia]. Little by little, things that happened in the studio became more prominent in the shaping of the music. Now I go in with a basic drum, bass, and piano chart sketch. When it comes to the other instruments, especially synthesizers, I never know what I want until I hear it. The recording process itself becomes part of the composition of music. I even work that way at home with my eight-track recorder and all the keyboards around me. I'll start off with an idea, do an overdub, and then see how things are coming out. I'll have to admit it makes me kind of lazy—I don't put too much down on paper anymore. Paper is slow. By the time I'd write some things down the idea would be lost.

Could you give me an example of something you've done recently?

One ballad which isn't titled yet is based on a musical spiral. There are four [different] chords in the song, but it's a five-chord [per chorus] song.*

[Using my eight-track recorder,] I started out with one note on the bottom and different chords on top. Then I started changing the notes on the bottom and came up with four chords I like, but the song still needed a fifth chord. Just to experiment, I went back to the first chord and then started the second eight-bar phrase with the second chord. I played it back [on tape], and it worked. Every chorus uses the same sequence but a different permutation of it. The tape I have at home is compositionally a perfect spiral with no stops. On the album you'll notice that there's an introduction and a little variation so that it doesn't become boring.

What do you keep in mind when you use the studio to edit or alter the music? Doesn't it hurt you as a jazz musician to cut into improvised solos, say, in order to shorten something down for AM airplay?

I can write longer compositions for an album, but nobody's ever going to hear them [on the radio]. People's span of attention stretches three to five minutes. After that they'll change the station.

When you cut, the tendency is to save all the hot parts. But that doesn't work. If you put all the hot parts together, you lose the contrast, you don't get the tension and release, and it decreases the heat of the hottest parts. It used to

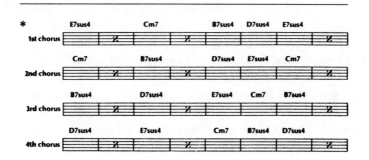

be like cutting off a piece of my body. Now, I say, "Go ahead, cut out my solo. I don't care." I'm not married to it as much as I used to be, and I think that's good. You can become self-indulgent if you're not careful. To think every moment in your music is something people want to hear! *You* might want to hear it, but that doesn't mean that the guy next to you wants to hear all that crap. Do you see what I mean? You can become too personal about your own music, and I don't want to be that way.

Which of your electric instruments do you play strictly as keyboard instruments?

I think of them all as keyboards, though that's not really fair–the synthesizer isn't one. Occasionally I'll play it like a keyboard, but when I play it like, say, Patrick Gleeson, getting more into its sounds, then I'm using it as a synthesizer. I don't want to make the synthesizer sound like a keyboard instrument, but I'm still new to it, so I have a hard time avoiding it.

Do you consider the electric String Ensemble a keyboard?

No. It functions best sustaining a background note, sounding like background strings, but it's not a solo instrument at all.

Hohner Clavinet?

That's definitely a keyboard, which I use only for rhythm with the *wah-wah*. It's sort of a counterpart to the guitar.

Digital Sequencer?

I haven't had time to get into that yet, but it would be very helpful if I wanted to do an electric solo thing. I could use it for a bass line. You can also use it to trigger a series of notes. You play into it, and it records the number of times the notes are being hit, so whenever you want those notes struck in that sequence, you just hit the key and they come out at a predetermined speed.

What practical difference is there in your use of the ARP Soloist and the 2600?

The Soloist, like any synthesizer, is a single-note instrument, which has preset synthesized sounds that simulate acoustic instruments. The 2600 has no presets, so you can program the attack, the release, and the filtering. The Soloist is quick, though. If I want a flute sound, I just throw a switch. I guess the Soloist is more of a keyboard instrument because the sounds are preset. Of course, you can't play accents on it. You get the same volume no matter how hard you press the key. It does have a feature, though, where you can get a *wow* or *growl* effect by touch control.

What would be the best instrument to start out with if anyone wanted something more sophisticated than an electric piano?

I'd say the ARP Odyssey or the Mini-Moog. ARP also makes a new model, called the **AXXE**, which is simpler than the Odyssey. The 2600 is too sophisticated to start with, though.

Have you noticed any traps to watch out for in using electric instruments?

One would be to think of these instruments as replacements for any others. They each have separate functions. There's an awful lot of music that sounds good on acoustic piano, but not on electric, and vice versa. Another trap is overusing the colors you can get out of them. You can really ruin a piece of music with too much Echoplex, for example. You just have to be careful, and use musical sense, as always.

I also have to be careful not to get gimmicky because electronics do lend themselves to it. The only way I know to avoid it is to use your own musical taste. It's not the nature of synthesizers to be gimmicky, so it isn't fair to blame the machines. The machines just do what you tell them to.

I was happy to hear about your V.S.O.P. tour with Freddie Hubbard and your colleagues from the Miles Davis band. After so many years of playing funk, how did you feel about the audience's response?

The reaction was unbelievable. I think it shows another side of the value of jazz/rock. Not that it was done for this purpose, but fusion music has had the virtue of being the first type of jazz the general public could relate to. Listening to it has been a stepping-stone to hearing modern jazz. There is a larger jazz audience as a result, and they're young people in their twenties, the same people who were only listening to rock-and-roll a few years ago. Another thing I realized on the tour is that this new jazz public didn't feel V.S.O.P. was only the music of the sixties. They heard it as current, their applause was that deep. That was the surprise for me.

You have a duo piano concert tour with Chick Corea coming up [in 1978]. How are you preparing for that?

The main thing is getting my finger agility—I can't say *back*—but to where it's never been before. In electronic keyboard music the emphasis isn't on the technical difficulty of the playing because the instruments don't depend on your fingers for touch, tone, or power. Although that's true somewhat of the Rhodes [electric piano] and very much [true] of the Yamaha electric grand. Playing on the V.S.O.P. tour helped me a lot, but I just got out my Oscar Beringer scale book, the Chopin études, Hindemith's *Ludus Tonalis,* Bach's *Well-Tempered Clavier,* some Debussy and Ravel, and [Nicolas] Slonimsky's *Thesaurus of Scales and Melodic Patterns.* I've heard that McCoy Tyner and John Coltrane used to practice out of that. I'm trying to get in an hour or so a day of practice.

Do you think it's possible to develop a touch on electric keyboards?

Let's define it first. When we talk about "touch," even with acoustic instruments, we're talking about what we *hear* as a result of how the performer touches the instrument. So we're really talking about hearing, not touching. Keith Jarrett's touch is out of sight, okay. But I'm talking about what I'm *hearing* from the instrument as a result of the way he touches it. Let's take a synthesizer. There are no hammers, so whatever sounds like "touch" is not a result of the way anyone touches the instrument. It's a result of the way you programmed the envelope. But touch is just not the most important way of differentiating people. The most important thing—on any instrument—is *ideas*. That's what you're really hearing.

What about the difference in touch between McCoy Tyner and Bill Evans?

If Bill Evans played the same notes McCoy Tyner played, the difference would not be very great. There would be a difference, but you'd have to back away from placing that much emphasis on touch.

What about the possibilities of touch, or sound control, on the Rhodes electric piano?

You can control it with pressure from your fingers. You won't get all the nuances you can get on an acoustic, but the volume on the Rhodes can be controlled with your fingers. You can also set the timbre so it's halfway between bright and mellow, which will allow you to do more things with it.

Do you think your composing has come full circle? Your recent music sounds more like "Watermelon Man" than "Maiden Voyage," "Dolphin Dance," "Riot," and so on. Do you consider the kind of writing you did for the sextet passé?

I still like it, but I don't do it now because I don't have an outlet for it. If I were scoring a film, I might do it. Otherwise, I don't think there are many people who'd be into that style of music, compared with the number who are into what I play now.

If you did have a market for the composing you did in the sixties that was equal to the market you had for Headhunters, *would you write in the jazz genre?*

No, I'd be playing some funkier music. Maybe the music would have a more advanced harmonic quality than it does now. The reason the voicings aren't more advanced is that it would make it more difficult for my audience to really get into it. Some of my records, like *Sextant* and *Mwandishi,* were never played that much, even by people who owned them, because you can't listen to these records when you have something else to do. People tend to put on records less demanding of their attention. I am trying to develop my music in a way that will be more functional—that won't interfere with other things you're doing.

Are you playing down to your audience?

No, not really. There's another reason for my present style: I haven't found a way to do more advanced things harmonically without losing the funkiness of it. That's why I don't like a lot of jazz/rock fusion music. They lose the funkiness because they put more emphasis on harmony than rhythm.

Does the concept of background music offend you?

Not at all. I think music can be multifunctional. It should be interesting enough to be satisfying, if you listen to it, but not so demanding that it can't fit into the rest of your life.

Is this an argument for the value of commercialism?

Music, by itself, is not valuable. What makes music valuable is the positive effect on the people who are going to hear it. When I started thinking about the people more, I approached music from the perspective of their lives, rather than from the music itself.

Do you feel some critics interpreted that as commercialism on your part?

Yes, but it's commercial because it sells, not because there's anything condescending about it. If *Sextant* sold eight hundred thousand copies, it would be "commercial," too, by definition. I don't have any message to give anyone. I want to inspire people, just to do better at what they're doing. If I can make people feel good tonight so that tomorrow they'll go to work with smiles on their faces, then my music is valuable. It's people who determine value.

Do you feel generally misunderstood on this issue?

By critics, not by the listeners. Most critics use formal criteria in evaluating music, but you can't discuss the "harmonics of funk." It doesn't apply. You have to evaluate funk on the level of emotions, the projection of emotions, maybe rhythms. We just don't have the terminology to discuss funky music critically.

Selected Discography

Maiden Voyage (1965); BLP-4195/84195; Blue Note.

Miles Davis: Miles Smiles (1966); CS-9401; Columbia.

Speak Like a Child (1968); BST-84279; Blue Note.

Man-Child (1975, electronic keyboards); PC-33812; Columbia.

V.S.O.P.: The Quintet (1978); CS-34976; Columbia.

An Evening with Herbie Hancock and Chick Corea (1978, duets); PC-32965; Columbia.

JOSEF
"JOE"
ZAWINUL

July 7, 1932–

Zawinul, as he likes to refer to himself, is an Austrian-born pianist turned keyboardist. He is unique among synthesizer players in two respects: He uses combinations of synthesizers to simulate a one-man orchestra, and he strives to create original, electronically synthesized music that sounds *acoustic*. Since 1976 he has combined single-voice and polyphonic (or multivoice) synthesizers to weave a fabric of nearly orchestral richness. The context for Zawinul's multikeyboard accomplishments has been Weather Report, a popular fusion band that Zawinul cofounded in 1970 with saxophonist Wayne Shorter. Since 1976 Weather Report has included Jaco Pastorius on bass and Peter Erskine on drums. During the 1970's *Down Beat* readers voted Weather Report top band seven times and named five of its LP's Album of the Year.

Zawinul spent his childhood in war-torn Austria, where he and his family were sometimes so desperate that he was sent out to steal food from the occupying forces. After the war he acquired broad experience with versatile popular orchestras in Europe. In 1959, on the strength of a Shearing-style recording he made in his late teens, Zawinul earned a scholarship to study at the Berklee College of Music, in Boston.

Zawinul, however, was not the academic type; he dropped out of school within months to join Maynard Ferguson's band. His tenure there was brief because of a personality clash with the leader. Next Zawinul spent nineteen months accompanying the blues and jazz singer Dinah Washington, playing on her hit record "What a Difference a Day Makes." He then worked for Cannonball Adderley (1961–69) and he proved himself a talented composer of soulful melodies such as "Mercy, Mercy, Mercy," "Walk Tall," "Country Preacher," and "74 Miles Away." Zawinul's writing and bluesy hard bop soloing on piano were largely responsible for the Adderley quintet's popularity during the sixties. Miles Davis took an interest in adding the electric piano to his band after hearing Zawinul play it with the Adderley group at a concert in Mexico. Miles added Zawinul to the group, too, selecting his composition "In a Silent Way" as the title track of the band's next album. Zawinul played on four of Davis's jazz/rock albums between 1969 and 1971.

Zawinul composed prolifically for Weather Report throughout the seventies. His works range from haunting, simply stated melodies like "Scarlet Woman" (on *Mysterious Traveler)* to simulated big band riffs of infectious gaiety like the very popular "Birdland" (on *Heavy Weather).* Zawinul thinks like a composer when he plays; this is essential to his development as a multikeyboardist. Regrettably his interest in the acoustic piano–despite his protestations to the contrary–has dwindled to a negligible level. It remains a color on his keyboard palette but is no longer a medium in its own right. I interviewed Zawinul at his elegant Spanish-style home in Pasadena, where he lived with his wife and their two teenage children. Sitting by the swimming pool, we could look down into the stadium where the Rose Bowl game is played. Zawinul often seems as multilayered and complex as his music. He can speak in objective, abstract terms about his work and, moments later, brag like a shameless press agent about his band. He is overbearingly serious and adamantly claims that he never smiles. Whatever his immediate mood, Zawinul radiates intense energy and an athlete's appetite for hard work.

Settling down in the living room, where most of the interview was taped, we sat among two pianos, four or five synthesizers, and an assortment of percussion instruments. Zawinul's living room is where much of his composing takes place, with the aid of his four-track tape recorder. Before it is written down, Zawinul's music materializes in the interaction of all these keyboards. He assembles it layer over layer, testing the results by multitracking, as other composers might test a new piece by playing it on the piano. How Zawinul makes these electronic keyboards "speak" (a term that I use advisedly) is the main subject of the following interview.

When did you first start playing piano?

Actually I started on accordion and played it for several years. We didn't have a piano. Of course, in Austria during the war there wasn't anything going on musically. Later on I started learning to play the piano like everyone else. Nothing special. I played a lot of gigs like weddings and entertainment music. My academic training is a pretty dubious matter, although I had a great teacher once in Austria. Her name was Valerie Zschorney and she was a pupil of a Professor Weingartner, who was a pupil of Franz Liszt. I went once a week for a few years, but I didn't take it seriously. I was out there on the streets. When I was eighteen, I got into an orchestra where there was a lot of reading to do. The reading you do at home, where you can practice, is one thing, but going into an orchestra, where you get a score that's nothing but notes, is completely different. To be a musician in Austria, you've got to play a lot of different stuff. It's an international place. We used to play in nightclubs, walking around to the different tables playing horas and gypsy music. That was on accordion. I loved it.

When did you start to take music seriously?

Tomorrow.

Did you play any other instruments besides piano and accordion?

Oh, man, I played trombone, bass trombone, clarinet, trumpet. This was in Friedrich Gulda's band, one of the best jazz bands in Europe. In my home every real musician plays lots of instruments. In this band we played every-thing, even Strauss overtures. You can't play just one instrument in Europe and ever become what they call a *Muzikant*. Everybody had to learn all the instruments to be considered a real musician. I wrote arrangements down from Woody Herman and Dizzy Gillespie records. That's another way I learned. The more instruments you know, the better you write. You have to know what's possible on the instruments. I can get a clarinet sound from a syn-thesizer not because there's a button that says clarinet but because I can blow the thing myself.

How did you get interested in electronic keyboards—first of all, the electric piano you played in the sixties?

I was turned on by electric instruments for the first time in 1949, when I was playing in an American servicemen's club in Austria. They had a Ham-mond organ in the mess hall, and I played every afternoon when nobody else was around. I played a lot of organ in the fifties and made a record on it over there. After Maynard's band, I worked with Dinah Washington for two years, and we once went on a tour with Ray Charles. He carried a sixty-six-key Wurlitzer around, and he was really the first person I'd ever heard on electric piano. On a gig down South, we came across a really dead piano, so Dinah asked if we could use the Wurlitzer. It was beautiful. They had the same kind of Wurlitzer in the Capitol studio when I was recording there with Cannon-ball Adderley in the mid-sixties, so I recorded "Mercy, Mercy, Mercy" on it. I carried the Wurlitzer on the road for a while, until Victor Feldman told me that Rhodes made a piano that was really smokin'. I got one. Miles Davis heard me play on it and liked it, and then Herbie got one, and later we recorded [Miles Davis's] *In a Silent Way* and *Bitches Brew* using it.

What was your introduction to synthesizer?

I was reading about Milton Babbitt and wondering about people like Morton Subotnick and John Cage. I could hear that there was really something in those instruments, although their music always seemed sort of pulled out of a hat to me. At that time I was in Cannonball's band, just making enough to survive, so I couldn't afford anything new. Later on Weather Report went to Boston, and I met Roger Powell, who was working for ARP. He showed me some basics, and I've slowly been moving along since then.

What do you find you can do with the Oberheim 8-Voice?

It has sixteen oscillators. Having every two oscillators tuned to unison, I can play eight voices with more strength. I can also tune each single oscillator to my liking and record it on the memory bank. For example, I can set up woodwinds as you would in a symphony, running it right down: piccolo, flute, clarinet, oboe, English horn, bass clarinet. But it takes a while before you're able to mix correctly. On *Heavy Weather* there's one sound that's exactly like a saxophone section playing in the street, only quite differently recorded. But it's all keyboards. There are eight modules, and each module has a pair of oscillators which you can tune in unison or to any interval you choose. On the standard setup, all sixteen are tuned in unison. Then, because of the memory bank module with sixteen noiseless buttons, any sound you've prepared can be obtained instantly. You don't have to mess around upstairs [on the keyboard] anymore. I filter everything to exactly the shade I want and write it into the memory. I try to stay away from electronic sounds and go for natural sounds, instead. They don't have to be *known* natural sounds. On "Black Market," for example, the sound isn't one that's known—you wouldn't recognize it as anything else—but it is acoustic. It sounds like some kind of native instrument.

Why don't you use acoustic instruments where it's possible?

Because I'd need a whole orchestra to do what I'm doing—at least thirty people on acoustic instruments to make the *Heavy Weather* album. I've heard orchestral sounds my entire life, and now I can do it myself because of a machine.

Are we back to the idea of the pianist as a one-man band?

In a way you're a one-man orchestra. Besides, I couldn't find thirty people who could play as well as I can play alone, as far as the tightness of the music is concerned. We do need other musicians in the band, too, of course. Fortunately Jaco Pastorius gets a very acoustic sound from his electric bass, and with Wayne Shorter on sax, ours is a very acoustic-sounding band.

When you try to simulate other instruments, how much realism do you strive for?

When I play a trumpet part, I almost make a kind of embouchure with my lips to help me get the right attack. The trumpet attack is unique. It's very important that I once played trumpet because I know how the instrument is approached. You listen to "River People" [on *Mr. Gone*], the reaction is going

to be: "That's a hell of a trombone solo." It's an ARP 2600. There's no trombone player who could play that solo.

What are the advantages to the Prophet 5?

It's like a mixing board [a recording studio device that combines, adjusts, and balances the sounds of different recorded tracks]. You can store a sound, take it out of memory without disturbing the memory, and rememorize it in the synthesizer. With other synthesizers, you have to start all over again to change things. The only handicap is that all the voices sound the same. Getting an oboe, clarinet, saxophone, and so on is possible on the Oberheim 8-Voice, but the Prophet 5 imitates only one instrument in the five voices. But that way I can create a trumpet section. Each instrument has its own function. The Prophet and Oberheim together are an orchestra.

You inverted the voltages on one of your ARP 2600s so that the upper register of the keyboard played the lower sounds and vice versa. Why?

Because it was a challenge for me to play in a mirrored system. It's good for the mind. If you improvise on chords, for example, you've got to transpose, and your mind has to be very, very fast. I was recording one day at home on the inverted setup, and that's when the song "Black Market" [on *Black Market*] was put together. After listening to it, I played the melodies on the straight keyboard, and it didn't sound as good as it did the mirrored way. Then I had to write the melody down and relearn it on the inverted keyboard because at first it was improvised. Onstage I play the first melody of the song with the right hand on the inverted keyboard, and the left hand accompanies on the Rhodes until after the first six notes into the bridge. Then the right hand plays the contrapuntal chord voicings on the polyphonic [Oberheim] synthesizer. The left hand continues the melody where the right hand stopped, putting a chord or two on the Rhodes into the spaces. It takes a little while to get used to thinking in the mirrored system. Only C and F sharp are the same as on the straight keyboard. B becomes C sharp, B flat becomes D, A becomes E flat, and so on. I also play chords on the bridge of "Black Market" on the Oberheim. The chord is going upward and the melody is going downward—in contrary motion. It's beautiful to challenge yourself visually. It makes you play new things.

How do you write music? Do you use the piano, synthesizers, or paper?

I don't start out on paper. I compose by improvising the melody on tape. Then I'll put it away for a few days before I start listening again. After hearing it a dozen times, I improvise the leading countervoices and overdub them. That's when I sit down with paper and work out an orchestration. If you're going to orchestrate with six-note chords, each voice making its own melody, there's no way you can avoid writing it all down. "Nubian Sundance" [on *Mysterious Traveler*] was a twenty-two-page score.

I wrote "Young and Fine" [on *Mr. Gone*] by humming it and accompanying myself on the piano. Then I had my son play the melody on trumpet while I imagined the background melody on the Oberheim and Prophet, and I think that orchestration could stand alone as a tune. That's how I work: Every leading voice should be a melody that can stand alone as a tune. You'll hear it better on the final mix [of separately recorded tracks] because overdubbing gives us a clearer separation of voices. And that's the *only* reason we overdub. If you don't have that magic in there, no amount of overdubbing will improve your record. I can still play all this live. The only reason to overdub is to get the clarity of the voices.

With all that overdubbing, don't you lose the spontaneity in your improvising?

I did overdub a solo on Jaco's [composition] "Punk Jazz." We started off with a click track [just rhythm] running on the digital sequencer in perfect mathematical time. Then we put on the bass line and harmony. I let it play and paced the studio. We started talking about something that reminded me of home, something my father once told me. I had the engineer turn the lights down to create some atmosphere. Boom! The solo hit me. Man, I could never sit down, tell the engineer to back it up three bars, and fill in a solo. You'd never get any magic in the music that way. You've got to play every part like you're a separate individual. That's where you get the power in electronic music.

Do you have any other observations about soloing?

If you play every part the same, you get sterile, nothing. Most people who play electronic instruments sound funny, like something's wrong. It's because everything is the same. The trouble with most electronic music is that it *sounds* electronic. I think our records are going to make a difference in the attitude of people toward electronic music.

When we're onstage, it's always different. On "Scarlet Woman" soloing on the ARP [2600, single-voice] I just work off the A minor chord, and I play something different every night. Jaco and I listen to each other so well we can go almost anywhere we want. On "A Remark You Made" [also on ARP] we used only two chords, just as on the *Heavy Weather* album. I'm playing in unregimented time; then there are a few violin effects—I'm a frustrated violinist—but I'm telling the story. There are sentences, short and long.

Are you saying that the melodic rhythm—that is, the rhythm of the melody itself— imitates speech? That's an element of great improvising in my opinion. You can hear it in people like Parker and especially Eric Dolphy. They play speech patterns.

Yeah, that's it. That's right. In fact I was at a New Year's Eve party with Herbie, at Wayne's house, and he was asking me how we got that effect, without using those words. Miles has it, too, in his articulation.

Did you have any problem acclimating yourself to the different keyboard touches?

No, no problem. On the spinet piano at my house there are metal bars nailed onto the hammers. The action is so heavy you can break your fingers if you're not used to it. Herbie Hancock played on it once, and he was really complaining. I feel like a fighter who's been training with heavy gloves under bad conditions, punching with weights on, you know. When he comes out into the ring, he's going to feel light. That's why I never had a problem with the different resistances of the keyboards. The metal bars have worn down a little now. They've been on there for thirteen years.

Do you still practice on it? If so, how regularly?

Yes, I still play scales, but I don't arrange my life in that regular sense. I do play piano every day. I don't just play simple scales, I do things in seconds, fourths, sixths, and so on—and some scales with one finger, to get every finger to be an individual. I have to be able to play all the tunes with my left hand alone. Sometimes I have to play chord arrangements in the left hand alternating between two keyboards and do something against that rhythm in the right hand. That orchestral thing always has to be there. Sometimes you have three or four movements you have to make in a fast tune, and you have to be quick to find spaces where you can do the changing. It's not just a matter of pushing a button. It's like a magic act. What do they call it? Sleight of hand. That's what it's like using at least three keyboards in every tune.

Has the acoustic piano lost any of its appeal to you?

Not at all. On the new album I use it on every tune. There's nothing more beautiful than a Rhodes and an acoustic piano hitting some things together. You have the openness and attack of the acoustic and the beauty of the Rhodes with maybe a little phaser added. Or synthesizer and acoustic piano together are really beautiful. I rate the Oberheim and the ARP's on melody playing just as high as the acoustic piano.

But can you get the nuances and subtlety on the synthesizer?

Definitely. Even more, in fact. On acoustic piano you can do only so much with one note. I can do a lot of shading on acoustic because I use the pedals, but it's nowhere near what I can do with one note on the ARP or the Oberheim. I can twang it, lower it, put some action on it. I think the synthesizer is an equalizer—it's going to show more than any other instrument where a musician is at.

In what way?

It'll show what's in you. There's so much variety you can get, it'll show either a great amount of imagination, a great ear, or . . . whatever is in you will be revealed. See, with an acoustic piano, you can get away with a lot of shit. I know, because I've been playing it all my life. When I hear people play, I know whether they're getting away with something. On acoustic piano, regardless of all the touch, dynamic, and chordal variations, you have to be concerned with only one sound. And to me, every acoustic player has a different sound, just as every electric player does. You can hear Keith Jarrett's sound, McCoy Tyner's sound, Herbie's sound, my sound. But on synthesizer you cannot just lay on this one sound; if you do, you're just lame. If you're playing a whole piece on synthesizer, it'll show how much you can really put into it.

It reveals the scope of your imagination?

Yes, and your scope as a musician.

On "Milky Way" [from Weather Report*], all that can be heard is the resonance of the strings, without any plucking or striking sounds. How did you achieve that effect?*

Well, I think there are certain things that should be left alone, left unsaid.

Okay, we'll call it sleight of hand. Do you have any advice for players who want to play two keyboards simultaneously?

Yes. Practice everything with the left hand. Right now, I'm even doing my handwriting left-handed. If you want it to look good and sound good, the two hands should become completely equal.

Would you consider performing an unaccompanied keyboard concert?

Eventually, but I think we're about two or three years away. I think we have to get faster and work with memory banks some more, but there is no reason why this can't be done. You know, I think Malcolm Cecil is a master, the way he built all those synthesizers together to create TONTO [The Original New Timbral Orchestra—a synthesizer studio]. What I'd like to do is open for a symphony orchestra. I would play alone on keyboards, and then the orchestra would give their concert. I don't like this electric/acoustic division because it is all one music. It really is. Some people like to hold onto things and defend them. I was never a holder-on. I always want to keep on moving.

Selected Discography

The Cannonball Adderley Quintet: Coast to Coast (1962); M-4703; Milestone.

Mercy, Mercy, Mercy (1965, with Adderley); SN-16153; Capitol.

In a Silent Way (1969, with Miles Davis); CS-9875; Columbia.

Zawinul (1970); SD-1579; Atlantic.

Weather Report (1971, electric piano); C-30661; Columbia.

Heavy Weather (1977, synthesizers); C-34418; Columbia.

Night Passage (1981, synthesizers); JC-36793; Columbia.

KEITH
JARRETT

May 8, 1945–

During the 1970's Keith Jarrett was the enfant terrible of jazz piano. He commanded the highest fees ever for solo performances, many of which were staged at opera houses and concert halls that had previously been the exclusive turf of classical artists. He played the role of prima donna to the hilt, sometimes complaining to the audience that the piano or the sound system was inadequate. His smug, quasi-philosophical pronouncements, which might interrupt a concert at any time, elicited ooohs and ahhhs from some fans but probably embarrassed those with less impressionable minds. When Keith Jarrett played the piano, he broke every rule in the book of good form. Never mind hand position—he did not even sit down much of the time. In especially rhapsodic passages, which abound in his seamless improvised compositions, his genuflecting and gyrating in front of the keyboard made Elvis Presley look like a mannequin.

Nevertheless, Jarrett made the piano sing a new song, and nearly everybody loved it. No one did more to stimulate interest in jazz piano among a broad audience than Jarrett did in his decade of prominence. His *Köln Concert* album of lengthy solo improvisations was a major factor in establishing the viability of the ECM label. Its sales of a quarter million units or so revived confidence in the commercial potential of the piano in jazz. Most important, Jarrett's spontaneous structuring of his music, his ability to incorporate and express basically European ideas in the jazz idiom, and the ecstatic heights to which he pushed his tone and melodies opened up new territory for other pianists to explore.

One of five children, Jarrett began piano lessons at the age of three and was judged to be a prodigy by some of his teachers. At seventeen he enrolled in the Berklee College of Music in Boston, but he soon moved to New York, where he and his wife lived in Spanish Harlem. Keith studied drums and soprano saxophone, instruments he continues to use on records. A jam session at the Village Vanguard led to four months of work in 1965 with Art Blakey and the Jazz Messengers. But Jarrett's passionate and soulful soloing ripened noticeably when he played with the Charles Lloyd Quartet (1966–69), one of the few jazz groups of the sixties to find a broad audience. With drummer Jack DeJohnette, his colleague from the Lloyd group, Jarrett joined Miles Davis's band in 1970. He formed his own quartet in 1972 with Dewey Redman on tenor sax, Charlie Haden on bass, and Paul Motian on drums.

Since 1973 Jarrett has maintained virtually three careers at once: bandleader, composer, and piano soloist. Inspired by diverse influences–Ornette Coleman, Bill Evans, Paul Bley, and modern classical music–Keith has synthesized his sources into a new and bold individuality. No other pianist has dared play entire concerts of spontaneous improvisations. Few could bring them off successfully if they tried.

The following conversation was taped in the general manager's office of KJAZ radio in Alameda, California. After an on-air interview, the customarily reticent Jarrett revealed his views on the piano, the creative process, and the subtle differences between composing and improvising.

How do you feel about the recent trend toward multiple keyboards?
The keyboard idea is one of the immense illusions in music at the moment. The keyboard is being used like a Parker Brothers game, a version of three-dimensional chess which they can sell to people who can't play two-dimensional chess. To simplify: People are making the problem of getting something out of themselves into an exterior problem of finding the right instruments to get it out with. It's like saying the reason I can't paint a masterpiece is that I don't have the right paints.

Should I infer that you don't think there's any good music being made on electric keyboards?
You can infer that, but not from this. It's a matter of what electricity really is. The world is electric to begin with. The very fact that we move around is because of electric impulses, and we're not plugged in, so obviously there's a bigger kind of electricity than the kind you plug in. I live in the electric world, and making it *electronic* would be less strong.

You once said, "My first experience in composing involved adding a note to the last chord of a Mozart concerto." Is that composing or improvising? How do you distinguish between the two in terms of your solo concerts?
Well, there's no distinction between the two in the way I deal with it, although there are many differences in the two processes. You might call it spontaneous composition, which would connect the two. When you write something on paper, no matter how preconceived it is, it's still spontaneous because you can always change your mind when the pencil is about to touch

the paper. Even if you edit three hundred times, it's still spontaneous each time.

The difference for me is that when I'm composing, I can concentrate on each of the lines separately. See, no matter what anyone says, the human ear cannot hear more than two lines at the same time. As a composer, perhaps I can arrange them so the listener has the illusion he can hear all the lines. For example, there is a certain way of playing Bach's piano music when he has four lines going at once in which—if the timing is just off precision—you can hear each line more clearly. If you played them exactly as they were on paper with a metronome, you could hear only one line at a time. Your ear makes the choice. In improvising there's no time to deal with that. But there's a feeling you can get while improvising that makes up for that problem. You can do it spontaneously if you can sit far enough back from your own playing, if you don't identify with your own playing and are not what people call completely involved in your music. If you're aware of what you're playing as a listener, you're waiting to be able to distinguish all the lines. Then, as a player, you can give yourself that as a listener.

I had a hard time deciding whether "A Pagan Hymn" on In the Light *was a spontaneous composition or written away from the piano.*

It was composed completely away from the piano, but that's a good example of the distinction being blurred.

Where do you see yourself within the pianistic tradition? Do you feel influenced by bebop, stride, the romantic classics?

I rarely see myself as a continuation of a pianistic tradition, except to the extent that I use the piano. I have to identify myself with what the piano has made people aware of. If Chopin wrote piano music that no one conceived of before him, I must consider Chopin an influence. But I don't feel influenced by him musically to the extent that I feel like part of a tradition. In the case of jazz pianists, the tradition is improvisation. I was influenced by the need these people had to improvise—improvise something valuable enough to last for years and years.

Who are some of the improvisers that have impressed you?

The funny thing is that it's the process of improvising that impressed me. That's more important than the product. The people who influenced me were people I never heard, which may sound a little strange.

Yes, it does.

I once went to a "blindfold test" in Paris, and I knew who Bud Powell was, even though I never listened to his records. Well, maybe I heard them without realizing it.

Were there other pianists you recognized without ever hearing them before?

Yeah, there were. When I was at Berklee, someone said I sounded a lot like Bill Evans. I'd never heard him. See, the spirit that actually motivates music to come out of somebody has nothing to do with other musicians that have played before.

Do you think you'd play differently if you had been born one hundred years ago?

Of course, but the spirit would be the same. For that matter, I play different in a basement from in an attic. But these are unconscious influences that are inescapable. I guess that's not what you had in mind.

Are there composers who have influenced your music?

Yes, but mostly because of what they were *trying* to do, not so much because of what they *did*. I feel very close to [Charles] Ives, and the reason is his supposed eccentricities, which were the only ways he could get out what he wanted to get out.

Your own piano playing technique is a bit eccentric, standing in front of the keyboard and so on. Is this a looseness you'd recommend? Do you recommend any particular way to acquire technique?

If someone studied piano playing by watching me play—or making films of my playing—he'd make a disastrous mistake. I play the way I do out of necessity, not because it's the best way in the world for anyone to play the piano. It's the only way I can get the piano to do what I want it to do. If I know *what I want it to do,* that's what's important.

I'd say anyone who wanted to play piano should start where the piano started in order to learn what people have done. Once they know what's been done, they're more capable of dealing with what they can hear. I don't know of many people who are as unaware of the tool they're using as pianists, which is reflected in the idea of keyboards. "A keyboard attached to a piece of wood that has strings on it and a cast-iron frame that goes out of tune more than they like" is probably what they know about it.

You've mentioned that the tone quality you're looking for can be elicited only from certain pianos. Which ones?

Hamburg Steinways. Occasionally the New York Steinway. The Bremen and Lausaune concerts were on seven-foot and nine-foot Steinways. I'd never do a group recording in a studio on a nine-foot Steinway. The *Facing You* album is on a five-foot-ten-inch Steinway.

You do get unique tone production, which seems characteristic of improvisers with a strong identity. Is there some way that tone can be worked on?

No, you don't work on that. You do the opposite. If you think about it, you're making a mistake. That's what's happening all over in music. People are asking too many questions, thinking that the answer will be laid on them. You go to hear someone who knocks you out and then go backstage with some earthshaking question that will change your life, if someone answers it. I don't remember ever having those questions to ask of anybody, like: "How do you do this or that?" It's part of the exteriorization process–like electronic instruments. It's a guru thing. You try to find someone who'll tell you what you should have been doing when you weren't "in." Meanwhile, you stay "out," which makes it harder to get back "in," which is where you live.

That's going to make my next question suspicious, but I'll ask it anyway. Do you think playing directly on the piano's strings, as you did in Charles Lloyd's band, is an effect that can be cultivated and practiced?

No. I stopped doing it because I saw people taking it that way. It was just part of the music I was playing. Anything can be used–you can learn a whole new set of things to *do* on a piano. That's not the problem. The problem is *why*! Are you doing it because you can't do something else or because you have to do it? There's a difference. People I've heard playing on the strings now–it's not an organic part of their music. It's a divorced effect. When you don't know what else to do, you might do that.

Maybe it's a type of experimentation.

All the experimenting I've done is between concerts. I don't experiment when I play. Experimenting is practicing being conscious. I know I can be conscious when I'm playing music. Playing is the least important thing. It's the most important to the audience, but the least to the artist. It's the end product, and–this may sound negative, but I don't mean it that way–it could be called the waste product: the waste product of the activity of being musical. Being musical with a capital *M* could simply mean living a harmonious life with your own organism and projecting that to other people. That's why we need music. You can't project being in harmony with yourself without using a medium, and music is the medium which comes closest to showing it.

Do you listen to much music?

I do, although not a lot of music that's being played now. I know what's happening. I have a barometer inside me. I feel responsible for knowing what's going on, so I dip quickly into things that are happening now and wait for something to impress me. When it doesn't, I also feel responsible not to pretend.

What's your feeling about the music business?

I feel disassociated from any business. I deal with it as though I were into it, but I'm not. I have a responsibility to my audience to make myself available somehow. If I have to do it by using the music business, I will in some ways. In other ways I won't. I won't go on the Johnny Carson show.

You have to draw the line somewhere.

The line comes a lot earlier than that.

Is there anything you'd like to express that we haven't covered?

Now that we're at the end, I'd like to say something about words. Everything I've said has been a response to something you've said or to the subject matter of the interview. It's not based on thinking I can transmit anything through words. The feeling I have at the end of every interview is: "I didn't say it!" because I can't say it in words.

Selected Discography

Forest Flower: At Monterey (with Charles Lloyd, 1968); AT-1473; Atlantic.*

Miles Davis: Live/Evil (1970); CG-30954: Columbia.

Solo Concerts: Bremen/Lausanne (1973); 3-1035; ECM.

The Köln Concert (1975); 1064/65; ECM.

Concerts: Bremen/Munich (1981); 3-1227; ECM.

With Quartet:

Fort Yawuh; AS-9240; Impulse.

Backhand; ASD-9305; Impulse.

Survivors' Suite; 1-9084; ECM.

CECIL
TAYLOR

March 15, 1933–

Cecil Taylor has challenged, confused, and ultimately expanded the concept of improvised piano music. Taylor grew up in a middle-class neighborhood in Corona, New York. He began playing the piano at five and also studied drums with the wife of a tympanist who lived across the street. In his teens Cecil was a fan of the bands led by drummers Chick Webb and Gene Krupa, but he listened most of all to the music of Duke Ellington, who was a favorite of his parents. He studied classical piano and played with some local bands around New York. In 1951 Taylor visited Boston, where he had relatives, and moved there the following year to study at the New England Conservatory of Music, where he was profoundly influenced by modern and atonalist composers, such as Igor Stravinsky, Béla Bartók, Arnold Schoenberg, Alban Berg, and Anton Von Webern. He emulated two distinctive piano styles during the 1950's: the intellectual styles of Brubeck and Tristano and the intense, blues-based playing of Bud Powell and Horace Silver. But Cecil was to turn out like no other player in the history of jazz piano. As early as 1961 Taylor was using virtually atonal clusters of notes rather than chords. One of many derogatory jokes about his music depicts him playing with a tennis ball clutched in his hand. It is likely that part of the cynicism and bitterness he expresses in the interview ahead is his reaction to the years of rejection and struggle he has endured. This attitude may also derive from his acute sensitivity to the problems of being black in America, a subject on which he readily expounds. And Taylor's language—like his music—can be powerful, original, and difficult.

In the mid-sixties Taylor reached maturity as a bandleader, perhaps a decade before he reached full maturity as a pianist. In the Cecil Taylor Unit, Taylor does not accompany the horns, violin, and rhythm section, but rather engages the other instruments in a continuous dialogue. Some members of the group—such as alto saxophonist Jimmy Lyons and drummer Andrew Cyrille—have worked with him over two decades. Although the Unit's music is well planned and constructivist (a term explained in Part One), the improvising is free within the established structure.

During the seventies Taylor's soloing and virtuosity blossomed. He used the full length of the keyboard, sometimes traversing its breadth in a few seconds and unleashing a hailstorm of notes. His percussive technique added a new dimension to the sound of the instrument. With the perfection of his own iconoclastic style, and the increased understanding of jazz in the seventies, Taylor was generally acknowledged as a major historical figure. Unfortunately the size of his audience and income does not reflect his significance. Taylor has served on the faculties of the University of Wisconsin and Antioch College in Ohio, and he received a Guggenheim Fellowship for composing in 1973. Taylor's career remains a steep uphill climb, but one he is adamantly committed to continuing.

It will soon be obvious that the Cecil Taylor interview is unlike any other in this collection. The first of several encounters documented ahead took place over breakfast in the dining room of the Holiday Inn near Chinatown.

What approach did you use for developing finger dexterity, and what would you recommend that younger pianists do in that regard?

You've really asked me two questions. The answer to both is essentially that each player must decide for himself.

You've told me that you have had music students, and I assume some of them were pianists. What did you ask them to do?

I can't really answer the question the way you've presented it. The implications of music are larger than the compartmentalization of technique, form, or content. It's a matter of the ability to express.

What do you mean by musical expression? Expression of what?

What do you mean by it?

The realization, the creation, of what you hear.

If you hear it, why is there any need to play it? It exists as soon as you hear it.

You "hear" it metaphorically—not the way you hear my voice. I often "hear" music that I can't express, or play, on the piano.

Isn't it enough that it exists in your head?

No, it's frustrating, in fact. How did you develop your finger dexterity?

I don't have it. It's all comparative. Music isn't that special. It's just one of those things in the air, something I've done. It comes out of the history, environment, culture we're living in. That determines how we hear, what we hear, and the method we use to create the sound. It also determines the standards, goals, and aesthetic levels we achieve. To talk about technique as anything more than a minimal consequence of a larger order—I mean, civilization—is to give it more importance than it deserves. Music is just another activity of man. Technique is only part of that. The traditions of the civilization shape it.

Yes, we are always building on the past. We didn't reinvent the wheel in order to build the automobile. We're interested in what you built on? Whom did you listen to as a student?

You want me to talk about certain things, but I'm prepared to talk only about the things I think are important. I'm interested in the cultural importance of the life of the music. The instrument a man uses is only a tool with which he makes his comment on the structure of music. That's why the evaluation of what a cat says about how he plays music is not too far from the noninteresting things he does when he is playing. That person wouldn't have too profound an understanding of what has happened in the music and the culture. We have to define the procedures and examine the aesthetics that have shaped the history of the music. That's more important than discussing finger dexterity. We might as well discuss basketball or tennis.

Well, what does distinguish your approach to the music from other approaches?

The history of the people, the culture, even the things they forget consciously. The way they cook, speak, the way they move, dress, how they relate to the pressures around them. What you experience in life informs (in-forms) you. If you work on One Hundred Forty-fifth Street in Harlem and years later in Tokyo, where you are taken to see the sights, you experience . . . the environment, listen to the sounds, watch the movement.

You'll be able to see that there are not these separations between things. There are different aesthetic choices made. What happened in the latter part of the eighteenth century in Africa had a profound effect on painting. The concepts of musical organization now have to be broadened to accommodate the worldwide awareness of music. Things are not that simple. Last year thousands of people came to hear me, [saxophonist] Archie Shepp, and Count Basie in the middle of a town built in the fifteenth century. There were people as far as you could see, and their shapes were just visible in the mist. It was like New York's "Jazzmobile" magnified forty or fifty times. I can't ignore that.

[Our conversation took an entirely unexpected turn, establishing that both of us liked the architecture of Antonio Gaudí, an early twentieth-century Catalan architect. His buildings are highly expressive, complicated, sensuous structures. Taylor especially liked the cathedral in Barcelona and believed Gaudí to have been a fascinating person. It was a typical digression in that it illustrated Taylor's intense interest in all the arts: painting, architecture, poetry, and dance. I was struck by the parallel between the qualities of Taylor's music and Gaudí's buildings, which were also ahead of their time yet classical in form. Taylor then picked up the subject of music again.]

Given the history of America, the phenomenon of black people playing music a certain way is not surprising. If in 1969 I was asked to join a music faculty [University of Wisconsin], then this whole thing is not about music. There's at least a duality of things operating here. I had the largest class at the university—one thousand and eighty students! And only one teaching assistant, by the way. For their examination I asked them to create something: a painting, a dance, poems, or music. The Music Department was outraged. But the students fought for this creativity, so I was heartened and came back for a second year. In that year we formed an orchestra [the Black Music Ensemble] which further outraged the department. The academy is not interested in creating artists. They are interested in making the learning of music into a commodity which can be packaged. Therefore, the creative responses of young people are not encouraged.

Historically the sixties was a time when teaching concepts were being challenged. There was a reexamination of what kind of teaching was "relevant." A few people were also beginning to understand how exclusive a clientele was being informed by the college experience.

When I went to the conservatory, there was one order, a list of the titans of music, which was considered to be absolute. Why? André Malraux [novelist and once minister of culture of France] was considered a very sophisticated man. Yet at an audience he had with Mao Tse-tung he allegedly said, "But of course you read Shakespeare here." Now what could be more provincial than that? There is the abolutism of the conservatory. What must be seen is that there are certain conceptions in music which are never challenged. At least not in the schools. That is a very narrow perspective.

Did you ever work with any individuals in your class?

Yes. In fact, one of the people in the band is someone who came to me while I was teaching at Antioch in Ohio.

Who?

I'm more interested in your response. *Who?* Which one? Why is that important?

I didn't say it was important. I simply wanted to know. [It was trumpeter Raphé Malik.]

Art works in really mysterious ways. [This statement, connecting art with mystery, took on more significance when I learned later that Taylor's book in progress about music is called *Mysteries*.] Do you play an instrument, too?

I play piano, I started playing classical music when I was young and eventually studied improvising with Lennie Tristano.

What was that like?

Finding out what it was all about.

Name something that it's all about–linear dimension, maybe? If you're talking about the top layer of music, which the ear responds to first, there's all kinds of movement, not just linear. I've heard Lennie play many times. What music do you listen to?

That's what I was going to ask you.

I once went to meet Lennie and went through a lot of nonsense just to get in to see him. What did you learn from him?

I remember playing left-hand chords to "You Go to My Head," trying to get a countermelody going with the thumb of my left hand. He had asked me to learn the song from Billie Holiday's recording of it. At one point my countermelody didn't work with the right-hand melody, and Lennie was quick to point out that it was wrong. "Yeah, I know," I admitted. "You only know it in your head," he told me, "but I'm not concerned with what you know in your wig." What I learned was that there are other ways of knowing something in music.

Like what?

Knowing in your hands or ears.

Now you're talking about what works and what doesn't work.

I'm talking about a separate cognitive process, knowing what you're doing musically. Making sense musically. That's not something you can learn intellectually. You can only develop the instinct you already have. . . . Why do I feel like you're interviewing me?

If intellectual cognition isn't enough, what else is music made up of?

Feelings.

What are they?

Why must I define my terms when you aren't willing to clarify your answers. That doesn't seem fair.

Does fairness amount to much?

Yes, it does. What's your concept of technique? . . . Isn't that where we began?

I don't know what language you speak or what you're prepared to hear. If we're going to talk, I need some idea of who you are. You might write anything. How do I know?

I'm trying to tell you.
Well, I thank you.

When I saw Cecil again, he was chain-smoking, pacing backstage at the
Zellerbach Auditorium on the Berkeley campus of the University of California.
"I always get nervous before I play," he said. "I practiced four hours today, but
that didn't help. Then I played on this Mason and Hamlin downstairs for
about fifteen minutes, but it wasn't any good. If you can't play, you can't
play."

Taylor was wearing a sleeveless undershirt with a towel draped over his
shoulders. It seemed obvious that he exercised regularly. "A body has to stay in
shape to play," he commented. As we sat down to talk, he cooled off with
occasional swigs from a bottle of imported beer. Taylor's exercise regimen
consists primarily of running around his loft in New York City. He does quite
a few laps, though he can't say how many because he counts the steps instead.

Taylor is a dance *aficionado.* In fact, he choreographed a work for thirteen
dancers while directing his play *A Rat's Mass* in New York. "At least I
thought of it as dancing," he quipped, "though I know a few people who
didn't." The play had a short run.

Just then the solo playing of Paul Bley, who had preceded Taylor on the
bill, became audible through the backstage monitors, a Bley much more romantic than usual. "Sort of a *bluesy* romanticism," Cecil said, correcting me. "I
remember hearing Paul play when he first came to New York. At the time I
thought he was technically very interesting. Youth demonstrates its strength
in terms of its technical prowess. But when players reach their maturity . . .
hmmm, you know he [Paul] is playing everything he wants to play. It's
interesting how the past has an influence on the music's continuance. The
blues flavor . . . those tenths he's playing in the left hand right now—that's
Teddy Wilson. It's funny that the roots show more in one's maturity than in
youth. Which probably makes me a genius. It's a reflection of a greater understanding of the history of the music."

"How does that make you a genius?

"Because I've continued to expand the realm of the piano in terms of what
I attempt to do."

"How does that relate to the past?"

"Ah, that's the mystery. Anyway, a lot of people feel it doesn't [relate to
the past], but the past is always with it."

"I don't think your playing is out of the context of tradition."

"I don't either." He recalled a recent duo piano performance with the sixty-eight-year-old Mary Lou Williams, who personifies the jazz piano tradition. His assessment of these duets was completely ambiguous to me. "One could write a small book about my experience of it," he said.

"What would the title of the book be?"

"*The Wrong Embrace.* Perhaps *The Misunderstood Embrace.* A lot of the critics thought it didn't work. The liner notes to the album [*Embraced,* on Pablo] was my answer to those people." Taylor stood abruptly to prepare for his appearance onstage.

"Why do you have an aversion to discussing the mundane realities of playing the piano?"

"When you get older, you get into the realities because you're trying to survive. One begins to understand what one's limits are."

Several days passed before we met for what I suspected would be the last time, at least in the context of this project. He was now in the midst of a San Francisco club date at the Keystone Korner opposite pianist Randy Weston. We sat on the lawn of Union Square Park. I had decided on a new tactic of quoting statements Taylor had made to other interviewers, and then asking him to defend, explain, or recant them. Naturally things did not go as planned.

In 1965 you said that "electronic music divorces itself from human energy." You've also told me that many of your attitudes have changed over the years. Has that one changed?

People put their emotions to all sorts of ends. I don't know that I've changed my opinion, but the area of human emotion can be perverted and subverted in a lot of ways. I'm answering your question, by the way.

You once said that musical notation can be used as a point of reference, "but the notation does not indicate music, it indicates direction." Could you explain how you use notation to communicate a piece of music to your band?

I don't know what I meant by saying that. I don't know if I said it . . . you know that old Rita Hayworth song "Put the Blame on Mame"?

Do you have a view on the usefulness of musical notation?

Now who'd be interested in that?

People interested in your music.

Who would they be? They aren't responsible for me making any money all these years. It's all right for them to love the idea of abstract pleasure which they get out of some intellectual preoccupations. Maybe that absolves them of their responsibility.

Do you feel an obligation to communicate what you know of your art to those people who are working in the same art form?

[Taylor laughed and indicated that I should say so. "Damn right I laughed," he added. After a few moments he continued.] That's not what your magazine does. You can't give anyone anything, or make choices for them. It takes long enough to be satisfied with choices you've made for yourself.

Are you satisfied with the choices you've made for yourself?

I accept the responsibility of having made them. I'm talking about the small part I'm playing in the evolution of the music, the gift that has been given to me, to have seen spiritualized the mysteries of the music at an early age. This made my actions predestined. One has to become aware of the force, both realistic and spiritual. It's about hard work, which is about living to the full extent of one's capabilities.

You once said that the recording procedure obscured a musician's sound rather than clarified it. Must it be so deceptive? Is there no such thing as "high fidelity" in recordings today? Are you dissatisfied with your own records?

Of course, I like ninety-eight percent of the records I've made, but that doesn't alter the fact that the engineers don't know how to record the music.

How could they improve their work?

If I had part of their salary, I might tell them.

Is money the only thing that would motivate you to—

Who's giving me money?

Your music and, indirectly, a lot of people who have affection for it.

Affection or curiosity? If they come to hear me play, it's not like coming to hear Bill Evans play. They have to work at it. I don't expect people who listen to Emerson, Lake, and Palmer to come hear me. I accept that reality. They are victims of a situation they don't even know exists. To produce music of this tradition is work, and I should be paid for it. Are the people who love my music responsible for paying my rent? If that's true, they're getting off light because I don't live all that well. Not like Peter Duchin does, although I play four times as much piano as he does.

What I really should be talking about is the cultural discrimination that exists in Europe and America—in the West. That's all right, though. The Third World is coming alive; their art is growing even through Western Europeans are trying to decimate it, like those barbarians in South Africa.

I can understand your being bitter about a lot of things, but not about the genuine affection many people feel for your music. Don't you believe they really feel that?

You say I appear to be bitter. That can't be inferred from anything I say because I don't feel that an audience has any responsibility other than to be there or not to be there. There's nothing personal between me and the audience at all. Liking the music is not personal. They're responding to sounds which they would just as soon dissociate from the person making the sounds. Otherwise, things would not be the way they are historically. They feel about me the way their parents felt about Louis Armstrong, although the nature of the oppression has been more subtle over the passage of time. You seem to think one should be grateful that there are these people who get emotionally involved. I'm also saying that there are certain levels of the relationship . . . well, it's not necessary to speak about them. There's no need to talk about the most important things in our lives, unless you want to write a poem about them. Listen, you can tell if an audience is there or not, or if one or two people are moved. I'm not going to pretend that there is cultural justice in America.

There may not be, but that doesn't mean each and every person is unjust.

You keep trying to defend what is historically endemic—the disease that consumes the vectors, or activity, which determine what people buy.

I'm saying that history is not totally endemic or determined. People can rise above their past.

The myth that there is [social] progress, which makes you comfortable, has no reality. The percentage of unemployed teenagers among blacks is getting larger, not smaller. Benny Goodman was the King of Swing, but he had Teddy Wilson, Lionel Hampton, and Mary Lou Williams working for him. The Beatles and the Rolling Stones were brought over here and made the Americans give them millions of dollars, but everyone knows who created that music. That's a manifestation of the disease. You know . . . Mick Jagger. Nothing's changed. It's just more subtle.

Obviously my importance does not have anything to do with the nature of the forces that have tried to hinder that development. The ability to sustain myself is made up of things that are not as negative as the things I see when I walk out my door. It's a gift of the knowledge of my ancestors' great accomplishments. I can do without appearing on Johnny Carson's show. I'm perfectly content to do what I do. I have a very interesting band now.

Selected Discography

In Transition (1955, 1959); BN-LA458-H2; Blue Note.
Cecil Taylor/Buell Neidlinger (1961); JAZ-5032; Jazz Man.

The New Breed: The Dedication Series, Vol. VIII (1961, with Archie Shepp); IA-9339/2; Impulse/ABC.

Unit Structures (1966, with Jimmy Lyons, Andrew Cyrille); BST-84237; Blue Note.

Silent Tongues (1974, solo); AL-1005; Arista.

3 Phasis (1978; Jimmy Lyons, Raphé Malik, Ramsey Ameen, Ronald Shannon Jackson); NW 303; New World.

Cecil Taylor (1978, personnel as above); NW 201; New World.

APPENDIX

The following discography does *not* include the twenty-seven pianists whose discographies appear in Part Two. An asterisk (*) indicates that the selected album is out of print.

Anthologies: *Piano Giants, Vol. 1;* P-24052; Prestige
   Masters of the Modern Piano (1955–1966); VE2-2314; Verve.
   Parlor Piano, 1917–1927; BLP-101Q; Biograph.
   The Modern Jazz Piano Album; SJL-2247; Savoy/Arista.
   One Night Stand: A Keyboard Event; KC2-37100; Columbia.
   A Jazz Piano Anthology; KG-32355; Columbia.
   Ragtime Piano; RF-33; Folkways.
   They All Played Ragtime (classic ragtime); JCE-52; Jazzology.
   Barrelhouse Piano, 1927–1936; 1028E; Jazzology.
   Boogie-Woogie Rarities, 1927–43; M-2009; Milestone.
   Bill Evans Tribute; PA-8028; Palo Alto Jazz.

Abrams, Muhal Richard. *Live at Montreux, 1978: Spiral;* AN-3007; Novus/
   Arista.
Albany, Joe. *Birdtown Birds;* IC-2003; Inner City.
Allison, Mose. *Mose Allison: Seventh Son;* P-10052; Prestige.
Ammons, Albert. *Boogie Woogie and the Blues;* XFL-15357; Commodore/CBS.
Barron, Kenny. *Sunset to Dawn;* 5018; Muse.
Basie, William "Count." *The Best of Count Basie;* MCA2-4050; MCA. *Satch and
   Josh* (with Oscar Peterson); 2310-722; Pablo.
Beirach, Richie. *Hubris;* ECM-1104; ECM.
Blake, Eubie. *The 86 Years of Eubie Blake;* C2S-847; Columbia. *Rags to Classics;*
   EBM-2; Eubie Blake Music.
Bley, Carla. *Musique Mecanique;* 9; Watt.
Bonner, Joe. *Impressions of Copenhagen;* T-114; Theresa.
Brackeen, Joanne. *Ancient Dynasty;* JC-36593; Columbia.

Bryant, Rusty. *Solo Flight;* 2310-798; Pablo.

Buckner, Milt. *Plays Chords;* 68047; MPS.*

Cables, George. *Cables' Vision;* 14001; Contemporary.

Cole, Nat. *King Cole Trio: Capitol Jazz Classics, Vol. 8;* M-11033; Capitol. *From the Very Beginning;* MCA2-4020; MCA.

Coltrane, Alice. *Transfiguration;* 2WB-3218; Warner Bros.

Cowell, Stanley. *Waiting for the Moment* (solo); GXY-5104; Galaxy.

Dameron, Tadd. *Memorial Album;* P-7842; Prestige.

Darch, Bob. *Ragtime Piano;* VAL-3120; United Artists.

Davis, Anthony. *Episteme;* GR-8101; Gramavision. *Lady of the Mirrors* (solo); 1047; India Navigation.

Duke, George. *The 1976 Solo Keyboard Album;* FE-38208; Epic.

Ellington, Duke. *Duke Ellington–1940;* R-013; Smithsonian Collection. *Duke Ellington, The Pianist (1966);* F-9462; Fantasy.

Ewell, Don. *Take It in Stride;* Chi-127; Chiaroscuro.

Fischer, Clare. *State of His Art* (solo); Rev-26; Revolution.

Flanagan, Tommy. *Ballads and Blues;* IC-3029; Inner City.

Frischberg, Dave. *You're a Lucky Guy;* CJ-74; Concord Jazz.

Galper, Hal. *Ivory Forest;* IC-3042; Inner City.

Garner, Erroll. *Concert by the Sea;* CS-9821; Columbia.

Guaraldi, Vince. *Jazz Impressions;* F-8359; Fantasy.

Guarnieri, Johnny. *Gliss Me Again;* Class-105; Classic Jazz.

Haig, Al. *Piano Time* (solo); 1006; Sea Breeze.

Hakim, Sadik. *Charlie Parker: Bird/The Savoy Recordings* (one track only); SJL-2201; Savoy/Arista.

Hanna, Roland. *Sir Elf* (solo); 1003; Choice.

Harris, Barry. *Live in Tokyo;* 130; Xanadu.

Hart, Clyde. *Charlie Parker: Bird/The Savoy Recordings* (four tracks); SJL-2001; Savoy/Arista.

Hawes, Hampton. *For Real;* 7589; Contemporary. *Charlie Haden & Hampton Hawes;* AH-4; Artists House.

Henderson, Fletcher (as accompanist). *Bessie Smith: Empty Bed Blues* (five tracks); CG30450; Columbia.

Heywood, Eddie. *The Biggest Little Band of the Forties;* XFL-15876; Commodore/CBS.

Hill, Andrew. *Nefertiti;* IC-6022; Inner City.

Hines, Earl. *Louis Armstrong and Earl Hines, 1928;* R-002; Smithsonian Collection. *Another Monday Date* (solo/trio); P-24043; Prestige.

Hodes, Art. *Down Home Blues* (solo); JCE-74; Jazzology.

Holmes, Richard "Groove." *Groovin' with Jug;* LN-10130; Pacific Jazz.

Hope, Elmo. *All Star Sessions;* M-47037; Milestone.

Hyman, Dick. *Genius at Play* (solo); 7065; Monitor-Everest.

James, Bob. *One on One: Bob James & Earl Klugh;* FC-36241; Columbia.

Johnson, James P. *Giants of Jazz: James P. Johnson;* J-19; Time-Life Records.

Johnson, Pete. *Boogie-Woogie Mood,* MCA-1333; MCA.

Jones, Hank. *Solo Piano;* SJL-1124; Savoy/Arista.

Joplin, Scott. *Scott Joplin–1916* (piano roll); BLP-1006; Biograph. As composer: *Joshua Rifkin: Piano Rags by Scott Joplin, Vols. I, II,* and *III;* H-71248, H-71264, H-71305; Nonesuch. (Also see Morath, Max.)

Jordan, Duke. *Charlie Parker: The Very Best of Bird* (most tracks); 2WB-3198; Warner Bros.

Kellaway, Roger. *Trio;* P-7399; Prestige.

Kelly, Ed. *Ed Kelly & Friend* (with Farrell "Pharaoh" Sanders); 106; Theresa.

Kelly, Wynton. *Keep It Movin';* M-47026; Milestone.

Kenton, Stan. *Artistry in Rhythm (1945–50);* 1043E; Creative World.

Lande, Art. *The Eccentricities of Earl Dant* (solo); 1769; 1750 Arch Street Records.

Larkins, Ellis. *Smooth One;* 145; Classic Jazz.

Leviev, Milcho. *Piano Lesson;* 1025; Dobre.

Lewis, Meade Lux. *Barrel House Piano;* 268; Archive of Folk and Jazz.

Lipskin, Mike. *Harlem Stride Piano;* 001; Buskirk.

Makowicz, Adam. *From My Window;* 1028; Choice.

Mance, Junior. *That Lovin' Feelin';* M-9041; Milestone.

Mangione, Gap. *Suite Lady;* 4694; A&M.

Marmarosa, Dodo. *Trio;* 108; Spotlite.* *Charlie Parker: The Very Best of Bird* (two tracks); 2WB-3198; Warner Bros.

Matthews, Ronnie. *Freddie Hubbard: Breaking Point;* BST-84172; Blue Note.

McCann, Les. *Live at Montreux;* 2-312; Atlantic.

McKenna, Dave. *Giant Strides* (solo); CJ-99; Concord Jazz.

McShann, Jay. *Confessin' the Blues;* 128; Classic Jazz.

Monk, Thelonious. *Pure Monk* (solo); 47004; Milestone. *The Complete Genius* (quartet/compositions); LA-579;H2; Blue Note.

Montoliu, Tete. *Catalonian Folk Songs* (solo); 304; Timeless Muse.

Morath, Max. *The World of Scott Joplin;* SRV-310-SD; Vanguard.

Morton, Jelly Roll. *Giants of Jazz: Jelly Roll Morton;* STL-J07; Time-Life Records.

Newborn, Phineas. *Great Jazz Piano;* 7611; Contemporary.

Nichols, Herbie. *The Third World;* LA485-H2; Blue Note.

Parlan, Horace. *Musically Yours* (solo); 1141; Steeplechase.

Pearson, Duke. *Dedication;* 7729; Prestige.

Perkins, Carl. *Introducing Carl Perkins;* DL-211; Dootone.

Powell, Bud. *The Amazing Bud Powell, Vol. 1;* BST-81503; Blue Note. *The Genius of Bud Powell, Vol. 1;* VE2-2526; Verve.

Powell, Richie. *Clifford Brown: The Quintet;* EMS-2-403; EmArcy.

Previn, André. *Plays Vernon Duke;* 7558; Contemporary.

Price, Sammy. *Fire;* 106; Classic Jazz.

Pullen, Don. *Montreux Concert,* Atlantic.* *Mingus Moves: Charles Mingus;* AT-1653; Atlantic.

Roberts, Luckey. *Luckey and the Lion: Harlem Piano;* S-10035; Good Time/Contemporary.

Ruiz, Hilton. *Steppin' into Beauty;* SCS-1158; Steeplechase.

Russell, George. *Outer Thoughts;* M-47027; Milestone.

Sample, Joe. *Joe Sample, Ray Brown, and Shelly Manne: The Three;* IC-6007; Inner City.

Scott, Shirley. *Blue Seven;* 7376; Prestige.

Smith, Jimmy. *The Incredible Jimmy Smith;* BST-81525; Blue Note.

Smith, Willie "The Lion." *The Original 14 Plus Two, 1938–1939;* XFL-15775; Commodore/CBS.

Stacy, Jess. *Benny Goodman: Carnegie Hall Jazz Concert–1938;* CSL-160; Columbia.

Strayhorn, Billy. *The Golden Duke* (duets with Ellington); P-24029; Prestige.

Sullivan, Joe. *Joe Sullivan: Piano;* 2851; Folkways.

Sutton, Ralph. *Ralph Sutton: Bix Beiderbecke and Piano Portraits (1950);* XFL-16570; Commodore/CBS.

Tatum, Art. *The Tatum Solo Masterpieces, Vols. 1–8;* 723, 729, 730, 789, 790, 791, 792, 793; Pablo. *Art Tatum Trio;* FJ-2893; Folkways.

Thornton, Argonne. See Hakim, Sadik.

Timmons, Bobby. *Moanin';* M-47031; Milestone.

Tristano, Lennie. *Requiem;* SD2-7003; Atlantic.

Turner, Joe. *King of Stride* (solo); 147; Chiarascuro.

Vukovich, Larry. *Blue Balkan;* IC-1096; Inner City.

Waldron, Mal. *Mingus Lives* (solo); 3075; Enja.

Waller, Fats. *Piano Solos, 1929–1941;* AXM2-5518; Bluebird/RCA.

Wallington, George. *Our Delight;* P-24093; Prestige.

Walton, Cedar. *Piano Solos;* 704; Clean Cuts.

Wellstood, Dick. *Alone;* JCE-73; Jazzology.
Williams, Jessica. *Orgonomic Music.* 703; Clean Cuts.
Yancey, Jimmy. *In the Beginning* (solo); JCE-51; Jazzology.
Young, Larry. *The Tony Williams Lifetime: Emergency;* 25-3001; Polydor.*
Zeitlin, Denny. *Expansions;* 1758; 1750 Arch Street Records.

INDEX

Len Lyons is one of today's foremost authorities on jazz and the author of *The 101 Best Jazz Albums,* a comprehensive listeners' guide to jazz on records. He has produced records, written liner notes, appeared on jazz radio shows across the country, and contributed numerous articles to national magazines. In 1976 he received the Ralph J. Gleason Memorial Fund Award for Jazz Criticism. A player himself, Lyons studied improvisation and theory with the legendary pianist and teacher Lennie Tristano. Lyons lives in Berkeley, California, with his wife and their two children.

Veryl Oakland, a photographer of jazz musicians for fifteen years, is a contributor to Leonard Feather's *Encyclopedia of Jazz in the Seventies* and Joachim Berendt's *Jazz: A Photo History.* His work regularly appears in internationally acclaimed publications, such as the Japanese jazz magazine *Swing Journal.*